O'Sullivan (*Ó Súilleabháinn*)
The Earliest Irish Royal Family
History and Genealogy
Third Edition

By William Randolph McCreight

CLEARFIELD

Front Cover: Donal Cam O'Sullivan, Prince of Eóganachta, Lord of Beare and Bantry.
Courtesy of Creative Commons License

Back Cover: The O'Sullivan Beare Dunboy Castle (Caisleán Dhún Baoi) after its destruction in 1602 by Sir George Carew. Courtesy of Creative Commons License

ISBN 978-0-8063-5647-1

Photographs in this book are by the author and members of his family unless otherwise credited in the captions.

Published for Clearfield Company by
Genealogical Publishing Company
Baltimore, Maryland, 2013

Made in the United States of America

Dedicated to my great-grandfather
Charles Pleasant Washington Sullivan (1859-1946)
and his daughter, my grandmother,
Sarah Katherine Sullivan (1886-1959)

And a very special thanks to Cheryl M. Killian and Sandra Phillips for proofreading, editing and advice that made this a far better book than I could have done without their help.

Table of Contents

Table of Photographs, maps and documents

Preface

Thinking of my great-grandfather Charles Sullivan brings back fond memories, but unfortunately, I only knew him until I was six years old. I remember him as a spry old man who walked with a cane and was very hard of hearing. The family called him Grandpa. My family lived in an eleven-room house in Newton, North Carolina, across the street from the Catawba County Courthouse. My great-grandparents, my great-grandmother's sister, my grandparents with their seven children, my grandmother's sister and her daughter all lived together in this house. My parents probably also lived there in the early days of their marriage, because a newspaper picture showed us all in front of the house and the caption said five generations. The house in Newton is no longer there; a bank occupies the site.

Grandpa took me around with him to many places in Newton and gave me coins from an old-fashioned change purse to buy candy. My parents moved to Maryland, when I was six years old and I never saw Grandpa again. He died in 1946 when I was twelve years old, and we were living in Florida. My grandmother sent me his change purse, which still had a few coins in it, and a few years ago my aunt, his granddaughter, gave me his pocket watch as a memento.

I recently began looking into Grandpa's history and was surprised to learn what an interesting and adventurous person he was. His family had a plantation in South Carolina with a considerable amount of land. He was born before the Civil War and my grandmother, his daughter, told me stories about the Civil War and how they had to hide the horses, food and household silver in the woods when the Yankees came and took everything they could lay their hands on. Grandpa's father had an accident that left him an invalid in considerable pain. After the Civil War, the plantation overseer left. Some of the slaves left and some remained. His father said he could no longer manage the plantation and, at the age of twelve, Grandpa took over the plantation management, hired workers, and kept the plantation together for the family.

I knew Grandpa had a hotel in Camden, South Carolina, because a newspaper clipping said my grandparents' wedding reception was in the elegant Hotel Camden in 1910 and the affable proprietor Charles Sullivan was the host. When I began looking into his past, it surprised me to learn my great-grandfather was quite an entrepreneur. He had at least eight hotels in South Carolina, North Carolina, Florida and Virginia. According to newspaper articles, he renovated them and opened dining rooms, making them elegant and the best in the state. With the help of librarians in these states, I was able to locate pictures of five of these hotels.

Looking farther back, I found that Grandpa's 5th great-grandfather came from Ireland to Virginia when he was seventeen years old in 1655. That was only 48 years after the first permanent English settlement in North America at Jamestown, Virginia. There was a newspaper clipping in my great-grandmother's trunk that said the Sullivans were descendants of the kings of Munster in Ireland. I found that the family is well documented in Irish history and the first person to take the surname Súilleabháinn, anglicized to Sullivan, was born in 874 AD. The histories say the Sullivans were the kings of Munster and in 170 AD had a castle called Knockgraffon in County Tipperary. The English invaded Ireland in 1169 and the extensive O'Sullivans properties in Tipperary were confiscated in 1192. The entire clan went to a better-protected place in wild and rugged areas of Counties Kerry and Cork. The O'Sullivans fought the English invaders in 1169, 1192, 1569, 1598, 1601, 1602, 1641, and 1648 with devastating results. All of their 32 castles were destroyed and the land was ravaged. Most of the O'Sullivan nobles went to France, Spain, and America. In 1988, the O'Sullivans regained the ruins of Knockgraffon Castle and this may be the only case of a family that can document its relationship with a specific building for almost 2,000 years.

I decided to document this interesting story for my O'Sullivan relatives and my family in the form of this book.

William Randolph McCreight
December 2012

Acknowledgments

I would like to especially thank the following people:

- My wife Antje for proofreading and editing.
- Cheryl M. Killian for proofreading and editing.
- Sandra Phillips for proofreading and editing.
- My sister-in-law Janice Lee McCreight, née Taylor for pictures and documents.
- The Irish Office of Public Works and David Pollock for his archaeological reconstruction of Knockgraffon Castle.
- Ann and Barry Clifford of Castlecove, Caherdaniel, County Kerry, Ireland, and Ann's father Val Drummond for advice about the history of Kerry and pictures.
- Donald W. Moore, Certified Genealogist, for research in Virginia.
- Humphrey Bolton for a picture of the old bridge in Carrick-on-Suir.
- James Yardley for a picture of Ormond Castle.
- The Tuosist Community Development Group in Ireland for a picture of Ardea Castle before it was destroyed.
- Joep Laumans in Ireland for a 1992 picture of Cappanacuss Castle.
- Steve Ford Elliot for a picture of Redwood Castle.
- The Irish Department of Arts, Heritage and Gaeltacht for an archaeological reconstruction of Carriganass Castle.
- Dr. Gary B. O'Sullivan for a picture of Château du Gravier (Dunderry Castle).
- Christopher Finot for a picture of Château de Sully.
- Steve Tuttle and his team at the South Carolina Department of Archives and History for research and numerous documents.
- The United States Patent and Trade Mark Office for two patents of inventions by Charles Pleasant Sullivan.
- Pelham Lyles, Director of the Fairfield County Museum, South Carolina, for information and pictures.
- Richard Hyman for information about the Pelham family.
- Alex Floyd of the Catawba County Library in Newton, North Carolina, for a picture of the house on Court House Square.
- The Lancaster County, South Carolina, Society for Historical Preservation, for pictures and information and Lindsay Pettus, President of the Society.

- Greenville County, South Carolina, Library for various pictures of Greenville.
- Lauren Swain Mosely of the Jacksonville Florida Historical Society Archives, for research.
- Garry R. Freeze for his advice and his pictures.
- Richard Horwege of Donning Company Publisher for use of pictures.
- Raymond W. Neal, Gary Harris and Fritz Hamer at the Lancaster County Library, South Carolina, for research.
- Dyron Knick at the Roanoke Public Library, Virginia, for research.
- Howard Branham at the Camden, South Carolina Archives & Museum, for research and photographs.
- Barbara Davis at the Northampton County, North Carolina Memorial Library, for research.
- Alicia Clarke at the Sanford Museum, Florida, for research and pictures.
- Julie Stutts of the Aiken County, South Carolina County Registrar Mesne Conveyance (RMC) Office, for research.
- The High Point Public Library, North Carolina, for research and pictures.

Part I
O'Sullivan (Ó Súilleabháinn) History
Spain, Ireland, France, and America

Irish writers, in many genres, are world renown and Ireland has a rich literature that dates back to the 5th century. Much older traditional histories dating back to the first Irish settlers appear in the annals of Ireland written in monasteries. The O'Sullivans may be the oldest documented royal family on record.[1] The *Annals of Clonmacnoise* [2] describe the O'Sullivan's ancestors from 16th century BC. Some historians consider the early parts as mythical, but they certainly have core elements of truth, because there is archaeological, linguistic and DNA corroboration. From the 5th century AD, when writing was introduced into Ireland, the data is verifiable from other historical sources. The ruins of Knockgraffon Castle (*Cnoc Graffon or Raffon*), near Cashel in Tipperary, Ireland, is the earliest of thirty-two known castles of the O'Sullivan clan. It is listed in the *Book of Rights (Lebor na gCeart),*[3, 4] and the *Book of Munster (An Leabhar Muimhneach)*[5] says Knockgraffon was the residence of Crown Prince Eoghan, born in 170 AD. But it is

Ruins of the Clonmacnoise monastery and school, where the Annals were written. Courtesy of Creative Commons License.

[1] The kings of Munster were the oldest hereditary rulers, but the Irish have not ruled since Queen Elisabeth I of England declared herself Queen of Ireland. The Japanese emperor is the oldest continuing hereditary monarch in the world. The *Nihon Shoki*, an 8th century Japanese history book, said the Japanese Empire was founded in 660 BC by Emperor Jimmu, whom mythology says was descended from the Sun Goddess. Most historians agree that it is unlikely that any of the recorded emperors existed until circa one millennium after Jimmu's recorded reign.

[2] *The Annals of Clonmacnoise being the Annals of Ireland from the earliest times to 1408 AD,* Dublin University Press, 1896, edited by Reverend Denis Murphy LLD MRIA, Vice President, Royal Society of Antiquities, Ireland, facsimile reprint Llanerch Publishers, 1993.

[3] *Lebor na gCeart (The Book or Rights), the Book of Lecan* and the *Book of Ballymotte*, lists rents and taxes paid in the area of Cashel in Munster, Ireland, compiled in 1390 from older sources, translated by John O'Donnovan in 1847, Celtic Society, Dublin.

[4] *Lebor na gCert (The Book of Rights)*, Translated by Dillon, Myles. Dublin: Irish Texts Society, 1962.

[5] *Eoghanacht Genealogies Book of Munster*, Reverend Eugene O'Keefe, 1703, based on works by Domhnall Ó

probably older than this. The first to be called Sullivan (Súilleabháinn) was Eochaid, son of Maolura, Lord of Knockgraffon, born in 874 AD. Knockgraffon remained the principal seat of the O'Sullivan clan until it fell to the English invaders in 1192 and was confiscated. Dr. Gary O'Sullivan, the present chief of the O'Sullivan MacCragh sept, bought Knockgraffon Castle in 1998 [6] from Donal Keating, a direct descendant of the invader who confiscated the Castle in 1192. The O'Sullivan MacCragh sept [7] is the oldest of the O'Sullivan royal bloodlines. There is probably no other family that can officially record its association with a specific building for almost 2,000 years.[8]

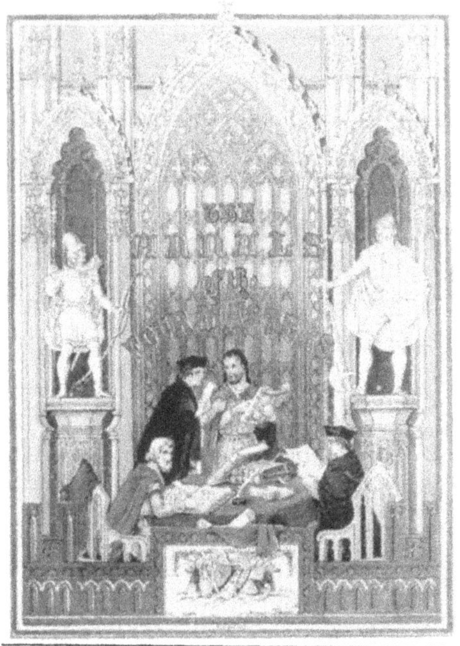

The Annals of the Kingdom of Ireland (Annála Ríoghachta Éireann) also known as The Annals of the Four Masters translated into English by Owen Connellan in 1846

Early Sources

The *Annals of Clonmacnoise* [9] *- Ancient Irish Chronicles from the earliest times to 1408* is an English translation of ancient Irish annals written in the Irish Gaelic language. The Abbey and School of Clonmacnoise is located on the Shannon River between Athlone and Banagher in County King, Ireland, which was renamed County Offaly in 1922. The original *Annals* contain information about ancient Irish families found in no other primary source. However, some pages were no longer legible from age and some pages were missing. Conell Mageoghagan completed the English translation on the 20th of April 1627 in Lemanaghan Castle, Offaly. It was published in Dublin in 1896. He believed the missing pages were removed because they embarrassed

Duinnin and Tadhig MacSáire Mheic Bhruaideadha.

[6] *The Oak and the Serpent*, Gary B. O'Sullivan MD FACOG FACS, Gold Stag Communications, 2007, pages 56, 111.

[7] A sept is a branch of an Irish clan.

[8] *The Oak and the Serpent*, Gary B. O'Sullivan MD FACOG FACS, Gold Stag Communications, 2007, page 111.

[9] *The Annals of Clonmacnoise being the Annals of Ireland from the earliest times to 1408 AD*, Dublin University Press, 1896, edited by Reverend Denis Murphy LLD MRIA, Vice President, Royal Society of Antiquities, Ireland, facsimile reprint Llanerch Publishers, 1993.

various families. The original Gaelic manuscript has been lost. The editor's preface said the original *Annals* were supposedly in the possession of Sir Richard Nagle, a descendant of the translator on his mother's side. It was believed some parts discredited his family and he would not allow it to be examined.

The Annals of the Kingdom of Ireland (*Annála Ríoghachta Éireann*), also known as *The Annals of the Four Masters* [10] (*Annála nag Ceithre Máistrí*), written in circa 1632, contain much of the same information as the *Annals of Clonmacnoise* and tell essentially the same story.

It was thought that John O'Hart's source for his book *Irish Pedigrees or the Origin and Stem of the Irish Nation,* [11] published in 1876, was the *Annals of the Four Masters*, but it covers the period from the biblical deluge (2,242 years after the creation) to 1616 AD, while the *Annals of Clonmacnoise* begins with the biblical creation and ends 208 years earlier in 1408. John O'Hart's work covers both of these periods and it appears he may have used both sources.

Many early chronicles were written by monks, based on ancient verbal histories, centuries after the events occurred. The monks typically listed generations beginning with Adam and Eve up to the Middle-Ages, for which there is no evidence, and they added Christian elements and divine events in times long before the people discussed knew anything about Christianity.

Writing was introduced into Ireland in the 5th century AD [12] in the form of funerary inscriptions engraved in Ogham.[13, 14] This was about the time when King Aodh Dubh of Munster and his successor King Finghin were born. There were 79 preceding generations of kings in *The Annals of Clonmacnoise.* However, it has been demonstrated that people in pre-literate societies, without written records, can remember their histories and genealogies for hundreds of years. There are several instances of historians discounting ancient annals as mythology and they were later proven by archaeologists to be basically true, discounting exaggerations for

---

10 *The Annals of Ireland Translated from the Original Irish of the Four Masters with Annotations* by Philip MacDermott, translator, Bryan Geraghty Verlag, 1846.

11 *Irish pedigrees; or, The origin and stem of the Irish nation*. John O'Hart. J. Duffy and Co. 1892.

12 The Celts, First Masters of Europe, Christiane Eluère, translated from French by Dauphine Briggs, Thames & Hudson, 1993, page 123.

13 Ogham is an old alphabet from Ireland consisting of lines and dashes vertically on rough standing memorial stones. It has fifteen consonants as lines touching or crossing an edge of the stone and five vowels as notches on the edge.

14 Merriam Webster Dictionary.

political reasons, superstitions and mystical elements commonly believed at the time. Examples are:

- Homer's [15] descriptions of the Trojan War in circa 1194 BC and the fall of Troy.
- The Vinland Saga [16] says Leif Ericsson settled in North America in circa 980 AD and the settlement lasted almost 500 years.
- The Saga of the Ynglings [17] says Scandinavia was populated by the migration of Óthin and his followers from the Sea of Asov near the Black Sea.

Like many early chronicles, *The Annals of Clonmacnoise* begins with Adam and Eve and lists Irish kings up to 1408. Because the early parts were passed on verbally for centuries some historians consider these parts mythical, but they certainly have core elements of truth. There is archaeological, linguistic and DNA evidence that supports the statements made in *The Annals of Clonmacnoise.* From the 5th century on, the information is supported by other historical accounts.

Before the Gaelic Celts arrived in Ireland

The Welsh historian Nennius [18] wrote in circa 796 AD that when the children of Israel crossed the Red Sea and the Scots came to Ireland, Ireland was uninhabited. Nennius was not correct. There were already inhabitants in Ireland long before the Gaelic Celts arrived. Ireland has a great many Mesolithic and Neolithic monuments, such as ring stones, standing stones, dolmens, ring forts, radial cairns etc. that are dated before 2500 BC.[19, 20] Archaeological sites revealed tools, weapons and household implement that show Ireland was inhabited in the Mesolithic period after the last ice age from circa 8000 BC. In the Neolithic period from 4000 BC to 2000 BC, agriculture and animal husbandry was practiced in Ireland. In the Bronze Age from 1200 to 700 BC, bronze weapons, tools and household goods were manufactured in Ireland. [21]

---

[15] *The Iliad*, Homer, William Benton Publisher, Best Books of the Western World, 1952.
[16] *The Vinland Saga,* translated from Nordic by Magnus Magnusson and Hermann Pálsson, 1965, Penguin Books.
[17] *The Saga of the Ynglings* in the *Heimskringala*, Snorri Sturluson, translated by Lee M. Hollander, University of Texas Press, 1964.
[18] *Historia Brittorum,* Nennius, circa 796 AD.
[19] *Exploring West Cork,* Jack Roberts, Bandia Publishing, 2009.
[20] *The antiquities of the Beara Peninsula,* Jack Roberts, Bandia Publishing, 2007
[21] *Ancient Ireland, Life Before the Celts*, Laurence Flanagan, Gill & MacMillan, 2000.

From where did the Celts come?

The *Annals of Clonmacnoise* say the Irish came from Scythia and travelled to Egypt, then to Spain. They then travelled from Spain to Ireland. The *Annals* say the Scots came from Spain and are the same people as the Irish. The ancient Scottish chronicles also say the Scots came from Spain, but the Irish were already there when the Scots arrived in Ireland.

Nennius wrote in circa 796 AD that the Scots came from Spain to Ireland and landed at Dalreita (the northwestern part of Antrim in Ulster). These versions are not mutually exclusive. The Scots did live in Northern Ireland for centuries until they migrated to the land of the Picts, present-day Scotland, in the 4th century AD. When Middle Age literature mentions Scotia, it means Northern Ireland.

There is some credibility in the *Annals of Clonmacnoise* statement that the Celts were in Scythia and Egypt and Spain. Until near the end of the 20th century, historians and archeologists believed the Urnfield Culture people [22] (1800 – 750 BC) were probably the ancestors of the Celts, or perhaps were proto-Celts. The remains of the earliest people definitely known to be Celtic were found in what is now Hallstatt [23], Austria. They lived there between 800 and 400 BC. Later the people of the La Tène Culture,[24] who emerged from the Hallstatt culture, lived in Switzerland and along the Rhine River. Celts migrated over most of Europe and into Asia Minor and have been called the first Pan-European culture. They encountered Alexander the Great and early Greeks, who gave them the name Celts. Celtic gold and other artifacts have been found in many parts of Europe, as far away as Russia [25] and the surrounding area. The Celtic Boii tribe was in Russia, Scythia, Syria and Egypt all in circa 300 BC.[26] These dates, from historians and archaeologists, do not exactly tally with the sequence of events the *Annals of Clonmacnoise* described, but it does show that Celts were in the places the *Annals of Clonmacnoise* said the Irish migrated.

---

[22] *Die Zeit der Kelten*, John Haywood, Thames & Hudson, translated into German from *Historical Atlas of the Celtic World*, 2001, page 30-31.

[23] Ibidem, pages 32-33.

[24] Ibidem, pages 34-35.

[25] I Celti, Gruppo Editoriale Fabbri, Comitato Amici di Palazzo Grassi, Presidente Feliciano Benevenuti, 1991, pages 778, 792.

[26] *Die Zeit der Kelten*, John Haywood, Thames & Hudson, translated into German from *Historical Atlas of the Celtic World*, 2001, page 37.

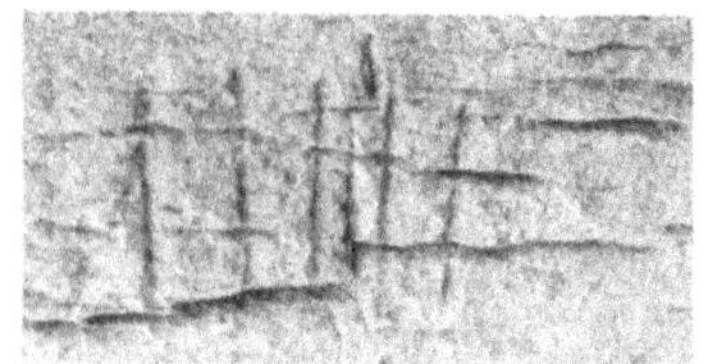

Ogham inscriptions are usually on standing memorial stones with 15 consonants as lines and five vowels as notches on the edge.

Neolithic stone axes, of porcellanite, from Tievebulliagh, Ireland. Courtesy of Creative Commons License.

Dolmen, near Waterville, County Kerry.

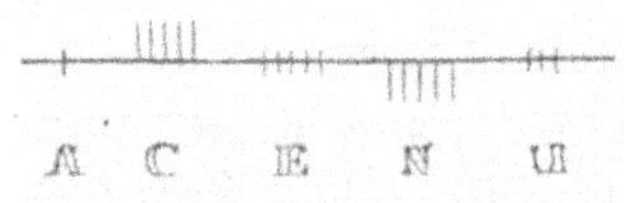

Translation of an Ogham inscription at Dunloe. Courtesy of Creative Commons License.

Ring fort near Waterville, County Kerry.

Ogham standing stone at Derrynane, County Kerry.

Staige ring fort near Castlecove, County Kerry, circa 2,000 years old, 30 meters in diameter, 6 meters high, 4 meter thick, without mortar.

Stone circle in Kenmare, County Kerry, circa 3,000 years old. The stones are aligned to predict astronomical events.

Did the Celts really begin with the Hallstatt people or were they much earlier? The above scenario originated with Herodotus [27], a Greek historian who lived from circa 484 to 425 BC. Herodotus wrote that the Celts lived at the source of the Danube River.

Herodotus knew about the Celts before 425 BC, but he did not know where the Danube originated. He thought the source of the Danube was in the Pyrenees Mountains, between what is now Spain and France. The source of the Danube is actually in southern Germany. This apparently caused historians to associate the remains found in nearby Hallstatt, Austria, with the beginning of the Celts and this idea persisted until near the end of the 20th century.

Evidence that the Gaelic Celts came from Spain

Several Celtic tribes were in Spain well before the Romans occupied it and written history of Iberia began. There is still a part of Spain called Galicia with a Celtic culture. It lies on the Atlantic coast in the north of the country. Celtic tribes, such as the Lusitani, Cantabri, Celtici, Vettoni, Vacciani, Callaici and Bracari are known to have been in Iberia in what is now north-western Spain well before 700 BC and some tribes had mixed with the aboriginal Iberians and are called Celtiberi.

Archaeological evidence

Until about 8,000 years ago, the sea level was lower and continental Europe, Ireland and the British Isles were one land mass. The North Sea and English Channel were dry land and Ireland did not become an island until circa 5000 BC. Professor Barry Cunliffe [28], an authority on the archaeology of the Atlantic coast of Europe, believes that over 7,000 years ago, in the late Mesolithic era, there was a cultural unity with extensive trading from west Scotland along the Atlantic coast to Spain and Portugal that persisted until modern times.[29] The genetic picture shows the Celts have been moving along the Atlantic coast from Spain and Portugal to Ireland and the western British Isles since the end of the last Ice Age.[30]

[27] *The Histories, Herodotus, Great Works of the Western World*, editor Robert Maynard Hutchins, 1952.

[28] Barry Cunliffe was professor of archaeology at Southampton University until 1972 when he became professor of archaeology at Oxford University. He has written extensively on the archaeology of the Atlantic coast of Europe.

[29] *The Origins of the British*, Stephen Oppenheimer, Constable & Robinson, 2006, pages 1-3.

[30] Ibidem, page 476.

Steve Olson [31] wrote that the number of Celts increased faster than their DNA. He questioned if we should call the Celts a culture rather than a people. This suggests other people joined them and were assimilated into their culture, possibly through marriage, for economic reasons or for protection. This happened with the Germanic tribes. For example: In his *Getica,* Jordanes [32] wrote in 551 AD that the Germanic Goths left Sweden in four boats and landed near the mouth of the Vistula River, now in Poland. Two hundred years later when they crossed the Danube River into Roman territory, they were a significant and threatening force. The tribe's growth was far too great to be accounted for only by reproduction, therefore they must have assimilated many others in their travels.

Linguistic evidence

Professor Colin Renfrew [33] wrote in 1987 that the Indo-European languages [34] emerged in Anatolia. When the Celts arrived in Spain the Celtic language had not yet separated as a new branch of the Indo-European language tree. [35] This is confirmed by new research in 2012 that shows the Indo-European language group originated in Anatolia and the Celtic language separated from the Balto-Slavic branch 5,000 years ago. Insular Celtic (Ireland and the British Isles) separated as a distinct branch of the Celtic language 4,500 years ago.[36] This places Celts in Ireland before circa 2500 BC. According to the *Annals of Clonmacnoise,* the early Gaelic explorers in Ireland were entertained by the local people and conversed with them. Therefore they must have spoken a similar language.

DNA Evidence

DNA research shows that Celts were in Ireland in the Neolithic period, and 88% of the Irish population today are descendants of people who arrived before the first farmers [37] who brought goats, sheep, and cattle from Spain to Ireland 4,500 years ago. Recent DNA studies show a clear relationship between the Irish and the

---

[31] *Mapping Human History,* Steve Olsen, Bloomsbury Publishing, 2002, page 184.

[32] *De origin actibusque Gestarum (The Origin and Deeds of the Getae),* commonly known as the *Getica,* Jordanes, 551 AD. Jordanes was an official and historian in the reign of the Gothic King Theodoric the Great, when he ruled Italy.

[33] Colin Renfrew succeeded Barry Cunliffe as professor of archaeology at Southampton University, when Barry Cunliffe received the professorship at Oxford University in 1972.

[34] The prototype language from which many European languages and others such as Sanskrit, Persian and Hittite emerged. The latest research indicates it originated in Anatolia.

[35] The Origins of the British, Stephen Oppenheimer, Constable & Robinson, 2006, pages 65, 99, 285-289.

[36] Quentin Atkinson, evolutionary biologist, et al, University of Auckland, New Zealand, *Science,* August 2012.

[37] *The Origins of the British*, Stephen Oppenheimer, Constable & Robinson, 2006, pages 470-472.

Basque.[38, 39, 40] The first historical mention of the Basque is by the Roman historians Strabo [41] and Plinius.[42] The Basque were probably the aboriginal people of the Iberian Peninsula and were in Spain well before the Celts arrived there.[43] The Basque language is not part of the Indo-European language group and evidence supports the idea that the Basque inhabited Spain before the spread of the Indo-European languages. [44] A DNA research report published in 2010 [45] indicates the R1b haplotype entered Europe in either the Mesolithic or Neolithic era. Other DNA studies show that the Irish [46, 47] and Basque [48, 49] share the highest percentage of R1b populations.This sets the dating of the origin of the Celts back thousands of years before the Hallstatt culture and is scientific proof of a long term connection between the Basques in Spain and the Irish Celts.

The arrival of the Celts in Ireland

The *Annals of Clonmacnoise* quote Collough O'Mór as saying 40 chiefs in 30 boats set out from Spain for Ireland and landed on the 17th of May 2934 (dated from the creation) one year before Christ's birth. *The Annals of the Four Masters* [50] says the party consisted of 150 people. Philip O'Sullivan Beare [51] writing in 1621 dated the migration 32 years later in the year 2966 (31 AD).

---

38 *The place of the Basques in the European Y-chromosome diversity landscape. European Journal of Human Genetics* 13 (12): 1293–302, Alonso, Santos; Flores, Carlos; Cabrera, Vicente; Alonso, Antonio; Martín, Pablo; Albarrán, Cristina; Izagirre, Neskuts; De La Rúa, Concepción et al, 2005.

39 Absher, D. M.; Tang, H.; Southwick, A. M.; Castro, A. M.; Ramachandran, S.; Cann, H. M.; Barsh, G. S. et al, 2008. *Worldwide Human Relationships Inferred from Genome-Wide Patterns of Variation.* Science 319 (5866): 1100–4.

40 *The place of the Basques in the European Y-chromosome diversity landscape.* Alonso *et al,* 2005. European Journal of Human Genetics 13 (12): 1293–1302.

41 *Geography Book III*, circa 17 AD, Strabo, Loeb Classical Library.

42 *Naturalis Historia*, Plinius (Pliny) 23–79 AD.

43 Spain and Portugal.

44 Spektrum der Wissenschaft, 4/2001, Luigi Luca Cavalli Sforza, page 22.

45 *A Predominantly Neolithic Origin for European Paternal Lineage,* Balaresque et al 2010.

46 *The Origins of the British – A Genetic Detective Story*, Stephen Oppenheimer, 2006, Constable and Robinson.

47 *Blood of the Isles: Exploring the Genetic Roots of Our Tribal History.* Brian Sykes, 2006, Bantam.

48 *The place of the Basques in the European Y-chromosome diversity landscape.* European Journal of Human Genetics, Alonso, Santos; Flores, Carlos; Cabrera, Vicente; Alonso, Antonio; Martín, Pablo; Albarrán, Cristina; Izagirre, Neskuts; De La Rúa, Concepción et al. 2005.

49 *Worldwide Human Relationships Inferred from Genome-Wide Patterns of Variation. Science,* Absher, D. M Tang, H.; Southwick, A. M.; Castro, A. M.; Ramachandran, S.; Cann, H. M.; Barsh, G. S. et al, 2008.

50 *The Annals of Ireland Translated from the Original Irish of the Four Masters with Annotations* by Philip MacDermott, translator, Bryan Geraghty Verlag, 1846.

51 *Historie Catholicae Hibernice Compendium*, Philip O'Sullivan.

Historians generally accept that the Celts came to Ireland after the time of Alexander the Great (356-323 BC) in circa 300 BC. But recent evidence shows Celtic people were certainly in Ireland before the Gaelic Celtic language developed into a separate stem of Celtic language thousands of years earlier. It is possible some Celts went to Ireland in 1 BC, as the *Annals of Clonmacnoise* said, but that does not account for King Milesius' birth date in 1046 BC and the statement that his sons founded the Irish kingdoms, unless the 300 BC, 1 BC and 31 AD dates are all incorrect.

If 150 Celts arrived in 30 boats, they were certainly greatly outnumbered by the indigenous population. DNA research by Professor Steven Oppenheimer [52] showed that 88% of the present population of Ireland are descended from the original founding lineage that arrived after the last Ice Age. For the British Isles as a whole, only 83% of the population are descendants of the first immigrants after the last Ice Age 20,000 years ago. Only 12% are descendants of the immigration 5,000 years later and 5% from all later immigrations. This can be explained by the fact the immigrants were probably small family groups and the earliest groups had a long time to multiply before later family groups arrived.

The Gaelic Celts dominated Ireland from their arrival until the 13th century. They must have either subjugated the indigenous people, or more likely merged with them. The *Annals of Clonmacnoise* does say when the thirty boats of settlers arrived, they were met with hostility. They met the King of Ireland at Taylten (now Teltown), fought a great battle and overthrew him.

> " ... *On the comeing of the sonns of Melitus of Spaine to this kingdom: of the overthroe they gave to [King] Twany de Dnan...* "

The O'Sullivan clan dominated its domain until the 16th century because they moved to a better-protected rough mountainous area in Kerry and Cork in circa 1192. The Gaelic Celts divided Ireland into four kingdoms: Munster, Leinster, Ulster and Connaught. There was a high king, but he had little authority over the provincial kings. The various tribes were virtually autonomous.[53]

---

[52] The origins of the British, Professor Stephen Oppenheimer, Constable & Robinson, 2006, page 470.

[53] *The Oak and the Serpent*, Dr. Gary B. O'Sullivan MD FACOG FACS, Gold Stag Communications, 2007, page 74-75.

Early history of the Irish

Rather than go through all of the many Irish kings who were ancestors of the O'Sullivans, I will mention only the major ones relevant to the Sullivan line after they arrived in Ireland. Readers interested in all of the Irish kings will find this information in:

- *The Annals of Clonmacnoise,*[54]
- *The Annals of Ireland,* aka *Annals of the Four Masters,*[55]
- *Irish Pedigrees or the Origin and Stem of the Irish Nation,*[56]
- *The Oak and the Serpent.*[57]

The Oak and the Serpent also describes the thirty-two known Sullivan castles and manors.

According to *The Annals of Clonmacnoise,* Milesius, born in 1046 BC, was king of the Celts in Spain and his sons led the migration to Ireland in 1 BC. Both of these dates cannot be correct.

Recent archaeological, linguistic, and DNA research confirms the events described in *The Annals of Clonmacnoise,* but the dates are probably in error.

Finghin, King of Munster and Lord of Cashel (born in 571 AD), was the 58th king and direct descendant of King Milesius. Finghin was the last King of Munster of his line and his primogeniture descendants became the O'Sullivan clan. When King Finghin died, his son was too young to be elected hence his younger brother Failbehe Flann was elected King of Munster. Flann's descendants, the MacCarthys, became kings of Munster.

Eochaid Súilleabháinn, born in 874 AD, was the descendant of King Finghin in the eighth generation. He was the first to be called *Súilleabháinn,* anglicized as Sullivan. His son Lorcan took the name Lorcan MacSúilleabháinn, (meaning son of

---

[54] *The Annals of Clonmacnoise being the Annals of Ireland from the earliest times to 1408 AD,* Dublin University Press, 1896, edited by Reverend Denis Murphy LLD MRIA, Vice President, Royal Society of Antiquities Ireland, facsimile reprint Llanerch Publishers 1993.

[55] *The Annals of Ireland Translated from the Original Irish of the Four Masters with Annotations* by Philip MacDermott, translator, Bryan Geraghty Verlag, 1846.

[56] *Irish pedigrees; or, The origin and stem of the Irish Nation,* 1892, John O'Hart, J. Duffy and Co.

[57] *The Oak and the Serpent,* Dr. Gary B. O'Sullivan MD FACOG FACS, Gold Stag Communications, 2007.

Map of Ireland. After the Gaelic Celts arrived in Ireland, they divided Ireland into four kingdoms: Leinster, Munster, Ulster and Connaught. Taken from *Pacata Hiberna*, by Sir George Carew, Lowney & Company, 1896.

Sullivan), and his son Baudhach took the name Buahdhach Ó Súilleabháinn. At that time, it was not a surname. It was a title indicating he was the Sullivan clan chief called *The O'Sullivan.*[58]

The *Annals of Clonmacnoise* lists Irish kings *"from the earliest times"* and say the O'Sullivans and the MacGillycuddys,[59] a sept of the O'Sullivan clan, are the surviving descendants of King Finghin of Munster who died in 618 AD. The MacGillycuddy sept fought the English and lost two major battles at Kinsale and Dunboy in 1602, yet managed to retain the clan's property until Oliver Cromwell's war against the Irish from 1649 to 1650. Their clan chief Donough burned his castle to keep it from falling into the hands of the English then fled to France.

The O'Sullivan clan in Historical times

The O'Sullivans had a castle called Knockgraffon (*Cnoc Graffon or Cnoc Rafann* or *Cnoc Rath Fionn,* Hill of Fort Fionn) before 170 AD, 1,022 years before they were defeated by the English in 1192. It is mentioned in the *Book of Munster* [60] that Eoghan (Owen), born in 702 AD, Crown Prince of Munster and tenth great-grandfather of King Finghin lived in Knockgraffon. But the family probably had a fortification there much earlier. Knockgraffon is not far from Clonmel on the river Suir and near Cashel, both in Tipperary.

The Rock of Cashel of Tipperary, published by Dúchas, says Cashel Castle dates back to the 4th century AD.[61] King Cor of Munster, born in 340 AD, 5th great-grandfather of King Finghin, left Knockgraffon Castle and built Cashel Castle of oak on a 30-meters-high (98.42 feet) limestone rock in the Golden Vale of Tipperary. It was later called the Rock of Cashel (*Carraig Phádraig).* This became the traditional seat of the Kings of Munster, one of the original four kingdoms of Ireland. Cashel's greatest king, Brian Boru, later became High King of Ireland. Little of the old castle has survived and the current buildings were built in the 12th and 13th centuries.

The Eóghanacht nobles, who became the O'Sullivan clan, continued to reside at Knockgraffon Castle. The O'Sullivans had considerable wealth and power and their

---

[58] *The Oak and the Serpent*, Gary B. O'Sullivan MD FACOG FACS, Gold Stag Communications, 2007, pages 53-60, The Clan Master's Genealogical Chart.

[59] MacGillycuddy is a sept of the O'Sullivan clan.

[60] *Eóghanacht Genealogies Book of Munster,* 1702, The Reverend Eugene O'Keefe, Doneraile, North Cork.

[61] The Rock of Cashel in Tipperary, Dúchas Heritage Service Department of Arts, Heritage, Geeltacht and the Islands, page 5.

lands included Clonmel, Cahir, Carrick-on-Suir and Cashel. GioUa-na-Neev O'Heerin, who died in 1420, wrote:

> *" ... O'Sullivan, who delights not in violence*
> *rules over the extensive Eóghanacht of Munster,*
> *about Knockgraffon broad lands he obtained,*
> *won by his victorious arms, in conflicts and battles... .*

The Sullivan clan chief was called *The O'Sullivan Mór* (The Great Sullivan) and this title was passed on to the eldest son until Cragh, born in 1375. When Cragh O'Sullivan died in 1410, his younger son Rory was elected clan chief.

From the death of Cragh on, the Irish chose their leaders under the law of tanistry, where all of the adult male relatives of the clan chief, including cousins and uncles, voted for the wisest and most competent of the clan chief's relatives to lead the clan as the chief's successor. The successor, called the *Tanist,* was chosen in the clan chief's lifetime in the event of unexpected death. Tanistry often resulted in wars and feuds and was declared illegal in 1667, during the first year of King James I of England's reign.

Cragh's eldest son Donal never had any title, breaking the tradition of Brehan law [62] that had existed since the time of King Milesius. Donal was called Donal O'Sullivan MacCragh (son of Cragh) creating a new sept[63] of the clan.

The O'Sullivan MacCragh sept is the oldest bloodline of the Irish Royal family. It was still recognized as a royal bloodline and its eligibility to be elected was accepted and honored.[64] Rory O'Sullivan's bloodline continued in the O'Sullivan Mór leaders until The O'Sullivan Mór died without legitimate sons in 1768 and the chieftainship reverted to the line of Cragh's eldest son Donal O'Sullivan MacCragh.

Two other main branches of the O'Sullivan clan are descended from King Finghin: The O'Sullivan Mór and O'Sullivan Beare. The O'Sullivan Beare descends from

---

[62] The inheritance part of Brehan law was similar to the English law of primogeniture where the eldest son inherited the title and all property.

[63] A sept is a branch of an Irish clan.

[64] *The Oak and the Serpent*, Gary B. O'Sullivan MD FACOG FACS, Gold Stag Communications, 2007, pages 138, 149.186-188.

Giolla na bhFlainn, son of Donal O'Sullivan Mór.[65] The O'Sullivan Mór sept descends from his brother Giolla Mochuda.[66]

"Bheiṫ gan Finġin, beiṫ gan Móir,
Do Chaiseal is adhbhar bróin,
Is ionann is beiṫ gan ní,
Más é Failbhe Flann bus rí."

"To be without Finghin, to be without Mor,
To Cashel is cause of sorrow,
It is the same as to be without anything
If Failbhe Flann be the King."

The Book of Rights, complied in 1390 from earlier sources, describes dissatisfaction with King Failbhe Flann of Munster.

The Eóganachta princes were not satisfied that King Finghin's younger brother, Failbhe Flann, was elected king of Munster and the O'Sullivan clan had a more valid claim to the throne. In 1214, this dissent became more acute because King Dermot MacCarthy accepted the authority of the English king and the lords regarded this as treachery. They demanded that Donal O'Sullivan Mór assume the throne. King Dermot was advised to eliminate this threat. He invited all of the adult male O'Sullivans nobles to a banquet at Raithin na nGaradhthe and massacred them all, including the clan chief's eldest son Giolla Mochoda O'Sullivan. Only two O'Sullivans with a claim to the throne did not attend the banquet and therefore survived: Donal's younger son Giolla na bhFlainn and Donal's grandson Dunlong . [67] This is mentioned in the *Annals of Clonmacnoise:* [68]

> " ... *MacArthy gave a great overthrow to the O'Sulevans. He killed O'Sulevan the Bald and two sons of O'Sulevan the Great, Owen and Conner O'Sulevan Beare and many others ... .*"

The Annals of the Four Masters, book 4, page 272 reported the same event.[69]

---

[65] *Materials for a History of the Family of John Sullivan of Berwick, New England: and of the O'Sullivans of Ardea, Ireland 1893,* taken from the works of Sir Bernard Burke, by Gertrude Euphoria Meredith and Thomas Coffin Amory, Page 90.

[66] Ibidem, Page 90.

[67] *The Oak and the Serpent*, Gary B. O'Sullivan MD FACOG FACS, Gold Stag Communications, 2007, page 1.

[68] *The Annals of Clonmacnoise being the Annals of Ireland from the earliest times to 1408 AD,* Dublin University Press, 1896, edited by Reverend Denis Murphy LLD MRIA, Vice President, Royal Society of Antiquities Ireland, facsimile reprint Llanerch Publishers, 1993.

[69] *The Annals of the Kingdom of Ireland (Annála Ríoghachta Éireann)* also known as *The Annals of the Four Masters (Annála nag Ceithre Máistrí)*, 1632, annotations by Philip MacDermott, translation by Bryan Geraghty, 1846, M1398.17.

Maiḋm mór aḋbal la Mág Carṫaiġ Cairbreaċ for Ua Suilleaḃain, ⁊ da ṁac uí Shuilleḃain, Eoġan ⁊ Concoḃar do marḃaḋ is in ccaiṫġliaḋ sin, ⁊ soċaiḋe imaille friú.

Quotation from the Annals of the Four Masters: "... A very great defeat was given by MacCarthy of Carberry to O'Sullivan, and the two sons of O'Sullivan, Eoghan [Owen] and Coner, together with many others, were slain in the conflict..."

The MacCarthy king of Munster was the nominal overlord of the O'Sullivan clan, but in fact since 1169, the O'Sullivan chiefs were princes of the Eóganachta nation and were virtually independent of the King MacCarthy Mór of Munster.

The colonization of Ireland by England

The reign of King Henry II of England, 1154 to 1189 [70]

In 1155, King Henry II of England wrote a letter to Pope Adrian IV, who was also English, seeking permission to invade Ireland *to reform the church.* Ireland was Catholic and not in need of reformation, but Pope Adrian issued the *Laudabiliter Bull* authorizing King Henry to invade Ireland under certain conditions. One of these conditions was that Ireland and all other Christian islands came under the jurisdiction of the pope. Since this included England, King Henry did not invade Ireland at that time. [71]

King Henry II had permission to invade Ireland from Pope Adrian IV and landed a large force at Waterford in 1171. Courtesy of Creative Commons License.

Ireland originally had four kingdoms, but in the 12th century, Ireland was divided politically into many kingdoms with fluid borders, competing against one another for control of the island. The Lords O'Sullivan Mór were the principal rulers of the kingdom of Munster.

Michael Richter [72] wrote that Diarmaid MacMurrough (*Diarmaid Mac Murchada*) invited the Cambro-Normans [73] of Wales, into Ireland in 1166 to help him regain

[70] The Kings & Queens of England and Scotland, Edmund Swinglehurst, 2002, S. Webb & Son Ltd, pages 48-49.

[71] New England Historical and Genealogical Register, volume XIX, October 1865, Number 2, page 289.

[72] *Milestones in Irish History*, Mercer Press, Ireland, 1986, chapter 4, The Norman Invasion of 1169 by Michael Richter, pages 41-51.

[73] The Normans invaded and conquered England in 1066. Cambro-Normans were Norman knights who settled in Wales after the Norman invasion.

Knockgraffon Castle. The Sullivans had Knockgraffon Castle from before 170 AD until they were defeated by the English in 1192 when it was confiscated. Only the ruin of the tower house remains. Courtesy of Creative Commons license.

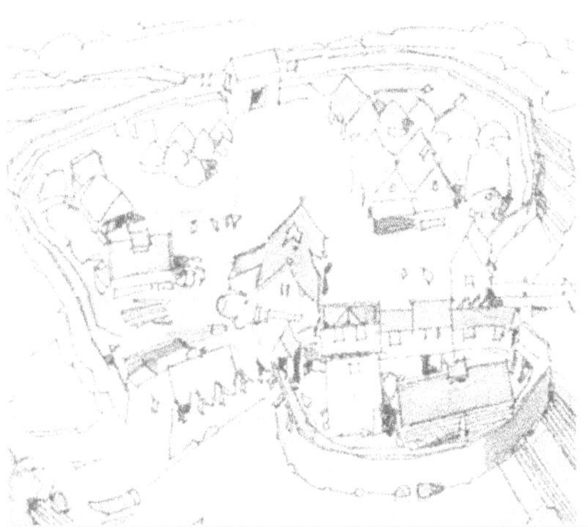

Archaeologist reconstruction of Knockgraffon Castle. how it probably looked before 1192. Courtesy of David Pollock and the Irish Office of Public Works.

The ruin of the abbey at Knockgraffon. The cemetery is still in use.

The Rock of Cashel. King Cor of Munster built Cashel Castle of oak, called the Rock of Cashel in circa 300 AD. It became the traditional seat of the kings of Munster. The surviving buildings are from the 12th and 13th centuries. Courtesy of Creative Commons License.

Clonmel town wall west tower in 2010. Courtesy of Creative Commons License.

The city of Cashel in 2012.

Cahir Castle, one of the largest castles in Ireland was built on an island in the River Suir in 1142, in O'Sullivan territory, by Conor O'Brian, Prince of Thomond. In 1375, the English granted it to James Butler, Earl of Ormond.

Cahir Castle in 1845, from *Concise History of Ireland*, by P. W. Joyce LLD, pubished in 1903.

Ormond Castle in Carrick-on-Suir was built before 1315 and in 1316 was granted to the Butler Family of England. James Butler was later created 1st Earl of Ormond. Courtesy of James Yardley, Creative Commons License.

Carrick-on-Suir Tipperary, old bridge. Courtesy of Humphrey Bolton, Creative Common License.

the kingdom he lost because he abducted Dervor Giolla, wife of Tiernan O'Rourke. After Muircheartach MacLochlainn, High King of Ireland, died in 1166, Diarmaid MacMurrugh, was exiled by his successor, Ruaidhrí Ó Conchobhair.

He fled to Normandy and obtained permission from King Henry II of England to use his subjects to regain his kingdom. In 1167, MacMurrough gained the support of the Cambro-Norman Lord Richard de Clare, 2nd Earl of Pembroke, aka [74] Strongbow.[75]

Richard fitzGodbert de Roche was the first Norman knight to arrive in Ireland in 1167 and in 1169 the main force of Normans and Welsh mercenaries landed in Loch Garman, Wexford and Leinster. They quickly captured several key towns. Diarmaid gave Strongbow his daughter Aoife in marriage and in 1170, Strongbow became Dairmaid's son-in-law and heir to his kingdom.

This is a blunder repeated throughout history. The historian Niccolò di Bernardo de Machiavelli (1469-1527) wrote the book *The Prince*.[76] The purpose was to explain how successful kingdoms were run. One of his pieces of advice was: *Never invite a foreign army into your kingdom.* There are numerous disastrous examples of this advice not being followed which changed the course of history:

- In 297 AD, the Germanic Goths [77] became Roman federates and entered Roman territory to protect their borders against other Germanic tribes and the Huns. The Romans made other Germanic tribes federates, for example early Frankish kings were governors of Roman Belgae. The Germanic Frankish Confederation ultimately controlled most of the Roman Empire and the Goths the rest.

- In 420 AD, the Romans invited the Visigoths [78] into Spain to drive out the Vandals and Alans. The Visigoths later ruled Spain until 711 AD when they were conquered by the Muslims.

- In 449 AD, the Briton King Vertigern [79] invited the Germanic Angels, Saxons and Jutes into his kingdom to defend against the Scots and Picts. These Germanic tribes eventually controlled all of England. The name England and the name of the English language comes from the Angels. The Anglo-Saxons ruled England until the Norman invasion in 1066.

---

[74] Also known as.
[75] New England Historical and Genealogical Register, volume XIX, October 1865, Number 2, page 289.
[76] *The Prince,* Machiavelli, Penguin Classics, 2003, translated by George Bull.
[77] *History of the Goths*, Herwig Wolfram, translated from German by Thomas J. Dunlap, University of California Press, 1988, page 59.
[78] *The Goths in Spain*, E. A. Thompson, Oxford Clarendon Press, 1969, page 2.
[79] *The Anglo-Saxon Chronicles, Winchester Manuscript*, year 449, translated by Michael Swanton, Phoenix Press, 1996, page 12.

Because of Diarmaid MacMurrough's blunder of inviting an Anglo-Norman [80] army into his country, Ireland did not recover its partial independence from England for 754 years until 1921 and full independence for 782 years in 1949.

Ireland was almost the only country in Europe that had never been dominated by the Romans and overrun by Germanic and Slavic barbarians after the fall of the Roman Empire. Ireland did not suffer through the Dark Ages when classical knowledge was lost in circa 400 AD during the rule of the invading tribes. Europe did not recover from the Dark Ages until the Renaissance, which began in Italy in circa 1350 and later in the rest of Europe. Until the Norman invasion in 1169 Ireland remained a purely Celtic [81] culture with a high level of learning and literature, while in Europe the lost knowledge of the Greeks and Romans was only preserved in the great Arab libraries of Alexandria, Cordoba, Toledo and Sicily. The invaders were a product of the Dark Ages with a feudal culture inferior to the Irish at that time.

King Henry II feared a rival Norman state in Ireland. He already had Pope Adrian IV's authority to invade Ireland through the *Laudabiliter papal Bull* of 1155. In 1171, Henry landed a large fleet at Waterford and was the first king of England to enter Ireland. He_proclaimed Dublin and Waterford Royal Cities and in 1172, Pope Alexander III, Adrian's successor, granted Irish lands to Henry. Henry gave the title *Dominus Hiberniae* (Lord of Ireland) and his Irish territories to his younger son John. John succeeded Henry and Ireland became the property of the English crown.

Many Irish kings accepted King Henry because they saw it as weakening the kingdom of Leinster and the Hiberno-Normans [82] who supported Diarmaid and Strongbow, but Henry could not control the Normans. The Anglo-Norman John de Courcy invaded and captured most of East Ulster, and in 1177, Raymond FitzGerald captured Limerick and North Munster. Other Anglo-Normans created their own kingdoms. The Anglo-Normans colonized Ireland and the invading lords were awarded vast tracts of land, confiscated from the Irish lords. They were called *undertakers* because they undertook to resettle the land with English, Scottish, and Norman tenant farmers. Ireland was democratic with a barter system, but the

[80] Anglo-Normans were descendants of the Normans who ruled England after the Norman invasion in 1066.

[81] With the exception of some Norse and Danish Viking settlements in coastal areas. The first Viking raids in Ireland were in 798 AD. There were settlements in Dublin, Wexford and Cork from 853 until the settlers were defeated in 980.

[82] The Hiberno-Normans were Norman lords who settled in Ireland and adopted Irish customs, clothing, married Irish women and showed little fealty to the Anglo-Norman settlers.

foreign land lords wanted a feudal system with profitable commercial enterprises. Some Irish lords were reduced to peasant tenant farmers.

The reign of King Richard I of England, 1189-1199 83

After a long resistance against the English, in 1192 during the reign of King Richard I, clan chief Donal O'Sullivan Mór was decisively defeated and he lost his territory in Tipperary. The entire O'Sullivan clan moved to Counties Cork and Kerry in the south, which was a wild mountainous area easier to defend.

King Richard I. In the reign of King Richard I, the Lion Hearted, Donal O'Sullivan Mór was decisively defeated and lost his territory in Tipperary. Courtesy of Creative Commons License.

The reign of King Edward I of England, 1272-1307 [84]

In 1301, the papal taxation register was compiled. It was the first Irish census and it listed properties and their taxation value, similar to the Doomsday Book of William the Conqueror in England. During the 14th century, Gaelic lords rebelled with surprise raids against resources as well as garrisons. Henry III and Edward I were too distracted by events in England, Wales, Scotland, and their domains in France to support the Norman colonists in Ireland and as a result the Normans began to ally themselves more with the Irish than with England.

The reign of King Edward II of England, 1307-1327 [85]

In 1315, Edward de Brus, younger brother of King Robert de Brus (Robert the Bruce) of Scotland, invaded Ireland and the Irish lords rallied around him, but he lost the battle of Faughard after his troops had caused considerable destruction. Nevertheless the Irish lords won back large amounts of land.

The Hiberno-Normans began to adopt the Irish language and customs, intermarried with the Irish and sided with the Irish in conflicts with England. In 1367, the Irish

[83] The Kings & Queens of England and Scotland, Edmund Swinglehurst, 2002, Webb & Son, pages 52-53.
[84] Ibidem,64-65.
[85] Ibidem, pages 68-69.

King Edward I. In the reign of King Edward I, a papal taxation register listed all property and its taxable value. Courtesy of Creative Commons License.

King Edward II. In the reign of King Edward II, a law was passed forbidding the English from adopting Irish customs and marrying the Irish. Courtesy of Creative Commons License.

King Edward III. In the reigns of Edward III and Henry VII, England was distracted by events in England and France and they delegated their authority to the Earls of Kildare. Courtesy of Creative Commons License.

parliament was concerned about the *Gaelicisation* of Ireland and passed legislation banning people of English descent from speaking the Irish language, wearing Irish clothes or marrying the Irish. But the government had little direct authority outside the major towns, and the ban could not be enforced.

King Henry VII of England. Courtesy of Creative Commons License.

The reigns of King Edward III of England 1327-1377 [86] to King Henry VII, 1485-1509 [87]

During the reign of ring Edward III, through the reign of King Henry VII, the English kings were distracted by a long series of other problems and paid little attention to Ireland:

- The Hundred Years' War, from 1337 to 1454, during the reigns of Kings Edward III, Richard II, Henry IV, Henry V and Henry VI.
- The Peasant's Revolt in 1381.
- The plague in 1381, killed more urban Normans and

[86] The Kings & Queens of England and Scotland, Edmund Swinglehurst, 2002, S. Webb & Son Ltd, pages 74-75.

[87] Ibidem, pages 108-109.

English than rural Irish.

- The War of the Roses in the reigns of Kings Henry VI, Edward IV, Richard III and Henry VII from 1455 to 1485.

The English kings delegated their authority to the FitzGerald Earls of Kildare. English authority was also weakened in Ireland by famines that killed a large part of the population. During this period the Irish lords won back more of their land.

In 1404, a war broke out between the MacCarthys and the O'Sullivans and they were at war with one another off and on until the invasion by Queen Elizabeth in 1580. *The Annals of the Four Masters* said: [88]

> " ... *A war broke out between MacCarthy and O'Sullivan Boy. Turlough Meith MacMahon, who was at this time MacCarthy's chief maritime officer, came up at sea with O'Sullivan and the sons of Dermot MacCarthy, who were aiding O'Sullivan against MacCarthy; and he drowned O'Sullivan, and made a prisoner of Donnell, the son of Dermot MacCarthy, on this occasion. ...* "
>
> And in 1451 " ... *Dermot, the son of Teige, son of Cormac MacCarthy, was slain; and Dermot, the son of O'Sullivan More, was slain in revenge of him. ...* "
>
> And in 1498 " ... *Thomas Oge, the son of Thomas the Earl, son of Garrett the Earl, and Cormac Oge, the son of Cormac, son of Teige MacCarthy, followed Owen, the son of Teige, son of Cormac MacCarthy, in pursuit of a prey. On this occasion Owen himself, and his two sons; O'Sullivan Beare, i.e. Philip, the son of Dermot, with his son, Teige-an-Chaennaigh; Brian Oge MacSweeny, with many others, were slain by them. ...* "
>
> And in 1563 " ... *O'Sullivan Beare (Donal, the son of Dermot, son of Donnell, son of Donnellson of Dermot Balbh) was slain by a bad man, namely, MacGillycuddy; and if his father, Dermot, was a man of great renown, this Donnell was a worthy heir of him. His kinsman, Owen O'Sullivan, took his place. ...* "

[88] *The Annals of the Kingdom of Ireland (Annála Ríoghachta Éireann)* also known as *The Annals of the Four Masters (Annála nag Ceithre Máistrí)*, 1632, Annotations by Philip MacDermott, translation by Bryan Geraghty, 1846, M1404.12, M1451.13, M1498.10, M1463.2.

The reign of Queen Elizabeth I, 1558 to 1603 [89]

The most brutal and savage wars in Ireland were fought in the reign of Queen Elizabeth I when England practiced a scorched earth policy, killing men, women, children, prisoners, destroying crops, and everything that could be of any use. The policy was to terrorize colonial populations to discourage rebellions.

Queen Elizabeth I. The most savage wars against the Irish were fought in the reign of Queen Elisabeth I. Courtesy of Creative Commons License.

The O'Sullivan Mór (Ó Súilleabháinn Mór)

After a long resistance against the English, in 1600 O'Sullivan Mór lands were reduced to 459,270 acres (35 by 20 miles) in County Kerry. The O'Sullivan Mór resided in Dunkerron Castle, which lies two miles west of the town of Kenmare (founded 1670) on the Sneem Road. The castle was built by Owen O'Sullivan Mór in 1596 on a rock. The O'Sullivan clan was prominent in Kerry for centuries and Dunkerron Castle was an O'Sullivan Mór stronghold, but today lies in ruins.

In 1595, King Donal MacCarthy Mór, the last MacCarthy king, died with no heir. A person who said he was an illegitimate son claimed the throne, but the elders refused to coronate him. King MacCarthy Mór's son-in-law claimed the throne, but Queen Elizabeth I of England opposed him and the English Crown took over the inheritance and the kingship, proclaiming herself Queen of Ireland. Under both Irish Brehan law and the English law of primogeniture, the O'Sullivans had a better claim to the throne than any of the MacCarthys.[90]

The O'Sullivan Mór coat of arms.

[89] The Kings & Queens of England and Scotland, Edmund Swinglehurst, 2002, S. Webb & Son Ltd, pages 128-129.

[90] *The Oak and the Serpent*, Dr. Gary B. O'Sullivan MD FACOG FACS, Gold Stag Communications, 2007, page 279.

After the Cromwell revolution, between 1653 and 1658, the English confiscated Owen O'Sullivan Mór's lands and gave them to Sir William Petty with the title Baron of Dunkerron, but this was granted by an invading nation and was not regarded by the Irish as a valid title.

The O'Sullivan Beare (Ó Súilleabháinn Bhéarra)

The O'Sullivan Beare territory measured 656,100 acres (50 by 20 miles) in County Cork and included the Bay of Bantry, which is 10 miles wide at its widest point. The O'Sullivan Beare resided in Dunboy Castle (Caisleán Dhún Baoi) on the Beara Peninsula near Castletownbere (*Baile Chaisleáin Bhéarra)* in County Cork. The castle defended the harbor (Beare Haven) allowing the O'Sullivan Beare to control the Irish coast and collect sizeable taxes. Lord Dermod O'Sullivan Beare, the clan chief, built Dunboy castle in circa 1473. Queen Elizabeth I granted Sir Eoghan (Owen) O'Sullivan Beare the chief rents of the castle, town, and lands of Dunboy, with 57 *carrucates* [91] of other lands. In 1585, Sir Eoghan attended Perrot's Parliament in Dublin. King James I granted Sir Eoghan's son and heirs forever the chief rents of Dunboy. Colonel Donal O'Sullivan Beare, lost these estates for supporting the Stuarts, but in 1660, King Charles II of England restored them.

The O'Sullivan Beare coat of arms.

Lord "Red" Hugh O'Donal's signature, Aodh Odanihnaill, contracted as Aodh Odonin, from the *Ulster Journal of Archaeology*, II., PL. I., No 9.

The O'Sullivan Beare clan fought in the first Desmond Rebellion against Queen Elizabeth I, from 1569 to 1573, led by the Earl of Desmond. They were defeated by the English on the 23rd of February 1573. In 1594, during Queen Elizabeth I's reign while England was at war with Spain, Hugh O'Neill, Earl of Tyrone revolted against the English and Spain backed the Irish revolt. The English were unable to put down the revolt and in 1599, Queen Elizabeth I put Robert Devereau, 2nd Earl of Essex in charge. He was unsuccessful and returned to England in defiance of Queen Elisabeth's orders. In 1601, Queen Elizabeth I replaced him with Charles Blount,

[91] A *carrucate* is 100 acres; approximately the land that can be worked by one plough team in a year.

Dunkerron Castle had four carved stones over the chimney piece that are no longer there. The plaque pictures below were published in the *Journal of the Kilkenny and Southeast of Ireland Archaeological Society*, volume 2, 1858-1859. The inscription says: *This work was made on the 20th of April 1596 by Owen O'Sullivan Mór and Sily ni Donoguh MacCarthy Reagh* [wife of Owen]. It was reported that the stones are now over a well near the castle, but if so, they are no longer visible.

The ruins of Dunkerron Castle, the main stronghold of the O'Sullivan Mór.

The well near Dunkerron Castle.
The carved stones are not to be seen.

Plaque Inscription

Probably Owen O'Sullivan Mór.

Heraldic fugures.

Probably Owen O'Sullivan Mór's wife Sily.

Baron Montjoy and Earl of Rochester as Lord Deputy to Sir George Carew, 1st Earl of Totnes. In 1601, Lord Hugh O'Donal led a rebellion against the English supported by Spain. Several Irish clans took part in the rebellion, namely the O'Sullivan, O'Donal and O'Neill clans.

Spain committed 5,000 troops, but a Spanish Army of 3,500 troops, commanded by Don Juan del Águila, landed in Kinsale Harbor on the 23rd of September 1601 on the wrong side of the bay, and fortified themselves in Rincorran Castle.

The English had about 7,500 troops, with 6,800 infantry and 622 cavalry under command of the Lord Deputy. On the 16th of October, Montjoy marched towards Kinsale with only 4,300 able soldiers and with other reinforcements nearby on the way, camped on the north side of Kinsale.

There are no muster lists for O'Neill, but it is believed he had approximately 6,000 infantry and 520 cavalry. In terms of numbers and quality of troops, the advantage was clearly on the side of the Irish.[92]

The Battle of Kinsale (Cionn tSáile)

Sir George Carew, 1st Earl of Totnes was appointed President of Munster in 1600 and Montjoy was his lord deputy. Sir George Carew led the attack on Kinsale. He wrote that Don Juan del Águila left a captain with 150 men at Rincorran Castle near Kinsale and promised to relieve them if they were attacked, or bring them off in boats. When the Spanish discovered the English presence, they tried to evacuate their troops by boat at night, but were repelled by Captain Button with shots from his ship. The English began to bombard Rincorran Castle with two culverins [93], but after three shots, one carriage broke and by 2:00 PM, the other developed a defect. The Spaniards fired back killing two and destroying two of the lord deputy's hogsheads [94] of beer. Every Spanish shot fell near the lord deputy's tent. The Spanish tried again to relieve their men by boat and were beaten off. The repaired culverins were put into action, but after a few shots broke an axel. After it was repaired, a canon was added and a continuous bombardment began.

[92] English Warfare, 1511-1642 Mark Charles Fissell Routledge, 2001, page 227.
[93] Originally a crude musket, in the 16th and 17th centuries it became a long 18 pound cannon with serpent shaped handles.
[94] A barrel holding 54 U.S. gallons or 64.85 imperial gallons.

Sir George Carew had been a ship's captain in the Royal Navy and an artillery officer. He was dissatisfied that the shots were scattered and he told his Lord Deputy Montjoy to leave it to him. By 6:00 PM, the Spanish sounded a drum to indicate the wish to negotiate. They wanted to surrender the castle and leave with their arms. This was refused and the bombardment began anew. In the dark, the Spanish made a sortie with 1,500 men to overrun the English trenches and spike [95] the guns, but were driven back. English reinforcements continued to arrive and the six Spanish ships in the bay of Kinsale could not break through with reinforcements, supplies, and artillery. At 2:00 AM, a weak place appeared in the walls and the drum again sounded. Again the terms were denied and some tried to escape. The wall was breached and 2,000 English troops stormed the castle. Twenty-three Spanish, a great many *churls,* [96] women, and children were taken. Not an armed Irishman was found. All being "*good guides*", [97] vanished except Dermod (aka Dermond) MacCarthy, who was a prisoner of the Spanish.

Hugh O'Neill and Robert Devereau, 2nd Earl of Essex, the title page of *History of Ireland*, by Thomas Moore, published in 1835.

The English insisted on disarming the Spanish, but Don Páez would rather be buried in the rubble of Rincorran Castle than give up his sword. It was agreed that all Spanish would be disarmed except Don Páez. He could leave the castle with his sword and give it up personally to Sir George Carew.[98]

Red Hugh O'Donal marched to assist the Spanish in Kinsale, but was delayed by rains that created boggy roads. But a frost froze the bogs and O'Donal crossed the Slieve Felim Mountains, marched the 40 English miles and arrived the next night. This was remarkably quick considering he was encumbered by his baggage on muddy roads. [99]

[95] Driving a spike into the hole for the fuse of a cannon made it useless.
[96] A peasant or a freeman without rank.
[97] Good guides was Sir George Carew's words, meaning they knew the land and how to escape.
[98] *Pacata Hiberna,* Sir George Carew, Lowney & Company, 1896, chapter XIII page 1-7.
[99] *A Concise History of Ireland*, P. W. Joyce LLD, page 259, Longman, Green & Co., 1903.

The battle turned against the English, because O'Donal's army was on one side and the Spanish were in the town on the other side. The English found themselves besieged in bad weather, lacked enough food and they lost men every day to cold and illness. [100] O'Neill arrived with four thousand men the next day and encamped north of the town at Belgooly, circa five kilometers (3.1 miles) from the English. [101] Six thousand English had already been killed or died of exposure and illness and O'Neill preferred not to attack them. He preferred to let their army simply melt away. A war council overruled him and an Irish and Spanish attack was planned for the night of the 3rd of January 1602. But an Irish traitor informed the English of the plan.

O'Neill attacked, but lost his way in the fog. When the fog cleared, he found himself near the English lines and the English were waiting for him. O'Neill was in a bad position, but attacked anyway. The Spanish did not attack as planned and surrendered the town and the castles of Baltimore and Castlehaven. The Irish lost the Battle of Kinsale. The English lost 10,000 men at the Battle of Kinsale and the Spanish lost 2,000.[102] [103]

The Irish decided to send Hugh O'Donal to Spain for more help and leave his army under command of his brother Rory. King Philip of Spain received him and promised to send an army much more powerful than Don Juan del Águila's. But Red Hugh O'Donal heard of the fall of Dunboy Castle and fell ill of "*sickness of heart*" at Simancas, near Salamanca in Spain. He died on the 10th of September 1602 at the age of twenty-nine. [104] [105]

The Lord Deputy received intelligence that six Spanish ships, with 2,000 men, laden with great store of ordinance and munitions were landing at Castlehaven. Another six were scattered in a storm and their locations were unknown. Castlehaven was a strategic position commanding the harbor.

---

[100] Idibem, page 260.
[101] Ibidem, page 260
[102] *Pacata Hiberna,* Sir George Carew, Lowney & Company, 1896, chapter IX pages 256, 256 footnote 1.
[103] *A Concise History of Ireland*, P. W. Joyce LLD, page 261, Longman, Green & Co., 1903.
[104] *Ibidem*
[105] *Early Irish History and Antiquities and the History of West Cork*, Reverend W. O'Halloran, 1916

The O'Neill Clan Chief Turlough Lynagh, predecessor of Hugh O'Neill. Taken from Pacta Hiberna, by Sir George Carew, Lowney & Company, 1896.

Map of Ireland. Made by Václav Hollar (Wenceslas in English), a Bohemian etcher who lived in England, shows Ireland as it was at the time of the battles of Kinsale and Dunboy. The Kerry and Beara peninsulas and the Kenmare and Bantry Bays are in the lower left quadrant. Courtesy of Creative Commons License.

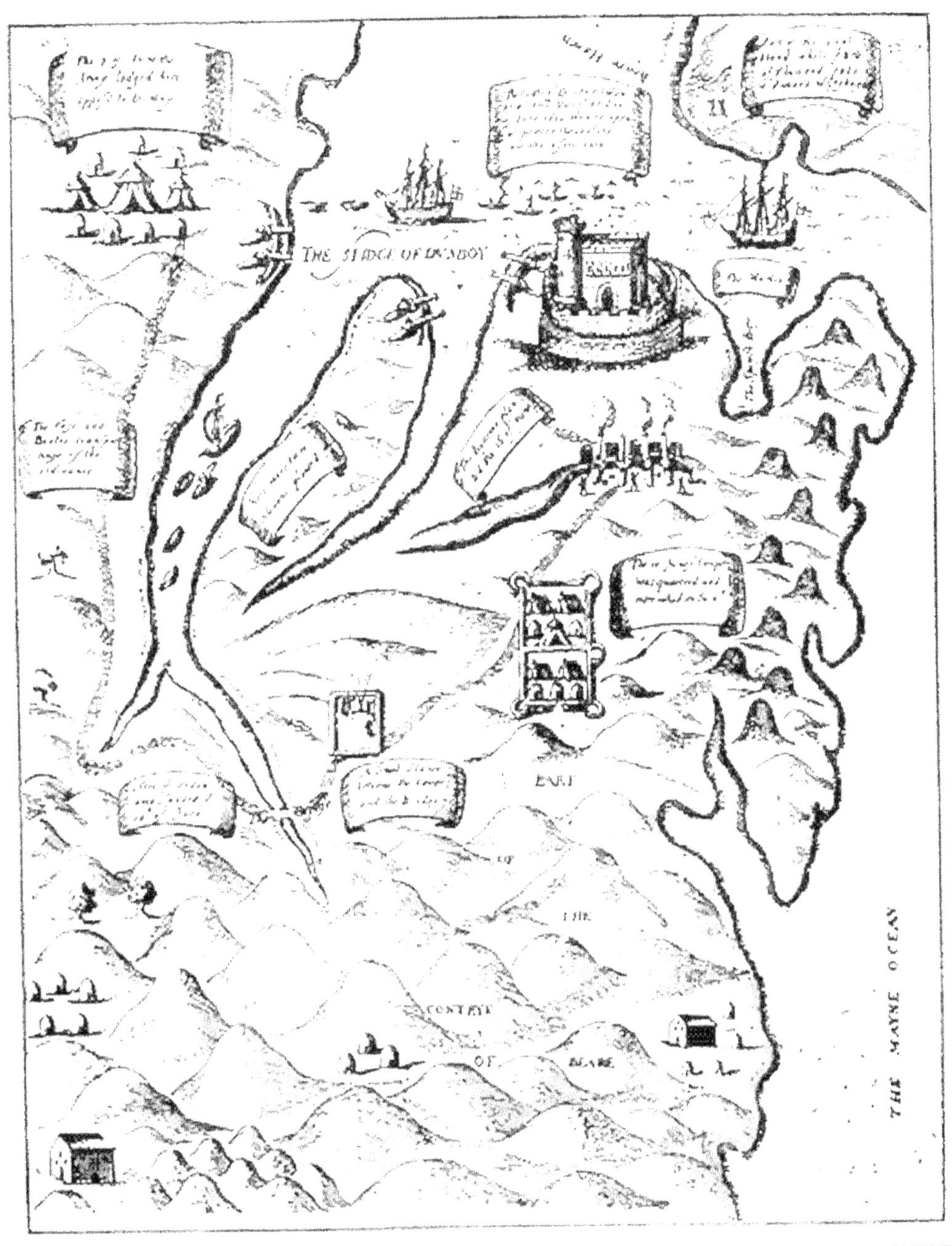

Sir George Carew's plan for the siege of Dunboy Castle. Dunboy Castle is shown in the upper right quadrant. Taken from Pacata Hiberna, Sir George Carew, Lowney & Company, 1896.

The siege of Dunboy Castle (Caisleán Dhún Baoi)

After the Battle of Kinsale, Lord Donal Cam O'Sullivan Beare allowed a Spanish garrison into Dunboy and other castles. Philip O'Sullivan wrote that his father Dermot conducted the Spaniard Vasco Sahavedro to Dunboy Castle and surrendered it to him on orders from the clan chief Prince Donal Cam O'Sullivan Beare.[106] Sir George Carew wrote:

> " ... *Donal O'Sullivan surrendered his strong Castle Dunboy, that absolutely commanded the Beare harbor, to the Spanish...* "

Don Juan sent 100 infantrymen, ten artillery pieces, and munitions to fortify Dunboy and ordered 100 men with eight artillery pieces, victuals, and munitions to remain at Castlehaven (*Gleann Bearcháin*). [107]

Sir George Carew ordered the Earl of Thormond to march with 2,000 infantry and 500 cavalry to Beare and determine the strength of Dunboy Castle. The actual expedition was 1,500 infantry and 50 cavalry. He expected the resistance to come from O'Sullivan and Richard Tyrrell. Richard Tyrrell was an experienced combat veteran. He positioned himself in the Glengarriff defiles and repelled the Earl of Thormond.[108] Sir George Carew also told the Earl of Thormond:

> " ... *Give all of the comfort you may to Owen O'Sullivan by whose means you know the affairs of those parts will be best composed...* "

Sir George Carew, 1st Earl of Totnes, was appointed President of Munster in 1600. He led the English attack on Kinsale in 1602 and on Dunboy Castle. Courtesy of Creative Commons License.

He was referring to, Owen grandson of the then deceased clan chief Sir Owen O'Sullivan [109]. Sir Owen's son Owen became clan chief and took over Carriganass Castle in 1563 after his father died.

---

[106] Ibidem, page 41.

[107] Ibidem, page 41, footnote 2.

[108] *Pacata Hiberna,* Sir George Carew, Lowney & Company, 1896, chapter II pages 148-153, 150 footnote 1, 153 footnote 1.

[109] Sir Owen's name was Eoghan. This name was anglicized to Owen or sometimes Eugene.

In 1540, clan chief Dermot O'Sullivan built Carriganass Castle. His eldest son was killed in a skirmish and his younger son Donal inherited the castle and was elected clan chief under the Irish law of tanistry.[110] Donal remained neutral in the Dermot revolt in 1569 and was jailed by the English. His younger brother Owen was elected clan chief because Donal's son, Donal Cam, was too young. When Donal Cam came of age, he believed he was the rightful clan chief and seized Carriganass Castle.[111] Owen surrendered his property, partly held by Donal Cam, to the English in return for a knighthood and under the condition his property would be re-granted. He was knighted and evicted his nephew Donal Cam from the castle.[112]

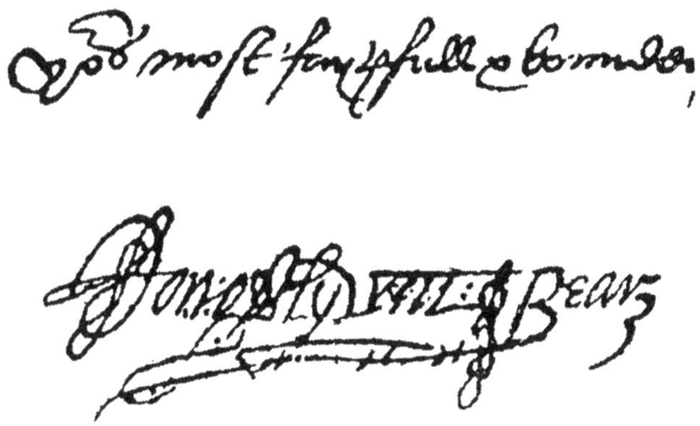

The signature of Donal Cam O'Sullivan Beare in 1601, with the inscription: *Yours most faythful and bounding, Don. Osulyvan Beare*, from *Gilbert's Fac-SIM. Nat. MSS.*

Sir Owen's nephew Donal Cam O'Sullivan appealed to the queen under the English primogeniture law [113], which does not recognize age for inheritance. Prince Donal Cam O'Sullivan of Eóganachta displaced Owen as clan chief. As the new clan chief, Donal Cam claimed Carriganass Castle and made it his main base. The title of Dunkerron Castle passed out of the O'Sullivan Mór hand to the O'Sullivan Beare and the O'Sullivan Mór had no choice but to move to Cappanacuss (sometimes spelled Cappanacush) Castle, the official residence of the O'Sullivan Mór Tanist.[114]

In 1593, Sir Owen appealed the decision. The English divided the estate and Donal Cam was given Beare, and Sir Owen received Bantry. After Sir Owen died, his son Owen became Lord of Bantry.[115] [116]

---

110 Tanistry refers to the Irish law whereby the next clan chief was elected during the lifetime of the existing chief. Until he became chief he was the Tanist.

111 *Early Irish History and Antiquities and the History of West Cork*, Reverend W. O'Halloran, 1916.

112 *The Oak and the Serpent*, Dr. Gary B. O'Sullivan MD FACOG FACS, Gold Stag Communications, 2007, page 273.

113 By the English law of primogeniture, the eldest son inherited his father's title and all of his estates.

114 The Tanist was the clan chief's elected successor.

115 *The Oak and the Serpent*, Dr. Gary B. O'Sullivan MD FACOG FACS, Gold Stag Communications , 2007, page 271, 273.

116 *Atlas and Cyclopedia of Ireland*, P. W. Joyce LLD, Murphy & McCarthy, 1900.

When the clan chief Hugh O'Neill revolted, to gain complete independence from England Donal Cam O'Sullivan, Lord of Beare, supported him [117] and marched west to Bantry and Beare Haven, but his cousin Owen, Lord of Bantry, supported the English. The younger Owen had decided the English would be the winning side and put himself forward as the Queen's O'Sullivan.[118]

A Spanish ship landed in Kenmare Bay at Kilmokilloc near Ardea Castle to determine if Dunboy Castle could be held. It brought munitions and a treasure of £12,000. Four boatloads of wine and munitions were unloaded and taken to Ardea Castle. The messenger was told the castle would hold until Michaelmas [119] at which time they required aid. The messenger said when he left Spain, 2,000 men had been assembled at Groyne on the northern Atlantic coast of Spain near Coruña. Donal Cam O'Sullivan distributed part of the treasure among his leaders. Part of the munitions and money was sent to Dunboy Castle to encourage the defenders.[120]

For the siege of Dunboy, Sir George Carew had 4,400 foot soldiers and 325 cavalry. In his *Pacata Hiberna,* he listed them all by numbers under the name of their captains. Nearly all of these captains were English, but nearly all of the men were Irish who had already been subjugated.[121]

Without authority, in return for favorable terms, the Spanish General Don Juan del Águila agreed to surrender Dunboy and other castles garrisoned by the Spanish to the English. Don Juan del Águila left Spanish garrisons in the castles and returned to Spain.[122] [123] [124] [125] [126] O'Neill and O'Donal decided that Donal Cam O'Sullivan was the best of the Munster allies and ordered that Donal Cam take command of the Munster forces. [127] [128] Donal Cam entered Dunboy Castle at night, disarmed the

---

[117] *Ibidem*

[118] *The Annals of the Kingdom of Ireland (Annála Ríoghachta Éireann)* also known as *The Annals of the Four Masters (Annála nag Ceithre Máistrí)*, 1632, annotations by Philip MacDermott, translation by Bryan Geraghty, 1846, M1602.11.

[119] Michaelmas is the feast day of the Archangel Saint Michael on the 29th of September. It is near the equinox and in the northern hemisphere is associated with the beginning of autumn.

[120] *Pacata Hiberna,* Sir George Carew, Lowney & Company, 1896, chapter VII pages 184-185.

[121] Ibidem, pages 154-156, 156 footnote 1.

[122] *Historiae Catholicae Hiberniae Compendium, Philip O'Sullivan, 1621, introduction by M. Kelly page vi.*

[123] *The Oak and the Serpent*, Dr. Gary B. O'Sullivan MD FACOG FACS, Gold Stag Communications, 2007, page 273.

[124] *Atlas and Cyclopedia of Ireland*, P. W. Joyce LLD, Murphy & McCarthy, 1900.

[125] *Pacata Hiberna,* Sir George Carew, Lowney & Company, 1896, chapter VII pages 184-185.

[126] *A Concise History of Ireland*, P. W. Joyce LLD, page 261, Longman, Green & Co., 1903.

[127] Ibidem

[128] *The Annals of the Kingdom of Ireland (Annála Ríoghachta Éireann)* also known as *The Annals of the*

Spanish, and seized their stores and artillery. He wrote an irate letter to King Felipe III of Spain complaining that Don Juan del Águila, without authority, delivered the castles into the hands of his enemies. He wrote that with the help of his own people he resolved to hold his castles until the king sent re-enforcements and retrieved the disaster caused by the cowardice of Don Juan Aqulia. [129] [130] Donal Cam sent his five-year-old son and heir, along with his cousin Philip and several other noble boys to Spain. They sailed from Castlehaven in February 1602 and landed in Coruña. They were well received by the Marquis de Caracena and he placed Philip under the care of the Reverend Patrick Synott, who arranged Philip's education at the Dominican monastery San Martiño Pinario (Saint Martín Pinario) in Santiago de Compostella, Galicia.[131]

The Irish were attacked by land and sea, hemmed in on the Beara Peninsula between the bays of Bantry and Kenmare. Lord Donal Cam O'Sullivan strengthened Dunboy Castle's defenses and left to meet Spanish reinforcements at Ardea Castle. He left Richard MacGeoghegan in command with 143 men. Donal Cam was at Ardea Castle when Dunboy Castle was attacked.

Sir George Carew began his siege of Dunboy Castle on the 6th of June 1602 and after a week, the castle wall was destroyed to rubble by cannon bombardment. An English force of over 2,000 men, stormed the castle slaughtering everyone they found, non-combatant men, women, and children. Twenty men who had surrendered were killed on the spot. Others tried to flee and jumped into the sea, but were killed with swords in the water. A few went into the powder cellars to blow themselves up with the gunpowder magazines, but were slashed to death before they could light the fuses. The Irish resistance was so fierce that it was admired even by Sir George Carew. Fifty-eight captives were executed in Castletown's market square the next day. Philip O'Sullivan wrote that half-murdered women and children were cast into the sea. [132] Sir George Carew even wrote about killing the survivors in his *Pacta Hibernia*: [133]

> " ... *Of the rebels, four were killed and two hurt, who with all of the rest were brought into the camp and afterwards executed ...* "

FourMasters (Annála nag Ceithre Máistrí), 1632, Annotations by Philip MacDermott, translation by Bryan Geraghty, 1846, M1602.14.

129 *Historiae Catholicae Hiberniae Compendium, Philip O'Sullivan, 1621, introduction by M. Kelly page vi.*

130 *Atlas and Cyclopedia of Ireland*, P. W. Joyce LLD, Murphy & McCarthy, 1900.

131 Ibidem, *page vii.*

132 *Historiae Catholicae Hiberniae Compendium, Philip O'Sullivan, 1621, introduction by M. Kelly page vii.*

133 *Pacata Hiberna*, Sir George Carew, Lowney & Company, 1896, page 196.

The Battle of Dunboy ended on the 17th of June 1602 and the castle was demolished with an explosion of gunpowder.[134] Sir George Carew was confident he had the rebellion under control and on the 1st of July at Bantry Abbey, he released two companies from duty. The English told Richard Tyrrell that he should:

> "*...do some acceptable service to save the lives of his men that their planned execution would be respited...*"

Tyrrell began negotiating his surrender. He was told he would be pardoned and he and his dependents would be at liberty. Nevertheless, twelve of Tyrrell's chief men were executed.

After Dunboy castle fell, O'Neill and O'Donal fled to Spain and their armies disbanded. Donal Cam O'Sullivan managed to muster 500 fighting men to carry on his resistance to the English.

On the 21st of August, Donal Cam besieged the O'Leary's Carrignacurra Castle. After a token resistance, the O'Leary people left the castle and joined Donal Cam's army. He then besieged Dundareike and they also joined Donal Cam's army. There was strong resistance at Carrickaphooka (sometimes spelled Carrickaphooca) Castle, owned by Tadhg McOwen MacCarthy, who was not in residence, but his wife was there. It too was finally subdued.

On the 30th of September, Cormac MacDermon escaped from the British and joined Donal Cam at Carrickaphooka Castle. The 500 men had grown to 1,500 and they moved to Macroom Castle. This was a force strong enough to be a threat to Sir George Carew, but Carew had the wife and daughter of Cormac MacDermon as hostages. On the 9th of October, Cormac MacDermon wrote a letter to Sir George Carew asking for forgiveness and mercy for his family. Donal Cam returned to Ardea Castle. A letter arrived from Spain claiming O'Donal had been poisoned by George Carew's spy James Blake of Galway. This caused the rebellion to collapse. The English took and garrisoned Bantry and Whiddy Island, which the Irish considered a last retreat. The castle was razed and the inhabitants butchered in such

[134] *Ibidem* chapter IX page 207.

Ruins of Ardea Castle in 2012. The castle was completely overgrown with bushes, vines and moss in 2012. It was one of the most important O'Sullivan castles on Kenmare Bay, built in 621 AD by Aodh Beanin. He was a maternal relative of the O'Sullivans and voluntarily gave the castle to the O'Sullivans in 1192 when they came from Tipperary to Counties Kerry and Cork.

The ruins of Ardea Castle tower in 1980. Courtesy of Creative Commons License.

Ardea Castle before 1602. Courtesy of Tuosist Community Development Group.

Kerry bog ponies. Histories describe large numbers of cavalry used by both the English and the Irish. Some Irish nobles imported horses from continental Europe, but most were probably these Kerry Bog Ponies. DNA research shows they are most likely descendants of horses brought to Ireland by Norse Vikings in the 9th and 10th centuries. They were later used for work in the peat bogs, but after demand for peat as a fuel diminished, they almost became extinct. In 2005, there were only 20 mares and eight stallions still living. In 2005, John Mulvuhill founded the Kerry Bog Pony Cooperative Society to save the breed from extinction. There are now 400 Kerry Bog Ponies. These particular ponies belong to Barry Clifford, one of the breeders. For readers interested in this topic see the excellent book: *The Story of the Kerry Bog Pony*, by Mary McGrath and Gay Keogh, Associated Editions, 2010.

Donal Cam O'Sullivan, Prince of Eóganachta, Lord of Beare and Bantry. Courtesy of Creative Commons License

Sir George Carew's battle plan map of Beare country. Dunboy Castle can be seen in the upper left quadrant. Taken *from Pacata Hiberna*, by Sir George Carew, Lowney & Company, 1896.

The ruins of Carrickaphooka Castle (Caisleán Carraig a' Phúcay). The castle was captured by Donal Cam O'Sullivan after he was joined by the O'Learys from Carrignacurra Castle. It was a five-story tower house castle built on a rock 6 kilometers west of Macroom, Cork in 1436 by Donal MacCarthy.

an atrocious manner that it was said generations later that women and children were half-murdered and cast into the sea.[135]

Dursey was ravaged twice and Sir George Carew himself described the massacre of non-combatants: [136]

" ... *They put the churles* [137] *to the sword that inhabited therein...*"

The *Churles* Sir George Carew said he had put to the sword were peasant tenant farmers with no land and no status. According to Philip O'Sullivan's history, this included their women and children. Philip O'Sullivan wrote: [138]

" ... *They here slew old men, woman and children. Drove them first into a Crowd and then shot and stabbed them all to the number of three hundred, most of them tenants of my father* ..."

The English began marching towards Glengarriff where Lord Donal Cam O'Sullivan expected to make his last stand. In late December 1602, Charles Wilmot, 1st Viscount Wilmot, camped near Glengarriff with an English force of 5,000 men.

Richard Tyrell had surrendered to the English and Lord Donal Cam O'Sullivan's other allies had fled to Spain, deserted or joined the enemy. Most Munster Irish had surrendered and were then against Donal Cam. The English were advancing from several sides and he was cut off from flight to Spain by English ships patrolling Bantry Bay. Yet, he still refused to surrender. Donal Cam decided to abandon his estates and seek asylum in Leinster with Brian O'Rourke of Brefney.[139, 140]

---

[135] *Historiae Catholicae Hiberniae Compendium, Philip O'Sullivan, 1621, introduction by M. Kellypage vii.*
[136] *Pacata Hiberna,* Sir George Carew, Lowney & Company, 1896, page ii, 563, 659.
[137] A peasant with no land or status.
[138] *Historiae Catholicae Hiberniae Compendium, Philip O'Sullivan, 1621, introduction by M. Kelly page vii.*
[139] *Ibidem.*
[140] *Pacata Hiberna,* Sir George Carew, Lowney & Company, 1896, chapter IX pages 282-283.

Recent writings said Cappanacuss Castle was in a grove of trees. The castle is now so overgrown with trees, vines and moss it is difficult to find, even if one knows where it is. The castle is in County Kerry about three miles from Kenmare on the way to Sneem near the end of a forestry road on the left.

Cappanacuss Castle in 2012. A closer view.

Cappanacuss Castle in 2012 is completely overgrown with trees, vines and moss .

Cappanacuss Castle in 20 years earlier in 1992. Courtesy of Joep Laumans.

Dunboy Castle (Caisleán Dhún Baoi) in 1980. In 1602, it was a stronghold of the O'Sullivan Beare, located on the Beara Peninsula near the town of Castletownbere. Courtesy of Creative Commons License.

Dunboy Castle as it looked in 2012. Vines, weeds, and grass have obscured the inner wall and almost obscured the remains of one building.

Castletownbere harbor in 2012

Castletownbere. Donoghue's pub in 2012. The painting of the Puxley Mansion on the wall, mislabeled as Dunboy Castle. See the Puxley Mansion picture below.

Castletownbere in 2012

Carriganass Castle in 2012 (Caisleán Charraig an Easa - The Castle on the Rock of the Waterfall). It is a tower house castle built in 1540 by Dermot O'Sullivan Beare 8 kilometers north-east of Bantry, near Kealkill, Cork. Some of the stones of the ruins of Carriganass castle were used to build Bantry House.

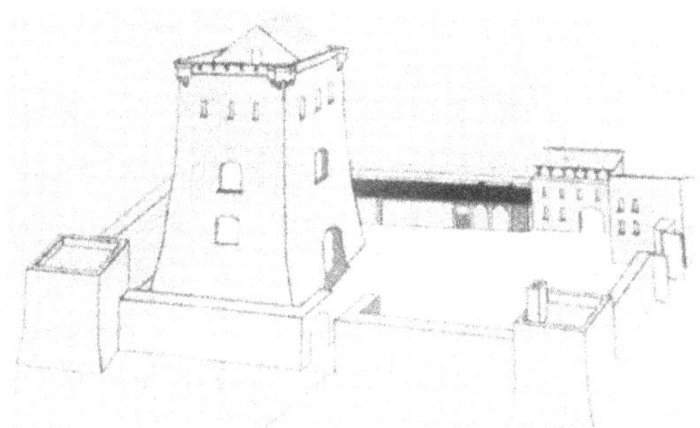

An archaeological reconstruction of Carriganass Castle. How it looked before its destruction. Courtesy of the Irish Department of Arts, Heritage and Gaeltacht.

Carriganass Castle in 1845, from *A Concise History of Ireland*, by P. W. Joyce LLD, published in 1903

Derryquin Castle, near Sneem built in the 18th century by Miles Mahoney. His eldest son, Kean, married the daughter of the O'Sullivan Beare. The family lived there until the 20th century and it was destroyed by the Irish Republican Army in 1921.

Bantry House was originally called Blackrock. It was built in circa 1700 south of Bantry Bay and its land totaled 80,000 acres (320 square kilometers). Some stones of Carriganass Castle were used to build Bantry House.

Donal Cam O'Sullivan Beare's epic march to Leitrim Castle in 1603

On the last day of 1602, Donal Cam O'Sullivan set out with 400 fighting men, and 600 women, children, and servants, among them Dermod (aka Dermond) and his wife, parents of Owen and Philip. [141] He left his sick and wounded behind who were all massacred the next day by the English. [142]At Muskerry, the next day they were attacked by the sons of Teg McOwen Carty that resulted in the loss of some men and their carriage. At Liscarcell, they were attacked by John Barry, brother of the viscount, at the ford of Bellaghan. They kept to the woods and the mountains that separate Kerry, Cork, and Limerick and marched 26 miles to Aghers on the first day.

Macroom Castle Donal Cam O'Sullivan mustered his troops here after his numbers increased to 1,500. This was enough to be a serious threat to Sir George Carew. Only a few walls of the original structure remain.

Donal Cam's wife carried and nursed his two-year-old son Donal on the march. They fought their way to Aherlow, near Tipperary and left their son with a trusted dependent, who reared him tenderly until he could be sent to his parents in Spain. [143] [144] They had no time to collect supplies because they were pursued and continually attacked by enemies. They had plenty of money, but the local people were afraid to sell them supplies. [145] [146] They had to fight their way past every castle on their way to Brian O'Rourke of Brefney's Leitrim Castle and most of those they fought were Irish lords attempting to gain favor from their English conquerors.

They fought their way north through the Barony Kilmanagh, over the Sliebh Feilim Mountains, to Ormonde and on the ninth day to the River Shannon, above Lough

[141] *Early Irish History and Antiquities and the History of West Cork*, Reverend W. O'Halloran, 1916

[142] *A Concise History of Ireland*, P. W. Joyce LLD, page 262, Longman, Green & Co., 1903.

[143] Ibidem pages 28-269.

[144] *Historiae Catholicae Hiberniae Compendium, Philip O'Sullivan, 1621, introduction by M. Kelly page vii, viii..*

[145] *Early Irish History and Antiquities and the History of West Cork*, Reverend W. O'Halloran, 1916

[146] *A Concise History of Ireland*, P. W. Joyce LLD, page 267, Longman, Green & Co., 1903.

Derg [147] [148] with their enemies hot on their heels. When they reached the River Shannon, it was flooded and there were no boats. On the advice of Dermod (aka Dermond), they killed sixteen of their horses to make *curraghs* [149] to cross the river.[150] [151] But they were attacked by Donogh MacEgan, Sheriff of Tipperary, who owned Redwood Castle.[152] Donogh MacEgan attempted to throw some of the women and children into the river, but *The O'Sullivan* killed him and many of his men. [153]

In County Galway, they were attacked at Aug hram and greatly outnumbered by Sir Thomas Burke, the Earl of Clanricard's brother, and Captain Malby. Donal Cam O'Sullivan rushed into the enemy ranks, beheaded Captain Malby's son and killed many others. When Captain Malby was killed, the attackers fled. Donal Cam won this battle mainly by his own skill and valor. [154] [155] [156]

Redwood Castle. When Donal Cam O'Sullivan and his followers reached the River Shannon it was flooded. They were attacked by Donogh MacEgan from Redwood Castle. Donogh MacEgan attempted to throw some of the women and children into the river, but *The O'Sullivan* killed him and many others. Courtesy of Steve Ford Elliot, Creative Commons License.

The O'Sullivans then marched into the safety of Brian O'Rourke territory.[157] On the 16th of January, after two weeks of starvation and fighting their way through hostile territory they were warmly welcomed by Brian O'Rourke at Leitrim Castle. Of the 1,000 who left two weeks earlier only thirty-five reached Leitrim Castle: Eighteen fighting men, sixteen

[147] Lake.

[148] *Early Irish History and Antiquities and the History of West Cork*, Reverend W. O'Halloran, 1916

[149] *Curraghs* are hide boats.

[150] *Historiae Catholicae Hiberniae Compendium, Philip O'Sullivan, 1621, introduction by M. Kelly page viii.*

[151] *A Concise History of Ireland*, P. W. Joyce LLD, page 269, Longman, Green & Co., 1903.

[152] *Pacata Hiberna,* Sir George Carew, Lowney & Company, 1896, chapter IX pages 183-184.

[153] *The Annals of the Kingdom of Ireland (Annála Ríoghachta Éireann)* also known as *The Annals of the Four Masters (Annála nag Ceithre Máistrí)*, 1632, Annotations by Philip MacDermott, translation by Bryan Geraghty, 1846, M1602.14.

[154] Ibidem, 1846, M1602.15.

[155] *A Concise History of Ireland*, P. W. Joyce LLD, page 270, Longman, Green & Co., 1903.

[156] *Early Irish History and Antiquities and the History of West Cork*, Reverend W. O'Halloran, 1916

[157] *Pacata Hiberna,* Sir George Carew, Lowney & Company, 1896, chapter IX page 284.

servants, and one woman, the wife of the chief's uncle, Dermot O'Sullivan. [158]
A few other survivors later straggled in. Donal Cam's wife was not among the survivors who reached Leitrim Castle, yet she does reappear later and it is not known how she escaped. She may have been left behind with other supporters and made her way to Spain. [159] Philip O'Sullivan wrote: [160]

> "... *I am astonished how my father, who was then near seventy years of age, and my mother, a delicate woman, could have so bravely borne these fatigues, which broke down so many men in the flower of their age and the prime of their strength* ..."

Lord Donal Cam O'Sullivan Beare, Dermod (aka Dermond), his wife, and three of their children soon joined the family members already in Spain. Donal Cam was assassinated on the 16th of July 1618 in Madrid. Philip fought a duel against a man who made an insulting remark against Donal Cam and took refuge from the Spanish police in the French embassy, but soon after was back at his post in the Spanish Navy. In April, Philip wrote a letter to Dermod (aka Dermond), Donal Cam's heir, consoling him on the death of his father and describing the Spanish naval action against the Turks in which his brother Daniel and several other Irish were killed. [161]
Sir George Carew remarked in his *Pacata Hiberna* that:

> " ... *All that are our [the Irish clan chiefs] had all sought mercy except O'Rourke and O'Sullivan and O'Sullivan is now with O'Rourke and these are obstinate only out of their diffidence to be safe of any forgiveness* ... "

But judging by the number of prisoners he executed, both soldiers and non-combatants, Sir George Carew was not exactly famous for forgiveness. Brian O'Rourke's castle was taken by the English and partly destroyed. In 1610, Roger Parke built a manor house castle on the site. He kept the original baun, [162] but demolished the O'Rourke tower house in the center. He used the stones of O'Rourke's tower to build the three-story manor house by the eastern wall. It is now known as Parke's Castle.

---

[158] *Early Irish History and Antiquities and the History of West Cork*, Reverend W. O'Halloran, 1916
[159] *A Concise History of Ireland*, P. W. Joyce LLD, page 268-269, Longman, Green & Co., 1903.
[160] *Historiae Catholicae Hiberniae Compendium, Philip O'Sullivan, 1621, introduction by M. Kelly page viii.*
[161] *Ibidem viii, ix.*
[162] A baun is the inner defensive wall surrounding an Irish tower house castle. It is the anglicized Gaelic word *badhún* which means a cattle-stronghold or a cattle-enclosure.

After the fall of Dunboy Castle to prevent another uprising, the English turned Southern Munster into a desert. They overran all of Beare and Bantry, destroyed all that was of use to the people, forcing them to withdraw to other parts of County Cork. In his *Pacata Hiberna,* Sir George Carew wrote: [163] [164] [165]

> " ... *Sir Charles with the English regiments overran all of Beare and Bantry, destroying all that he could find meet for the relief of his men so that the country was wholly wasted. He sent Captain Fleming and soldiers into Sullivan's Island and put the churls to the sword who inhabited therein ...* "

This was a terrible massacre and in fact was carried out twice on the island. Philip O'Sullivan wrote that 300 of his father's tenants, (men women. and children) were killed. Mark Charles Fissel wrote: [166]

> ... " *From 1570 to the 1590s the English strategy of occupation was based on destructive marches to succor garrisons and strike fear amongst the population. ...* "

As an English supporter Queen Elizabeth rewarded Owen O'Sullivan with his cousin Donal Cam O'Sullivan's property and he became the Lord of Beare and Bantry. But in fact the real rulers were the English. Owen was bitterly despised by the other O'Sullivans for his treachery and they called his line the O'Sullivan Galldha (foreigners). Owen abandoned Carriganass Castle and moved to Reenadisert Castle in County Cork between Bantry and Glengarriff. It was a walled tower house castle and was later badly damaged in Oliver Cromwell's war against the Irish (1649-1658) and remained uninhabited. It is now a ruin. [167]

King James I. In the reign of King James I, Owen O'Sullivan was awarded Dunboy Castle for supporting the English in their conquest of the Beara Peninsula. Courtesy of Creative Commons License.

[163] *Pacata Hiberna,* Sir George Carew, Lowney & Company, 1896, chapter IX pages 285-286.

[164] *A Concise History of Ireland,* P. W. Joyce LLD, page 272, Longman, Green & Co., 1903.

[165] *Early Irish History and Antiquities and the History of West Cork,* Reverend W. O'Halloran, 1916

[166] *English Warfare, 1511-1642,* Mark Charles Fissell Routledge, 2001, page 211.

[167] *The Oak and the Serpent,* Dr. Gary B. O'Sullivan MD FACOG FACS, Gold Stag Communications, 2007, page 287.

Brian O'Rourke's Leitrim Castle, now called Parke's Castle. Of the 1,000 men, women, and children who set out, only thirty-five reached Leitrim Castle. It was later confiscated by the English and given to the Parke family. They tore down the tower house and built a mansion by the east wall, which can be seen in the picture. Courtesy of Sytheston, Creative Commons License.

Ruins of Reenadisert Castle. After Owen O'Sullivan was rewarded with Beare and Bantry for supporting the English in the conquest of the Beara Peninsula, he left Cappanacuss Castle and lived in Reenadisert Castle.

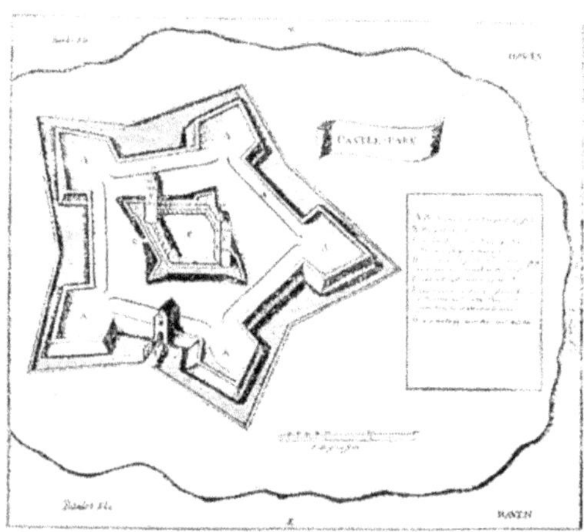

Leitrim Castle, now called Parke's Castle, was a star fort. This design became popular because all parts of the wall could be protected from within the castle. Taken from *Pacata Hiberna*, Sir George Carew, Lowney & Company, 1896.

Dunloe Castle is near Killarney on the grounds of a hotel by the same name. Dunlong O'Sullivan captured the castle in 1261 and the Irish controlled it for about 400 years. Only part of the tower house and fragments of the wall remain.

Cove Castle was a minor O'Sullivan castle. The ruins are near Castlecove beach in County Kerry.

Arabella House was built by the MacElligott family, a sub-sept of the O'Sullivan clan. Sir George Carew called it Castle Eliot. It is not a ruin, but is in a bad state of repair and is unoccupied.

The reign of King James I, 1603-1625 168 and King Charles I, 1625-1649 [169]

Hugh O'Neill surrendered in 1603, a few days after Queen Elizabeth I died. Spain and England signed a peace treaty soon afterwards.

In 1612, the 9th year of King James I of England's reign, Dunboy Castle was re-granted to Owen O'Sullivan. His son Owen Donal O'Sullivan joined the Irish Rebellion in 1641 during the reign of King Charles I. He was condemned and fled Ireland. His family scattered among relatives and friends, and some immigrated to America.

The rule of Oliver Cromwell, 1649-1658 [170]

Oliver Cromwell continued the *scorched earth policy* of his predecessors as a means of suppressing potential revolts in Ireland. Captive men women and children were killed and crops and anything of use destroyed.

Oliver Cromwell continued the scorched earth policies of Queen Elisabeth's reign, killing men women and children and destroying everything of use. Courtesy of Creative Commons License.

Oliver Cromwell [171] was elected to parliament in 1628 and led the English civil war from 1642 to 1649. He became the leader of the nation after the parliament voted to execute King Charles I in 1649. He established a new army model and banned all peers and members of parliament. Thomas Fairfax led the new army and Cromwell appointed himself second in command. Royalists in parliament objected so Cromwell broke up the group of dissenters and appointed himself in sole command. He reduced the number of parliamentary members to those who supported him and ruled England as a dictator. In 1653, he expelled the parliament and named

[168] The Kings & Queens of England and Scotland, Edmund Swinglehurst, 2002, S. Webb & Son Ltd, pages 158-159.

[169] Ibidem, pages 162-163.

[170] Ibidem, pages 166-167.

[171] *History of the kings and queens of England and Scotland*, E. Webb and Son, Booksmart Ltd, 2002.

himself *Lord Protector of the Commonwealth*. Cromwell died in 1658 and by 1660, the monarchy was restored to Charles II who returned from exile.

During Oliver Cromwell's war against the Irish, Owen Donal O'Sullivan Beare's wife Elisabeth (possibly his daughter Elisabeth) immigrated to Virginia with his minor son John Thomas O'Sullivan. They arrived on the 24th of October 1655. This was only forty-eight years after the first permanent English colony in North America was founded at Jamestown so it is likely they landed on the James River.

The reign of King George II, 1727-1760 [172]

In 1730, the English Crown granted the O'Sullivan lands in County Cork to the English Puxley family thereupon the O'Sullivan family placed a curse on the Puxley family that *cows would wander through their halls*.

King George II. In the reign of King George II the Puxley family was granted the lands of the O'Sullivan Beare where they built a vast mansion near the ruins of Dunboy Castle. Courtesy of Creative Commons License.

The Puxley family built a great mansion, called the Puxley Mansion, not far from the ruins of Dunboy Castle of the O'Sullivan Beare. The Puxley family was wealthy, partly through supporting smugglers along the Beara coast.

In 1866, Puxley began vast expansions to the mansion, but in 1872 his wife died in childbirth and the renovation of the mansion was never finished. In 1921, the Irish Republican Army burned the Puxley Mansion. The mansion is now a ruin and only its skeleton remains. The O'Sullivan curse came to pass, but the mansion is now being renovated to be a luxury hotel.

In 1768, the MacCarthy Mór clan chief

[172] The Kings & Queens of England and Scotland, Edmund Swinglehurst, 2002, S. Webb & Son Ltd, pages 198-199.

died without a legitimate male heir ending the Rory O'Sullivan line. The clan leadership reverted to the original Finghin royal line which became the O'Sullivan clan.

O'Sullivans in Spain and France [173]

After their final defeat, many of the O'Sullivans and other Irish nobles went to Spain, France, and America. This period was known as *the flight of the earls*. Both the French and the Spanish recognized the royal bloodlines of the O'Sullivans and gave them land, titles, and generous pensions. A number of O'Sullivans served in the French Army and the Spanish Navy. There are two castles in France that are still the homes of the descendants of the O'Sullivans:

- The O'Sullivan MacCragh at Château du Gravier (Dunderry Castle) in Gravier, Cher, Centre Region, France.
- The MacMahon O'Sullivan Beare at Château de Sully, near Beaune, Bourgogne Region, France. [174]

Other castles with Irish connections in France [175]

- O'Connor, Château du Bignon-Mirabeau
- O'Mahoney, Château de Pont Bellanger
- O'Kelly Farrell, Château la Soriniere
- Walsh, Château de Serrant
- Henessy, Château de St. Brice
- Phelans, Château Phelans-Segur
- O'Byrne, Château la Houringue
- Lynch, Château Lynch-Bages
- MacCarthy Reagh Château St. Gery

[173] *The Oak and the Serpent*, Dr. Gary B. O'Sullivan MD FACOG FACS, Gold Stag Communications , 2007, page 188.
[174] Ibidem
[175] Ibidem, Page 275.

The Puxley Mansion. In 1730, the English King George II granted O'Sullivan Beare's land to the Puxley family and they built a mansion near the ruins of Dunboy Castle. The Irish Republican Army burned it in 1921 leaving only the outer shell intact. It is now being renovated as a luxury hotel.

Puxley Mansion painting. The painting is on an outer wall of O'Donoghue's pub in Castletownbere advertising Murphy's Irish stout. It is labeled Dunboy Castle, but it is actually the Puxley Mansion.

Château du Gravier (Dunderry Castle). The castle in Gravier, Cher, France, is the international headquarters of the O'Sullivan MacCragh sept. This is the oldest Irish royal bloodline. Courtesy of DR. Gary B. Sullivan MD FACOG FACS.

The MacMahon O'Sullivan Beare Château de Sully near Beaune, Bourgogne, France. Not to be confused with Sully, Saône-et-Loire. John Mahon O'Sullivan was naturalized in France in 1749. He was a descendant of Sir Owen O'Sullivan Beare, 14th Lord of Beare and Bantry (1549-1594). He married Charlotte le Belin Dame d'Eguilly. In 1750, King Louis XV created him Marquis d'Guilly. His son, the 2nd Marquis, served in the American Revolutionary War. His grandson, Patrice de MacMahon served as a general in the Crimean War and the Austro-Sardinian War. The day after his victory at the Battle of Magenta, Napoleon III created him Duc de Magenta. He succeeded Adolphe Thiers, the first president of the Third Republic of France, when he resigned and on the 24 th of May 1873 he became the second president. These two titles, Marquis and Duke, still exist. Courtesy of Christopher Finot, Creative Commons License.

Patrice MacMahon, Duke of Magenta, second president of the Third French Republic, official portrait 1870 Courtesy of Creative Commons License.

The Dominican monastery San Martiño Pinario (Saint Martín Pinario)
The monastery is in Santiago de Compostella, Galicia, Spain. This is where Philip O'Sullivan was educated. He was the author of:

- *Historiae Catholicae Hiberniae Compendium,*
- *Chapters towards a history of Ireland in the Reign of Queen Elisabeth,* originally published in Spanish,
- *Brief relation of Ireland, and the Diversity of Irish in the Same, and Priests in Ireland and Gentlemen gone abroad,*
- *Natural History of Ireland.*

After he fled Ireland, he was an officer in the Spanish Navy and was created Count of Beare. Courtesy of Creative Commons License.

Scenes of Counties Kerry and Cork

View of Kenmare Bay as seen from the window of the home of Ann and Barry Clifford, Castlecove, Caherdaniel.

Castlecove

Cove near Portmagee

Priest's Leap

Ring of Beara near Ardea Castle

Part II
O'Sullivan (*Ó Súilleabháinn)* Genealogy

Introduction

The Irish migrated from Spain to Ireland and established four kingdoms. Munster was the southern most of these kingdoms. King Finghin of Munster, Lord of Cashel, born in 571 AD, was a direct descendant of King Milesius in Spain and King Finghin's line became the O'Sullivan clan. King Finghin's descendant Eochaid Súilleabháinn, born in 874 AD, was the first to be called *Súilleabháinn,* anglicized as Sullivan. His son Lorcan took the name Lorcan MacSúilleabháinn, (son of Sullivan), and his son Baudhach took the name Baudhach Ó Súilleabháinn, indicating he was chief of the Sullivan clan.

The other Irish clans recognized the O'Sullivan clan as the oldest bloodline of the Irish royal family and the O'Sullivan MacCragh sept [176] as the oldest of the Sullivan lines.

The names in various documents for the same people are sometimes different because Gaelic names were either anglicized or simply transliterated into English in different ways. The most common examples of the names in this book are: Eoghan became Owen, Donal became Daniel or Donald, Finghan became Florence.

This book documents six major O'Sullivan genealogical lines of the Mór, Beare and MacCragh septs. In the 9th generation, the O'Sullivan Mór divided into two lines. In the 10th generation, there was a 3rd line; in the 19th generation there was a 5th and a 6th line.

The format used is the New England Historical and Genealogical Society format developed in 1870. This genealogy includes six parallel Sullivan lines, descended from a common O'Sullivan ancestor, who went to France, Spain, Virginia, Maine, New Hampshire, Massachusetts, and New York.

The format has two disadvantages for this particular report:

[176] A sept is a branch of an Irish clan.

1. It lists generations sequentially and puts individuals in all lines under that generation heading. This genealogy has many names in most generations, with a maximum of twelve. This makes it difficult to follow any single line of descent.

2. Sometimes the same name appears more than once in different places. This is because people often married a relative, resulting in multiple lines of descent and several different relationships to the same ancestor.

The partial solution to the standard format is to follow each name with the entire genealogy going back to the first generation parenthesis in a smaller font size.

Despite due caution, in a database of this size, errors are bound to occur. I would be grateful to hear from readers who detect errors they can document from reliable sources at:

Info@McCreight.org

The superscript numbers after the names refer to documentary references in the endnotes for Part II. Some sources generally considered as authorities and widely referenced, nevertheless contain errors. When conflicts arise, readers should compare references, and select those that they believe are most credible.

Generation 1

1 **Eochaid Súilleabháinn, 8th Lord of Knockgraffon** [1, 2, 3, 4, 5, 6, 7].
Born in 874 AD.

Eochaid was the first to be called Súilleabháinn as a sobriquet (nickname), anglicized to Sullivan, and is the ancestor of the O'Sullivan clan. Eochaid Súilleabháinn was a direct descendant of Finghin, the 14th King of Munster and Lord of Cashel born in 571 AD, and a descendant of King Milesius.

In the 9th century, Danish Vikings began raiding the coast of Ireland and according to the *Annals of Ulster,* in the year 841, they over-wintered there. Soon after, they built a fortress at Dublin and called it the kingdom of Dyfin from the Irish name Dubhlinn. They later built other fortresses. In the mid-10th century, a council was held at Cashel to plan an attack to drive the Danes out of Ireland. Eochaid Súilleabháinn attended that council. A plan was made to attack the Danes in Limerick. At that time Eochaid Súilleabháinn was over 70 years old and his son Lorcan MacSúilleabháinn participated in the attack.

Eochaid Súilleabháinn, 8th Lord of Knockgraffon had the following known son:

2 i **Lorcan MacSullivan, 9th Lord of Knockgraffon** [1, 2, 3, 6, 7] was born in 914 AD.

Generation 2

2 **Lorcan MacSúilleabháinn (MacSullivan), 9th Lord of Knockgraffon** [1, 2, 3, 6, 7].
Born in 914 AD.

(Eochaid Súilleabháinn, 8th Lord of Knockgraffon-1)

Lorcan was the first to take his father's name as a surname MacSúilleabháinn (son of Sullivan), and founded the O'Sullivan clan.

In the mid-10th century, an army of approximately 1,000 Irish Eóghanacht troops attacked the Danish Vikings at Limerick. Lorcan was one of the leaders at the age of about 30 years. The Danes were asked to surrender and give hostages, but their response was to march out with circa 400 men. The Danes put up a fierce fight until their leader was killed and Lorcan killed the son of the Danish king. The Irish then captured Limerick. The Irish took gold and hostages in tribute and marched on to Cork without garrisoning Limerick. The Danes in Cork were holding hostages. The Irish scaled the wall, took the town, and freed the hostages. On the way back to Cashel, they were ambushed by Danes, but drove them off. Waterford was taken next, but King Gofraid MacSitriuc (in Danish Sitriucsson) and the other Danish leaders escaped in their ships to Dublin.

Lorcan MacSúilleabháinn (MacSullivan), 9th Lord of Knockgraffon had the following known son:

3 i Baudhach Ó Súilleabháinn (O'Sullivan), 10th Lord of Knockgraffon [1, 2, 3, 6, 7] was born in 954 AD.

Generation 3

3. **Baudhach Ó Súilleabháinn (O'Sullivan), 10th Lord of Knockgraffon** [1, 2, 3, 6, 7].
Born in 954 AD.

(Lorcan MacSullivan, 9th Lord of Knockgraffon-2, Eochaid Súilleabháinn, 8th Lord of Knockgraffon-1)

He was the first to be called Ó Súilleabháinn, anglicized to O'Sullivan. At that time, it was not a family name. It was the title of the chief of the clan. The title was *The O'Sullivan Mór*, which means the Great O'Sullivan. Baudhach translates into English as *the Victor.* He married a Macedonian woman named Veera née unknown. In 1023, he deposed King Tadhg MacCarthy of Munster.

Baudhach O'Sullivan, 10th Lord of Knockgraffon and Veera had the following known son:

4 i Aodh O'Sullivan, 11th Lord of Knockgraffon [1, 2, 6, 7] was born in 994 AD.

Generation 4

4 **Aodh O'Sullivan, 11th Lord of Knockgraffon** [1, 2, 6, 7].
Born in 994 AD.

(Baudhach O'Sullivan, 10th Lord of Knockgraffon-3, Lorcan MacSullivan, 9th Lord of Knockgraffon-2, Eochaid Súilleabháinn, 8th Lord of Knockgraffon-1)

Aodh O'Sullivan, 11th Lord of Knockgraffon had the following known son:

5 i Cathal O'Sullivan, 12th Lord of Knockgraffon [1, 2, 6, 7] was born in 1054.

Generation 5

5 **Cathal O'Sullivan, 12th Lord of Knockgraffon** [1, 2, 6, 7].
Born in 1054.

(Aodh O'Sullivan, 11th Lord of Knockgraffon-4, Baudhach O'Sullivan, 10th Lord of Knockgraffon-3, Lorcan MacSullivan, 9th Lord of Knockgraffon-2, Eochaid Súilleabháinn, 8th Lord of Knockgraffon-1)

Cathal O'Sullivan, 12th Lord of Knockgraffon had the following known son:

6 i Baudhach O'Sullivan, 13th Lord of Knockgraffon [1, 2, 6, 7] was born in 1074.

Generation 6

6 **Baudhach O'Sullivan, 13th Lord of Knockgraffon** [1, 2, 6, 7].
Born in 1074.

(Cathal O'Sullivan, 12th Lord of Knockgraffon-5, Aodh O'Sullivan, 11th Lord of Knockgraffon-4, Baudhach O'Sullivan, 10th Lord of Knockgraffon-3, Lorcan MacSullivan, 9th Lord of Knockgraffon-2, Eochaid Súilleabháinn, 8th Lord of Knockgraffon-1)

Baudhach O'Sullivan ,13th Lord of Knockgraffon had the following known son:

7 i MacCraith O'Sullivan Mór, 14th Lord of Knockgraffon [1, 2, 6, 7] was born in 1114.

Generation 7

7 **MacCraith O'Sullivan Mór, 14th Lord of Knockgraffon** [1, 2, 6, 7].
Born in 1114.
Died in 1176.

(Baudhach O'Sullivan Mór, 13th Lord of Knockgraffon-6, Cathal O'Sullivan, 12th Lord of Knockgraffon-5, Aodh O'Sullivan, 11th Lord of Knockgraffon-4, Baudhach O'Sullivan, 10th Lord of Knockgraffon-3, Lorcan MacSullivan, 9th Lord of Knockgraffon-2, Eochaid Súilleabháinn, 8th Lord of Knockgraffon-1)

In 1171, Dermot MacCarthy Mór, King of Munster, submitted to King Henry II of England. Many of the Eóghanacht chiefs demanded he abdicate in favor of MacCraith, who was *The O'Sullivan Mór*, or at least some other MacCarthy chief. MacCraith refused to support this movement and was killed in 1176 defending the Dermot MacCarthy Mór against his own son Cormac.

I question the name MacCraith, because it means son of Craith, and his father was Baudhach. But this comes from no less an authority than Sir J. Bernard Burke. He was the son of John Burke and the family was well-known genealogists for several generations. Their most famous work was *Genealogical and Heraldic Dictionary of the Peerage and Baronetage of the United Kingdom,* generally known as *Burke's Peerage*, first published in 1847. Sir Bernard sent a letter, dated the 7th of September 1887, including a detailed report on the O'Sullivan clan to Thomas Coffin Amory. This letter and the report were reproduced in *Materials for a History of the Family of John Sullivan of Berwick, New England and of the O'Sullivans of Ardea, Ireland (1893),* by Gertrude Euphemia Meredith and Thomas

Coffin Amory.

Dr. Gary Brian O'Sullivan, suggested two possibilities:

1. His father's name may have been Craith and had the sobriquet (nickname) Baudhach. A sobriquet is often recorded in the records and in fact the first time the name Sullivan (Súilleabháinn) was used it was a sobriquet for Eochaid Súilleabháinn, 8th Lord of Knockgraffon.
2. A generation may have been skipped in the records.

MacCraith O'Sullivan Mór, 14th Lord of Knockgraffon had the following known sons:

8 i **Donal O'Sullivan Mór, 15th Lord of Knockgraffon** [1, 2, 6, 7] was born in 1134.
ii Gila Padraig O'Sullivan, was killed by the Normans at the Battle of Ferdrium in West Cork.
iii Anad O'Sullivan was killed in battle by the Normans in 1201.

Generation 8

8 **Donal O'Sullivan Mór, 15th Lord of Knockgraffon** [1, 2, 6, 7].
Born in 1134.

(MacCraith O'Sullivan Mór, 14th Lord of Knockgraffon-7, Baudhach O'Sullivan, 13th Lord of Knockgraffon-6, Cathal O'Sullivan, 12th Lord of Knockgraffon-5, Aodh O'Sullivan, 11th Lord of Knockgraffon-4, Baudhach O'Sullivan, 10th Lord of Knockgraffon-3, Lorcan MacSullivan, 9th Lord of Knockgraffon-2, Eochaid Súilleabháinn, 8th Lord of Knockgraffon-1)

Donal O'Sullivan Mór avenged his father's death in 1176. He led a group of Eóghanacht lords who killed Cormac MacCarthy and restored Cormac's father Dermot to the throne of Munster.

Lord Donal O'Sullivan Mór was *The O'Sullivan Mór* (chief of the O'Sullivan Mór sept). He was the last Lord of Knockgraffon. He was decisively defeated by the English in 1192 and the O'Sullivan clan lost its extensive lands in Tipperary. The entire clan moved south to Counties Kerry and Cork, which was a wild rocky mountainous area where they succeeded in keeping their independence for 449 years.

Donal O'Sullivan Mór, 15th Lord of Knockgraffon had the following known sons:

9 i **Giolla Mochoda O'Sullivan Mór, clan chief** [1, 3, 7, 8]. was murdered at a banquet in 1214 by King Dermot Duna Droighneain MacCarthy Mór of Munster.
ii Giolla na Bhflainn O'Sullivan Mór[1, 3, 6, 7, 8, 9] was born in 1166. He escaped death in 1214 because he did not attend the banquet where King Dermot Duna Droighneain MacCarthy Mór of Munster murder all of the other O'Sullivan royal heirs.

Generation 9

9 **Giolla na Bhflainn O'Sullivan Mór** [1, 3, 6, 7, 8, 9].
Born in 1166.

(Donal O'Sullivan Mór, 15th Lord of Knockgraffon-8, MacCraith O'Sullivan Mór, 14th Lord of Knockgraffon-7, Baudhach O'Sullivan, 13th Lord of Knockgraffon-6, Cathal O'Sullivan, 12th Lord of Knockgraffon-5, Aodh O'Sullivan, 11th Lord of Knockgraffon-4, Baudhach O'Sullivan, 10th Lord of Knockgraffon-3, Lorcan MacSullivan, 9th Lord of Knockgraffon-2, Eochaid Súilleabháinn, 8th Lord of Knockgraffon-1)

In 1214, the Eóghanacht chiefs again demanded *The O'Sullivan Mór* assume the throne. King Dermot Duna Droighneain MacCarthy Mór was advised to eliminate the threat. In 1214, he invited the adult male O'Sullivans to a banquet at Raithin na nGaradhthe and murdered them all including the clan chief Giolla Mochoda O'Sullivan Mór. The only royal survivors were the two who did not attend the banquet: Dunlong, Donal's 14-year-old grandson and Giolla na BhFlainn, Donal's youngest son. Dunlong was the rightful heir to the throne of Munster. He was still a minor when the O'Sullivan clan moved to Kerry. Irish law required that a king, or clan chief, be the wisest to rule in peace and the strongest to lead in war. This ruled out minors and anyone with a physical defect.

Giolla na Bhflainn O'Sullivan Mór had the following known sons:

10 i **Philip O'Sullivan Mór**[1, 3, 6, 7].
11 ii **Dunlong O'Sullivan Mór** [9, 10] was born in 1200.

Generation 10

10. **Philip O'Sullivan Mór** [1, 3, 6, 7].

(Giolla na Bhflainn O'Sullivan Mór-9, Donal O'Sullivan Mór, 15th Lord of Knockgraffon-8, MacCraith O'Sullivan Mór, 14th Lord of Knockgraffon-7, Baudhach O'Sullivan, 13th Lord of Knockgraffon-6, Cathal O'Sullivan, 12th Lord of Knockgraffon-5, Aodh O'Sullivan, 11th Lord of Knockgraffon-4, Baudhach O'Sullivan, 10th Lord of Knockgraffon-3, Lorcan MacSullivan, 9th Lord of Knockgraffon-2, Eochaid Súilleabháinn, 8th Lord of Knockgraffon-1)

The O'Sullivan clan divided into two septs: The O'Sullivan Beare and the O'Sullivan Mór. Dunlongh was the clan chief, called *The O'Sullivan Mór, (The Great O'Sullivan).*

Philip O'Sullivan Mór had the following known sons:

12 i **Annaidh O'Sullivan Beare, 1st Lord of Beare and Bantry** [1, 3, 6, 7].
Annaidh was called *The O'Sullivan Beare.*
ii Dunlongh O'Sullivan Mór [1, 3] was born in 1200. Dunlongh was the clan chief, called *The O'Sullivan Mór, (The Great O'Sullivan).*
13 iii **Anaduff O'Sullivan Mór** [1].

11 **Dunlong O'Sullivan Mór** [9, 10] was born in 1200 [9, 10].

(Giolla na Bhflainn O'Sullivan Mór-9, Donal O'Sullivan Mór, 15th Lord of Knockgraffon-8, MacCraith O'Sullivan Mór, 14th Lord of Knockgraffon-7, Baudhach O'Sullivan, 13th Lord of Knockgraffon-6, Cathal O'Sullivan, 12th Lord of Knockgraffon-5, Aodh O'Sullivan, 11th Lord of Knockgraffon-4, Baudhach O'Sullivan, 10th Lord of Knockgraffon-3, Lorcan MacSullivan, 9th Lord of Knockgraffon-2, Eochaid Súilleabháinn, 8th Lord of Knockgraffon-1)

Dunlong was *The O'Sullivan Mór* (chief of the O'Sullivan Mór sept). By this time, the Normans had adopted Irish customs and married into Irish families until they were largely *more Irish than the Irish* and had rejected the feudal system of the English in Dublin. English influence was weakened because the plague of 1349 hit the Normans in urban areas harder than the rural Irish and because the Irish had learned the military tactics of the Normans. In 1259, the Norman Lord John FitzThomas took over land confiscated from the O'Sullivans and the MacCarthys. Within a few years there were many Norman castles in Cork and Kerry. In 1261, Lord John FitzThomas decided to wipe out all Irish resistance and marched with a large army on the Eóghanacht areas in Cork and Kerry. On the 24th of July 1261 the Irish ambushed and defeated his army in Callan Glen near Kilgarvan in the Roughty River Valley. The O'Sullivans and the MacCarthys took over all of the castles south of the Maine River. Dunlong O'Sullivan took over the castles Dunloe, Dunkerron, Cappanacuss and a number of minor keeps. The O'Sullivan clan controlled this area for the next 400 years.

Dunlong O'Sullivan Mór had the following known son:

14 i **Murtagh O'Sullivan Mór** [9, 10] was born in 1235 [9, 10].

Generation 11

12 **Annaidh O'Sullivan Beare, 1st Lord of Beare and Bantry** [1, 3, 6, 7].

(Philip O'Sullivan Beare-10, Giolla na Bhflainn O'Sullivan Mór-9, Donal O'Sullivan Mór, 15th Lord of Knockgraffon-8, MacCraith O'Sullivan Mór, 14th Lord of Knockgraffon-7, Baudhach O'Sullivan, 13th Lord of Knockgraffon-6, Cathal O'Sullivan, 12th Lord of Knockgraffon-5, Aodh O'Sullivan, 11th Lord of Knockgraffon-4, Baudhach O'Sullivan, 10th Lord of Knockgraffon-3, Lorcan MacSullivan, 9th Lord of Knockgraffon-2, Eochaid Súilleabháinn, 8th Lord of Knockgraffon-1)

Annaidh O'Sullivan Beare was the 1st Lord of Beare and Bantry and was called *The O'Sullivan Beare.*

Annaidh O'Sullivan,1st Lord of Beare and Bantry had the following known sons:

15. i **Amhiaffe O'Sullivan Beare** [1, 3, 6, 7].
ii Gilmochud O'Sullivan Beare.

13 **Anaduff O'Sullivan Mór** [1].

(Philip O'Sullivan Mór-10, Giolla na Bhflainn O'Sullivan Mór-9, Donal O'Sullivan Mór, 15th Lord of Knockgraffon-8, MacCraith O'Sullivan Mór, 14th Lord of Knockgraffon-7, Baudhach O'Sullivan, 13th Lord of Knockgraffon-6, Cathal O'Sullivan, 12th Lord of Knockgraffon-5, Aodh O'Sullivan, 11th Lord of Knockgraffon-4, Baudhach O'Sullivan, 10th Lord of Knockgraffon-3, Lorcan MacSullivan, 9th Lord of Knockgraffon-2, Eochaid Súilleabháinn, 8th Lord of Knockgraffon-1)

Anaduff O'Sullivan Mór and had the following known son:

16 i **Giolla Mohud O'Sullivan Mór**[1].

14 **Murtagh O'Sullivan Mór** [9, 10].
Born in 1235 [9, 10].

(Dunlong O'Sullivan Mór-10, Giolla na Bhflainn O'Sullivan Mór-9, Donal O'Sullivan Mór, 15th Lord of Knockgraffon-8, MacCraith O'Sullivan Mór, 14th Lord of Knockgraffon-7, Baudhach O'Sullivan, 13th Lord of Knockgraffon-6, Cathal O'Sullivan, 12th Lord of Knockgraffon-5, Aodh O'Sullivan, 11th Lord of Knockgraffon-4, Baudhach O'Sullivan, 10th Lord of Knockgraffon-3, Lorcan MacSullivan, 9th Lord of Knockgraffon-2, Eochaid Súilleabháinn, 8th Lord of Knockgraffon-1)

Murtagh was *The O'Sullivan Mór* (chief of the O'Sullivan Mór sept). Crofton Croker wrote a poem based on a legend that Murtagh O'Sullivan Mór, Lord of Dunkerron, married a *merrow* (mermaid) and in 1864, Henry Smart wrote a cantata, *Bride of Dunkerron,* based on the same story. The tradition is Murtagh and the merrow had children, before her father murdered him, and their Lords of Dunkerron descendants have royal meer-blood.

Murtagh O'Sullivan Mór had the following known son:

17 i **Bernard O'Sullivan Mór** [9, 10] was born in 1270 [9, 10].

Generation 12

15 **Amhiaffe O'Sullivan Beare** [1, 3, 6, 7].

(Annaidh O'Sullivan Beare, 1st Lord of Beare and Bantry-11, Philip O'Sullivan-10, Giolla na Bhflainn O'Sullivan Mór-9, Donal O'Sullivan Mór, 15th Lord of Knockgraffon-8, MacCraith O'Sullivan Mór, 14th Lord of Knockgraffon-7, Baudhach O'Sullivan, 13th Lord of Knockgraffon-6, Cathal O'Sullivan, 12th Lord of Knockgraffon-5, Aodh O'Sullivan, 11th Lord of Knockgraffon-4, Baudhach O'Sullivan, 10th Lord of Knockgraffon-3, Lorcan MacSullivan, 9th Lord of Knockgraffon-2, Eochaid Súilleabháinn, 8th Lord of Knockgraffon-1)

Amhiaffe O'Sullivan Beare and had the following known son:

18 i **Teige O'Sullivan Beare** [1, 3, 6, 7].

16 **Giolla Mohud O'Sullivan Mór** [1].

(Anaduff O'Sullivan Mór-11, Philip O'Sullivan-10, Giolla na Bhflainn O'Sullivan Mór-9, Donal

O'Sullivan Mór, 15th Lord of Knockgraffon-8, MacCraith O'Sullivan Mór, 14th Lord of Knockgraffon-7, Baudhach O'Sullivan, 13th Lord of Knockgraffon-6, Cathal O'Sullivan, 12th Lord of Knockgraffon-5, Aodh O'Sullivan, 11th Lord of Knockgraffon-4, Baudhach O'Sullivan, 10th Lord of Knockgraffon-3, Lorcan MacSullivan, 9th Lord of Knockgraffon-2, Eochaid Súilleabháinn, 8th Lord of Knockgraffon-1)

Giolla Mohud O'Sullivan Mór had the following known son:

19 i **Owen O'Sullivan Mór** [1, 11].

17 **Bernard O'Sullivan Mór** [9, 10].
Born in 1270 [9, 10].

(Murtagh O'Sullivan Mór-11, Dunlong O'Sullivan-10, Giolla na Bhflainn O'Sullivan Mór-9, Donal O'Sullivan Mór, 15th Lord of Knockgraffon-8, MacCraith O'Sullivan Mór, 14th Lord of Knockgraffon-7, Baudhach O'Sullivan, 13th Lord of Knockgraffon-6, Cathal O'Sullivan, 12th Lord of Knockgraffon-5, Aodh O'Sullivan, 11th Lord of Knockgraffon-4, Baudhach O'Sullivan, 10th Lord of Knockgraffon-3, Lorcan MacSullivan, 9th Lord of Knockgraffon-2, Eochaid Súilleabháinn, 8th Lord of Knockgraffon-1)

Bernard was *The O'Sullivan Mór* (chief of the O'Sullivan Mór sept). Bernard O'Sullivan Mór had the following known son:

20 i **Dunlong O'Sullivan Mór** [9, 10] was born in 1340 [9, 10].

Generation 13

18 **Teige O'Sullivan Beare** [1, 3, 6, 7].

(Amhiaffe O'Sullivan Beare-12, Annaidh O'Sullivan Beare, 1st Lord of Beare and Bantry-11, Philip O'Sullivan-10, Giolla na Bhflainn O'Sullivan Mór-9, Donal O'Sullivan Mór, 15th Lord of Knockgraffon-8, MacCraith O'Sullivan Mór, 14th Lord of Knockgraffon-7, Baudhach O'Sullivan, 13th Lord of Knockgraffon-6, Cathal O'Sullivan, 12th Lord of Knockgraffon-5, Aodh O'Sullivan, 11th Lord of Knockgraffon-4, Baudhach O'Sullivan, 10th Lord of Knockgraffon-3, Lorcan MacSullivan, 9th Lord of Knockgraffon-2, Eochaid Súilleabháinn, 8th Lord of Knockgraffon-1)

Teige O'Sullivan Beare had the following known son:

21 i Dermod (aka Dermond) Balluf O'Sullivan Beare[1, 3, 6, 7, 12].

19 **Owen O'Sullivan Mór** [1, 11].

(Giolla Mohud O'Sullivan Mór-12, Anaduff O'Sullivan-11, Philip O'Sullivan-10, Giolla na Bhflainn O'Sullivan Mór-9, Donal O'Sullivan Mór, 15th Lord of Knockgraffon-8, MacCraith O'Sullivan Mór, 14th Lord of Knockgraffon-7, Baudhach O'Sullivan, 13th Lord of Knockgraffon-6, Cathal O'Sullivan, 12th Lord of Knockgraffon-5, Aodh O'Sullivan, 11th Lord of Knockgraffon-4, Baudhach O'Sullivan, 10th Lord of Knockgraffon-3, Lorcan MacSullivan, 9th Lord of Knockgraffon-2, Eochaid Súilleabháinn, 8th Lord of Knockgraffon-1)

Owen O'Sullivan Mór had the following known son:

i Dermod (aka Dermond) O'Sullivan, Lord of Dunkerron Castle, was *The O'Sullivan Mór.*

22 ii **Donal na Sgreadaidhe O'Sullivan Mór** [11].

20 **Dunlong O'Sullivan Mór** [9, 10].
Born in 1340 [9, 10].

(Bernard O'Sullivan Mór-12, Murtagh O'Sullivan-11, Dunlong O'Sullivan-10, Giolla na Bhflainn O'Sullivan Mór-9, Donal O'Sullivan Mór, 15th Lord of Knockgraffon-8, MacCraith O'Sullivan Mór, 14th Lord of Knockgraffon-7, Baudhach O'Sullivan, 13th Lord of Knockgraffon-6, Cathal O'Sullivan, 12th Lord of Knockgraffon-5, Aodh O'Sullivan, 11th Lord of Knockgraffon-4, Baudhach O'Sullivan, 10th Lord of Knockgraffon-3, Lorcan MacSullivan, 9th Lord of Knockgraffon-2, Eochaid Súilleabháinn, 8th Lord of Knockgraffon-1)

Dunlong was The O'Sullivan Mór (chief of the O'Sullivan Mór sept).

During the rule of Dunlong, son of Bernard, King Edward III of England was alarmed at the *Gaelicization* of the Norman settlers in Ireland. In 1366, the Statutes of Kilkenny forbade Norman Irish settlers from speaking Gaelic, wearing Gaelic clothing, riding *Scythian style* (bareback) or marrying Gaelic women. This law was certainly not enforceable.

Dunlong O'Sullivan Mór had the following known sons:

23 i **Cragh O'Sullivan Mór** [9, 10] was born in 1375 [9, 10].

ii Rory O'Sullivan Mór. When Cragh died, his son was a minor and his younger brother Rory was elected The O'Sullivan Mór [10].

Generation 14

21 **Dermod (aka Dermond) Balluf O'Sullivan Beare** [1, 3, 6, 7, 12].

(Teige O'Sullivan Beare-13, Amhiaffe O'Sullivan Beare-12, Annaidh O'Sullivan, 1st Lord of Beare and Bantry-11, Philip O'Sullivan-10, Giolla na Bhflainn O'Sullivan Mór-9, Donal O'Sullivan Mór, 15th Lord of Knockgraffon-8, MacCraith O'Sullivan Mór, 14th Lord of Knockgraffon-7, Baudhach O'Sullivan, 13th Lord of Knockgraffon-6, Cathal O'Sullivan, 12th Lord of Knockgraffon-5, Aodh O'Sullivan, 11th Lord of Knockgraffon-4, Baudhach O'Sullivan, 10th Lord of Knockgraffon-3, Lorcan MacSullivan, 9th Lord of Knockgraffon-2, Eochaid Súilleabháinn, 8th Lord of Knockgraffon-1)

Dermod (aka Dermond) Balluf O'Sullivan Beare had the following known sons:

24 i **Donal O'Sullivan Beare, the Swarthy, 8th Lord of Beare and Bantry** [1, 3, 6, 12, 13, 14, 15, 16, 17, 18].

ii Dermod (aka Dermond) O'Sullivan Beare [1, 3].

25 iii **Philip O'Sullivan Beare, Lord of Beare** [1, 7].

iv Awiny O'Sullivan Beare [1].

v Owen O'Sullivan Beare [1].
vi Conor O'Sullivan Beare.

22 **Donal na Sgreadaidhe O'Sullivan Mór** [11].

(Owen O'Sullivan Mór-13, Giolla Mohud O'Sullivan Mór-12, Anaduff O'Sullivan-11, Philip O'Sullivan-10, Giolla na Bhflainn O'Sullivan Mór-9, Donal O'Sullivan Mór, 15th Lord of Knockgraffon-8, MacCraith O'Sullivan Mór, 14th Lord of Knockgraffon-7, Baudhach O'Sullivan, 13th Lord of Knockgraffon-6, Cathal O'Sullivan, 12th Lord of Knockgraffon-5, Aodh O'Sullivan, 11th Lord of Knockgraffon-4, Baudhach O'Sullivan, 10th Lord of Knockgraffon-3, Lorcan MacSullivan, 9th Lord of Knockgraffon-2, Eochaid Súilleabháinn, 8th Lord of Knockgraffon-1)

Dermod (aka Dermond), Lord of Dunkerron Castle, *The O'Sullivan Mór*, died and his younger brother Donal na Sgreadaidhe (the screamer) O'Sullivan Mór was elected *The O'Sullivan Mór*. Because Dunkerron Castle was the seat of the *O'Sullivan Mór*, Dermod's (aka Dermond) widow and children had to leave Dunkerron Castle and were moved to Cappanacuss Castle.

Donal na Sgreadaidhe O'Sullivan Mór had the following known son:

26 i **Donal O'Sullivan Mór, Lord of Dunkerron Castle** [11, 17]. He died in 1580 [11].

23 **Cragh O'Sullivan Mór** [9, 10, 224].
Born in 1375 [9, 10].

(Dunlong O'Sullivan Mór-13, Bernard O'Sullivan Mór-12, Murtagh O'Sullivan-11, Dunlong O'Sullivan-10, Giolla na Bhflainn O'Sullivan Mór-9, Donal O'Sullivan Mór, 15th Lord of Knockgraffon-8, MacCraith O'Sullivan Mór, 14th Lord of Knockgraffon-7, Baudhach O'Sullivan, 13th Lord of Knockgraffon-6, Cathal O'Sullivan, 12th Lord of Knockgraffon-5, Aodh O'Sullivan, 11th Lord of Knockgraffon-4, Baudhach O'Sullivan, 10th Lord of Knockgraffon-3, Lorcan MacSullivan, 9th Lord of Knockgraffon-2, Eochaid Súilleabháinn, 8th Lord of Knockgraffon-1)

Cragh was *The O'Sullivan Mór* (chief of the O'Sullivan Mór sept). He was the last *O'Sullivan Mór* of the senior Milesian line. Cragh died when his son was still a minor hence his younger brother Rory was elected *The O'Sullivan Mór*. Cragh's widow and children had to leave Dunkerron Castle and move to Cappanacuss Castle in the Templenoe parish. They had a large family and now a small estate, so many went abroad.

Cragh O'Sullivan Mór had the following known son:

27 i **Donal O'Sullivan MacCragh** [9, 10] was born in 1410 [9, 10].

Generation 15

24 **Donal O'Sullivan Beare, the Swarthy, 8th Lord of Beare and Bantry** [1, 3, 6, 12, 13, 14].

(Dermod (aka Dermond) Balluf O'Sullivan Beare-14, Teige O'Sullivan Beare-13, Amhiaffe O'Sullivan Beare-12, Annaidh O'Sullivan, 1st Lord of Beare and Bantry-11, Philip O'Sullivan-10, Giolla na Bhflainn O'Sullivan Mór-9, Donal O'Sullivan Mór, 15th Lord of Knockgraffon-8, MacCraith O'Sullivan Mór, 14th Lord of Knockgraffon-7, Baudhach O'Sullivan, 13th Lord of Knockgraffon-6, Cathal O'Sullivan, 12th Lord of Knockgraffon-5, Aodh O'Sullivan, 11th Lord of Knockgraffon-4, Baudhach O'Sullivan, 10th Lord of Knockgraffon-3, Lorcan MacSullivan, 9th Lord of Knockgraffon-2, Eochaid Súilleabháinn, 8th Lord of Knockgraffon-1).

Donal O'Sullivan Beare, the Swarthy, 8th Lord of Beare and Bantry had the following sons:

28 i **Dermod O'Sullivan Beare, 11th Lord of Beare and Bantry** [1, 3, 6, 12, 13, 15, 17, 18, 19, 20, 21, 22, 23, 24, 25, 26, 27, 28, 29, 30] was born circa 1500 in Dunboy Castle, County Cork, Munster, Ireland. He died in 1549 in Dunboy Castle, County Cork, Munster, Ireland.

ii Annalaigh O'Sullivan Beare, 12th Lord of Beare [1, 3, 20, 30]. He died in 1519 [19, 20]. He was Tanist (heir) to his brother Dermod (aka Dermond). He murdered his brother in 1519 and died in the same year.

iii Eochy O'Sullivan Beare[1, 2, 19, 20]. He died in 1601.

iv Teige O'Sullivan Beare [1, 19].

25 **Philip O'Sullivan Beare, Lord of Beare** [1, 7].

(Dermod (aka Dermond) Balluf O'Sullivan Beare-14, Teige O'Sullivan Beare-13, Amhiaffe O'Sullivan Beare-12, Annaidh O'Sullivan, 1st Lord of Beare and Bantry-11, Philip O'Sullivan-10, Giolla na Bhflainn O'Sullivan Mór-9, Donal O'Sullivan Mór, 15th Lord of Knockgraffon-8, MacCraith O'Sullivan Mór, 14th Lord of Knockgraffon-7, Baudhach O'Sullivan, 13th Lord of Knockgraffon-6, Cathal O'Sullivan, 12th Lord of Knockgraffon-5, Aodh O'Sullivan, 11th Lord of Knockgraffon-4, Baudhach O'Sullivan, 10th Lord of Knockgraffon-3, Lorcan MacSullivan, 9th Lord of Knockgraffon-2, Eochaid Súilleabháinn, 8th Lord of Knockgraffon-1)

Philip O'Sullivan Beare, Lord of Beare had the following known son:

i Teige O'Sullivan Beare [19]. He died in 1598.

26 **Donal O'Sullivan Mór, Lord of Dunkerron** [11, 17]. He died in 1580[11].

(Donal na Sgreadaidhe O'Sullivan Mór-14, Owen O'Sullivan Mór-13, Giolla Mohud O'Sullivan Mór-12, Anaduff O'Sullivan-11, Philip O'Sullivan-10, Giolla na Bhflainn O'Sullivan Mór-9, Donal O'Sullivan Mór, 15th Lord of Knockgraffon-8, MacCraith O'Sullivan Mór, 14th Lord of Knockgraffon-7, Baudhach O'Sullivan, 13th Lord of Knockgraffon-6, Cathal O'Sullivan, 12th Lord of Knockgraffon-5, Aodh O'Sullivan, 11th Lord of Knockgraffon-4, Baudhach O'Sullivan, 10th Lord of Knockgraffon-3, Lorcan MacSullivan, 9th Lord of Knockgraffon-2, Eochaid Súilleabháinn, 8th Lord of Knockgraffon-1)

Donal O'Sullivan Mór, Lord of Dunkerron Castle and **Mary Oge** married [11, 17, 31]. She died in 1593 [11, 17].

They had the following known children:

29 i **Owen O'Sullivan Mór, Lord of Dunkerron Castle** [11]. He died in 1623 [11].

ii Broght O'Sullivan Mór [11].

iii Connor O'Sullivan Mór [11].

iv Donal O'Sullivan Mór [11].

30 v **Ellen O'Sullivan Mór** [11, 13, 18, 19, 21].

vi Daughter O'Sullivan Mór [11].

27 **Donal O'Sullivan MacCragh** [9, 10, 223, 224].
Born in 1410 [9, 10].

(Cragh O'Sullivan Mór-14, Dunlong O'Sullivan Mór-13, Bernard O'Sullivan Mór-12, Murtagh O'Sullivan-11, Dunlong O'Sullivan-10, Giolla na Bhflainn O'Sullivan Mór-9, Donal O'Sullivan Mór, 15th Lord of Knockgraffon-8, MacCraith O'Sullivan Mór, 14th Lord of Knockgraffon-7, Baudhach O'Sullivan, 13th Lord of Knockgraffon-6, Cathal O'Sullivan, 12th Lord of Knockgraffon-5, Aodh O'Sullivan, 11th Lord of Knockgraffon-4, Baudhach O'Sullivan, 10th Lord of Knockgraffon-3, Lorcan MacSullivan, 9th Lord of Knockgraffon-2, Eochaid Súilleabháinn, 8th Lord of Knockgraffon-1)

Because Donal O'Sullivan MacCragh was only about ten years old when his father died, his uncle was elected as *The O'Sullivan Mór*. Due to this change in clan leadership, Donal and his mother were required to move from Dunkerron Castle (the seat of the clan) to nearby Cappanacuss Castle. However, Donal was still recognized as the senior line of the O'Sullivan clan and became chief of the O'Sullivan MacCragh sept. His title was *The O'Sullivan MacCragh* (son of Cragh). He was the first of the O'Sullivan MacCragh sept, which is the oldest of the Irish royal bloodlines. He was killed defending King Dermot MacCarthy against his son.

Donal O'Sullivan MacCragh had the following known son:

31 i **Conor O'Sullivan MacCragh** [9, 10] was born in 1444 [9, 10].

Generation 16

28. **Dermod O'Sullivan Beare, 11th Lord of Beare and Bantry** [1, 3, 6, 12, 13, 15, 17, 18, 19, 20, 21, 22, 23, 24, 25, 26, 27, 8, 29, 30].

Born in circa 1500 in Dunboy Castle, County Cork, Munster, Ireland.
Died in 1549 in Dunboy Castle, County Cork, Munster, Ireland.

(Donal O'Sullivan Beare, the Swarthy, 8th Lord of Beare and Bantry-15, Dermod (aka Dermond) Balluf O'Sullivan Beare-14, Teige O'Sullivan Beare-13, Amhiaffe O'Sullivan Beare-12, Annaidh O'Sullivan, 1st Lord of Beare and Bantry-11, Philip O'Sullivan-10, Giolla na Bhflainn O'Sullivan Mór-9, Donal O'Sullivan Mór, 15th Lord of Knockgraffon-8, MacCraith O'Sullivan Mór, 14th Lord of Knockgraffon-7, Baudhach O'Sullivan, 13th Lord of Knockgraffon-6, Cathal O'Sullivan, 12th Lord of Knockgraffon-5, Aodh O'Sullivan, 11th Lord of Knockgraffon-4, Baudhach O'Sullivan, 10th Lord of Knockgraffon-3, Lorcan MacSullivan, 9th Lord of Knockgraffon-2, Eochaid Súilleabháinn, 8th Lord of Knockgraffon-1)

Dermod (aka Dermond) O'Sullivan Beare, of Dunboy Castle, 11th Lord of Beare and Bantry, was called The Powdered (*an-Phudar*) because he died in a gunpowder explosion in 1549 that badly damaged his castle. The Annals of the Four Masters said:

> *" ... O'Sullivan [Dermot], a kind and friendly man to his friends, and fierce and inimical to his enemies, was burned by gunpowder in his own castle; and his brother, Auliffe O'Sullivan, took his place; and he also was killed soon afterwards. ..."*

He was described as:

> *"... Strong in War, formidable to his enemies and dear to his friends..."*

His treaty with the land deputy, Sir Anthony St. Leger, dated the 20th of September 1512, is printed in the state papers of King Henry VIII, volume III, page 422 and is mentioned in Sir George Carew's papers. In 1540, clan chief Dermod (aka Dermond) O'Sullivan Beare built Carriganass Castle. His eldest son was killed in a skirmish, thus his younger son Donal inherited the castle and was elected clan chief under the Irish law of tanistry.

He married **Lady Julia MacCarthy,** daughter of Donough MacFineere MacCarthy Reagh, Prince of Carbery, and Lady Eleanor FitzGerald [1, 3, 13, 18, 19, 21, 22, 25, 27, 28, 29, 32] , born in circa 1500 in Carbery, Ireland. Lady Julia died in circa 1550 in Dunboy Castle, County Cork, Munster, Ireland. If these documented birth and death dates are correct, it does not seem reasonable that she could be the mother of all of the children listed below.

Dermod O'Sullivan Beare ,11th Lord of Beare and Bantry and Lady Julia MacCarthy had the following known children:

32 i **Dermod (aka Dermond) O'Sullivan Beare** [12, 18, 19, 26, 33, 34, 35] was born in 1526 in Dunboy Castle, County Cork, Munster, Ireland [35].

33 ii **Donal O'Sullivan Beare, 13th Lord of Beare and Bantry** [6, 17, 18, 19, 21, 25] was born before 1537 in Dunboy Castle, County Cork, Munster, Ireland. He died in 1563 [25].

34 iii **Sir Owen O'Sullivan Beare, 14th Lord of Beare and Bantry** [15, 17, 18, 19, 23, 27, 35, 36, 37] was born before 1549 in Dunboy Castle, County Cork, Munster, Ireland. He died in 1594 in Dunboy Castle, County Cork, Munster, Ireland [17, 35].

35 iv **Sir Philip O'Sullivan Beare, Lord of Ardea Castle** [13, 18, 19, 21, 22, 26, 28, 32, 35, 38]. Died in 1606 [18].

v Johanna O'Sullivan Beare was born in Dunboy Castle, County Cork, Munster, Ireland.

vi Honora O'Sullivan Beare [18, 26] was born in Dunboy Castle, County Cork, Munster, Ireland.

36 vii **Conor O'Sullivan Beare** [19] was born in Dunboy Castle, County Cork, Munster, Ireland.

29 **Owen O'Sullivan Mór, Lord of Dunkerron Castle** [11].
Died in 1623 [11].

(Donal O'Sullivan Mór, Lord of Dunkerron O'Sullivan-15, Donal na Sgreadaidhe O'Sullivan Mór-14, Owen O'Sullivan Mór-13, Giolla Mohud O'Sullivan Mór-12, Anaduff O'Sullivan-11, Philip O'Sullivan-10, Giolla na Bhflainn O'Sullivan Mór-9, Donal O'Sullivan Mór, 15th Lord of Knockgraffon-8, MacCraith O'Sullivan Mór, 14th Lord of Knockgraffon-7, Baudhach O'Sullivan, 13th Lord of Knockgraffon-6, Cathal O'Sullivan, 12th Lord of Knockgraffon-5, Aodh O'Sullivan, 11th Lord of Knockgraffon-4, Baudhach O'Sullivan, 10th Lord of Knockgraffon-3, Lorcan MacSullivan, 9th Lord of Knockgraffon-2, Eochaid Súilleabháinn, 8th Lord of Knockgraffon-1)

John Perrott was appointed Lord Deputy of Ireland by Queen Elizabeth I. His main task was to begin the plantation of the southern province of Munster. The Crown's policy was to parcel out lands from estates confiscated from the Irish lords at rents. In particular, the estates of 600,000 acres, or 2,400 square kilometers, were confiscated from the recently defeated Earl of Desmond. The undertakers [developers] were to bring in English farmers and laborers to build towns and work the land. In 1685, Perrott convened a parliament in Dublin to be attended by the Gaelic lords. Owen O'Sullivan attended this parliament, but it proved to be a disappointment to the Gaelic lords.

He married **Julia MacCarthy Reagh,** daughter of Donough MacCarthy Reagh, Prince of Carbery. [11] She was documented as being alive in 1603 [11].

Owen O'Sullivan Mór, Lord of Dunkerron Castle O'Sullivan Mór and Julia MacCarthy Reagh had the following known children:

37	i	**Owen O'Sullivan Mór, of Dunkerron Castle** [11] was born after 1640 [11].
	ii	Mary O'Sullivan Mór [11].
	iii	Ellen O'Sullivan Mór [11].
38	iv	**Donal O'Sullivan Mór, Lord of Dunkerron Castle** [11].
	v	Dermod O'Sullivan Mór [11].
	vi	Julia O'Sullivan Mór [11].

30 **Ellen O'Sullivan Mór** [11, 13, 18, 19, 21].

(Donal O'Sullivan Mór, Lord of Dunkerron O'Sullivan-15, Donal na Sgreadaidhe O'Sullivan Mór-14, Owen O'Sullivan Mór-13, Giolla Mohud O'Sullivan Mór-12, Anaduff O'Sullivan-11, Philip O'Sullivan-10, Giolla na Bhflainn O'Sullivan Mór-9, Donal O'Sullivan Mór, 15th Lord of Knockgraffon-8, MacCraith O'Sullivan Mór, 14th Lord of Knockgraffon-7, Baudhach O'Sullivan, 13th Lord of Knockgraffon-6, Cathal O'Sullivan, 12th Lord of Knockgraffon-5, Aodh O'Sullivan, 11th Lord of Knockgraffon-4, Baudhach O'Sullivan, 10th Lord of Knockgraffon-3, Lorcan MacSullivan, 9th Lord of Knockgraffon-2, Eochaid Súilleabháinn, 8th Lord of Knockgraffon-1)

She married **Donal O'Sullivan Beare, Lord of Ardea Castle (45)** [11, 13, 18, 19, 21, 26] son of Sir Philip O'Sullivan Beare, Lord of Ardea Castle and Honora MacCarthy. Donal lived in Ardea Castle.

They had the following known son:

52 i **Philip O'Sullivan Beare, Lord of Ardea Castle** [18, 19, 26, 28].

31 **Conor O'Sullivan MacCragh** [9, 10, 223].
Born in 1444 [9, 10].

(Donal O'Sullivan MacCragh-15, Cragh O'Sullivan Mór-14, Dunlong O'Sullivan Mór-13, Bernard O'Sullivan Mór-12, Murtagh O'Sullivan-11, Dunlong O'Sullivan-10, Giolla na Bhflainn O'Sullivan Mór-9, Donal O'Sullivan Mór, 15th Lord of Knockgraffon-8, MacCraith O'Sullivan Mór, 14th Lord of Knockgraffon-7, Baudhach O'Sullivan, 13th Lord of Knockgraffon-6, Cathal O'Sullivan, 12th Lord of Knockgraffon-5, Aodh O'Sullivan, 11th Lord of Knockgraffon-4, Baudhach O'Sullivan, 10th Lord of Knockgraffon-3, Lorcan MacSullivan, 9th Lord of Knockgraffon-2, Eochaid Súilleabháinn, 8th Lord of Knockgraffon-1)

Conor was *The O'Sullivan MacCragh* (chief of the O'Sullivan MacCragh sept). Conor killed Cormach MacCarthy to avenge the murder of his father.

Conor O'Sullivan MacCragh had the following known son:

39 i Eoghan O'Sullivan MacCragh [9, 10] was born in 1474 [9, 10].

Generation 17

32 **Dermod (aka Dermond) O'Sullivan Beare** [12, 18, 19, 26, 33, 34, 35].
Born in 1526 in Dunboy Castle, County Cork, Munster, Ireland [35].

(Dermod O'Sullivan Beare, 11th Lord of Beare and Bantry-16, Donal O'Sullivan Beare, the Swarthy, 8th Lord of Beare and Bantry-15, Dermod (aka Dermond) Balluf O'Sullivan Beare-14, Teige O'Sullivan Beare-13, Amhiaffe O'Sullivan Beare-12, Annaidh O'Sullivan, 1st Lord of Beare and Bantry-11, Philip O'Sullivan-10, Giolla na Bhflainn O'Sullivan Mór-9, Donal O'Sullivan Mór, 15th Lord of Knockgraffon-8, MacCraith O'Sullivan Mór, 14th Lord of Knockgraffon-7, Baudhach O'Sullivan, 13th Lord of Knockgraffon-6, Cathal O'Sullivan, 12th Lord of Knockgraffon-5, Aodh O'Sullivan, 11th Lord of Knockgraffon-4, Baudhach O'Sullivan, 10th Lord of Knockgraffon-3, Lorcan MacSullivan, 9th Lord of Knockgraffon-2, Eochaid Súilleabháinn, 8th Lord of Knockgraffon-1)

Dermod (aka Dermond) was defeated by the English and fled to Spain where he received a pension of 50 gold pieces per month from the King of Spain. At that time, this was an enormous sum of money.

He married **Joan MacSweeny** [1, 18, 19, 26, 35]. She died before 1602 [32].

Dermod (aka Dermond) O'Sullivan Beare and Joan MacSweeny had the following known children:

40 i **Baronet John William O'Sullivan** [33, 34].
ii Philip O'Sullivan, Earl of Beare Haven [19, 39] was born in circa 1590 in

Dunboy Castle, County Cork, Ireland. He died in 1660 in Spain. Philip O'Sullivan was only twelve years old when Dunboy Castle was destroyed in 1602. He was sent to Spain and educated at the Dominican monastery San Martiño Pinario (Saint Martín Pinario) in Santiago de Compostella, Galicia, Spain. He was an officer in the Spanish Navy and the author of several books, including the *Historiae Catholicae Hiberniae Compendium*. He died at Coruña, Spain, in 1660 and his wife died soon after. Philip O'Sullivan Beare's *Historiae Catholicae Hiberniae Compendium* was published in Lisbon, Portugal in 1621. In 1850, it was republished with notes by Dr. Kelly of Maynooth. It contains a history of the English in Ireland from the Anglo-Norman Invasion to 1588, and a history of the O'Neill and O'Donal wars. The introduction said his mother was Johanna MacSweeny. She bore seventeen children, but all but four died before the fall of Dunboy Castle in 1602. Philip fought a duel against a man who made an insulting remark against his uncle, Donal Cam O'Sullivan, and took refuge from the Spanish police in the French Embassy. Soon after, he was back at his post in the Spanish Navy. In April, he wrote a letter to Dermod (aka Dermond), Donal Cam O'Sullivan's heir, consoling him on the death of his father and describing the Spanish naval action against the Turks in which his brother Daniel and several other Irish were killed. A letter from Father Peter Talbot, who later became Archbishop of Dublin, to the Marquis of Ormond, dated the 10th of January 1660, in Madrid said:

> *" ... The Earl of Beare Haven is dead and left only one daughter of twelve years to inherit his titles in Ireland and his goods here, which amount to 100,000 crowns ..."*

ii Leona O'Sullivan [19].
iii Daughter (name unknown) was a nun in Spain [19].

33 **Donal O'Sullivan Beare, 13th Lord of Beare and Bantry** [6, 17, 18, 19, 21, 25].
Born before 1537 in Dunboy Castle, County Cork, Munster, Ireland.
Died in 1563 [25].

(Dermod O'Sullivan Beare, 11th Lord of Beare and Bantry-16, Donal O'Sullivan Beare, the Swarthy, 8th Lord of Beare and Bantry-15, Dermod (aka Dermond) Balluf O'Sullivan Beare-14, Teige O'Sullivan Beare-13, Amhiaffe O'Sullivan Beare-12, Annaidh O'Sullivan, 1st Lord of Beare and Bantry-11, Philip O'Sullivan-10, Giolla na Bhflainn O'Sullivan Mór-9, Donal O'Sullivan Mór, 15th Lord of Knockgraffon-8, MacCraith O'Sullivan Mór, 14th Lord of Knockgraffon-7, Baudhach O'Sullivan, 13th Lord of Knockgraffon-6, Cathal O'Sullivan, 12th Lord of Knockgraffon-5, Aodh O'Sullivan, 11th Lord of Knockgraffon-4, Baudhach O'Sullivan, 10th Lord of Knockgraffon-3, Lorcan MacSullivan, 9th Lord of Knockgraffon-2, Eochaid Súilleabháinn, 8th Lord of Knockgraffon-1)

Donal O'Sullivan became 13th Lord of Beare and Bantry. In 1563, he was deposed in favor of his uncle Eochy, but was later restored. He was slain in 1563 by a MacGillycuddy. Donal had a son named Donal Cam, born in 1561, who became the 15th Lord of Beare and Bantry in 1593. His son Donal Cam opposed the English at the Battle of Kinsale and after several defeats, he refused to surrender and led 1,000 O'Sullivan Beare on an epic march to the castle of Brian O'Rourke.

He married **Margaret O'Brian,** daughter of Sir Daniel O'Brian ,Viscount of Clare and Catherine FitzGerald, Viscountess Clare [18, 19, 21, 25].

Donal O'Sullivan Beare,13th Lord of Beare and Bantry and Margaret O'Brian had the following known sons:

41 i **Donal Cam O'Sullivan Beare, Prince of Beare, 15th Lord of Beare and Bantry** [3, 6, 17, 18, 19, 21, 25, 40, 41, 42, 43, 44] was born in 1561 in Dunboy Castle, County Cork, Munster, Ireland [3, 19]. He died on the 16th of July 1618 in Madrid, Spain [3, 19].

42 ii **Dermod (aka Dermond) O'Sullivan Beare** [3] was born in Coruña. Spain.

34 **Sir Owen O'Sullivan Beare, 14th Lord of Beare and Bantry** [15, 17, 18, 19, 23, 27, 35, 36, 37].
Born before 1549 in Dunboy Castle, County Cork, Munster, Ireland.
Died in 1594 in Dunboy Castle, County Cork, Munster, Ireland [17, 35].

(Dermod O'Sullivan Beare, 11th Lord of Beare and Bantry-16, Donal O'Sullivan Beare, the Swarthy, 8th Lord of Beare and Bantry -15, Dermod (aka Dermond) Balluf O'Sullivan Beare-14, Teige O'Sullivan Beare -13, Amhiaffe O'Sullivan Beare-12, Annaidh O'Sullivan, 1st Lord of Beare and Bantry-11, Philip O'Sullivan-10, Giolla na Bhflainn O'Sullivan Mór-9, Donal O'Sullivan Mór, 15th Lord of Knockgraffon-8, MacCraith O'Sullivan Mór, 14th Lord of Knockgraffon-7, Baudhach O'Sullivan, 13th Lord of Knockgraffon-6, Cathal O'Sullivan, 12th Lord of Knockgraffon-5, Aodh O'Sullivan, 11th Lord of Knockgraffon-4, Baudhach O'Sullivan, 10th Lord of Knockgraffon-3, Lorcan MacSullivan, 9th Lord of Knockgraffon-2, Eochaid Súilleabháinn, 8th Lord of Knockgraffon-1)

Owen was elected, under the Irish law of tanistry, as the 14th Lord of Beare and Bantry when his brother Donal died without an heir of legitimate age (Donal's son Donal Cam was only two years old). Owen was arrested by the English for remaining neutral in a conflict with other Irish lords. When Owen's nephew Donal Cam came of age, he claimed as his inheritance Beare, Bantry, Ardea and all other castles in the domains including its harbor and Dunboy Castle. Donal Cam seized Carriganass Castle from Owen. Owen surrendered his property, partly held by his nephew Donal Cam, to the English in return for a knighthood and under the condition his property would be re-granted to him. He was released from jail and evicted his nephew Donal Cam from Carriganass Castle.

Donal Cam O'Sullivan appealed to Queen Elizabeth I under the English primogeniture law, which did not consider age as a factor in inheritance. Sir Owen was displaced again as clan chief. Donal Cam O'Sullivan became clan chief, and the 15th Lord of Beare and Bantry. As the new clan chief, Donal Cam claimed Carriganass Castle and made it his main base. In 1593, Sir Owen appealed the decision. The English divided the estate, giving Beare to Donal Cam and Bantry to Sir Owen. Owen was a member of the disappointing Perrott parliament in Dublin in 1585.

Sir Owen's son Dermod (aka Dermond) married Joan MacCarthy, daughter of Cormac MacCarthy Mór Lord Muscry and he died as Lord Beare and Bantry in 1617. Their son Dermod (Sir Owen's grandson) married Joan, daughter of Gerald FitzGerald, 16th Earl of Desmond. He succeeded his father and died in 1618. Marshall MacMahon, Duke of Magenta, second president of the Third French Republic, was one of his descendants.

Sir Owen O'Sullivan Beare, 14th Lord of Beare and Bantry married **Helena,** daughter of James, Lord Barry-Roe FitzGerald and Ellen MacCarthy Reagh [1, 18, 19, 27, 35, 37] in ca. 1570. She died after 1617. They had the following known children:

43 i **Owen O'Sullivan Beare, Lord of Beare and Bantry** [19, 23, 27, 35, 41, 45] was born in circa 1570 in Dunboy Castle, County Cork, Munster, Ireland. He died on the 31st of August 1616.

ii John O'Sullivan Beare [1, 19] was born in Dunboy Castle, County Cork, Munster, Ireland.

iii Donal O'Sullivan Beare, Lord of Dunkerron Castle, Lord of Bantry [1, 19] was born in Dunboy Castle, County Cork, Munster, Ireland.

iv Julia O'Sullivan Beare [1] was born in Dunboy Castle, County Cork, Munster, Ireland.

44 v **Gillycuddy O'Sullivan Beare** [1, 19] was born in Dunboy Castle, County Cork, Munster, Ireland.

vi Teige O'Sullivan Beare [19] was born in Dunboy Castle, County Cork, Munster, Ireland. Teige went to the low countries, where he served as a captain.

vii Honora O'Sullivan Beare [19].

35.. **Sir Philip O'Sullivan Beare, Lord of Ardea Castle** [13, 18, 19, 21, 22, 26, 28, 32, 35, 38]. Died in 1606 [18].

(Dermod O'Sullivan Beare, 11th Lord of Beare and Bantry-16, Donal O'Sullivan Beare, the Swarthy, 8th Lord of Beare and Bantry-15, Dermod (aka Dermond) Balluf O'Sullivan Beare-14, Teige O'Sullivan Beare-13, Amhiaffe O'Sullivan Beare-12, Annaidh O'Sullivan, 1st Lord of Beare and Bantry-11, Philip O'Sullivan-10, Giolla na Bhflainn O'Sullivan Mór-9, Donal O'Sullivan Mór, 15th Lord of Knockgraffon-8, MacCraith O'Sullivan Mór, 14th Lord of Knockgraffon-7, Baudhach O'Sullivan, 13th Lord of Knockgraffon-6, Cathal O'Sullivan, 12th Lord of Knockgraffon-5, Aodh O'Sullivan, 11th Lord of Knockgraffon-4, Baudhach O'Sullivan, 10th Lord of Knockgraffon-3, Lorcan MacSullivan, 9th Lord of Knockgraffon-2, Eochaid Súilleabháinn, 8th Lord of Knockgraffon-1)

He married **Honora MacCarthy,** daughter of Cormac MacCarthy, of Duhollow [13, 18, 19, 21].

Sir Philip O'Sullivan Beare, Lord of Ardea Castle and Honora MacCarthy had the following known children:

i Dermod (aka Dermond) O'Sullivan Beare, Lord of Ballygibbon [18, 19, 26].

ii Owen O'Sullivan Beare [18, 19, 26].

iii Ellen O'Sullivan Beare [18, 19, 26].
iv Julia O'Sullivan Beare [18, 19, 26].
45 v **Donal O'Sullivan Beare, Lord of Ardea Castle** [11, 13, 18, 19, 21, 26].

36 **Conor O'Sullivan Beare** [19].
Born in Dunboy Castle, County Cork, Munster, Ireland.

(Dermod O'Sullivan Beare, 11th Lord of Beare and Bantry-16, Donal O'Sullivan Beare, the Swarthy, 8th Lord of Beare and Bantry-15, Dermod (aka Dermond) Balluf O'Sullivan Beare-14, Teige O'Sullivan Beare-13, Amhiaffe O'Sullivan Beare-12, Annaidh O'Sullivan, 1st Lord of Beare and Bantry-11, Philip O'Sullivan-10, Giolla na Bhflainn O'Sullivan Mór-9, Donal O'Sullivan Mór, 15th Lord of Knockgraffon-8, MacCraith O'Sullivan Mór, 14th Lord of Knockgraffon-7, Baudhach O'Sullivan, 13th Lord of Knockgraffon-6, Cathal O'Sullivan, 12th Lord of Knockgraffon-5, Aodh O'Sullivan, 11th Lord of Knockgraffon-4, Baudhach O'Sullivan, 10th Lord of Knockgraffon-3, Lorcan MacSullivan, 9th Lord of Knockgraffon-2, Eochaid Súilleabháinn, 8th Lord of Knockgraffon-1)

Conor O'Sullivan Beare had the following known son:

i Teige O'Sullivan Beare [19]. He died in 1598.

37 **Owen O'Sullivan Mór, Lord of Dunkerron Castle** [11].
Born after 1640 [11].

(Owen O'Sullivan Mór Lord of Dunkerron Castle-16, Donal O'Sullivan Mór, Lord of Dunkerron O'Sullivan-15, Donal na Sgreadaidhe O'Sullivan Mór-14, Owen O'Sullivan Mór-13, Giolla Mohud O'Sullivan Mór-12, Anaduff O'Sullivan Beare-11, Philip O'Sullivan Mór-10, Giolla na Bhflainn O'Sullivan Mór-9, Donal O'Sullivan Mór, 15th Lord of Knockgraffon-8, MacCraith O'Sullivan Mór, 14th Lord of Knockgraffon-7, Baudhach O'Sullivan, 13th Lord of Knockgraffon-6, Cathal O'Sullivan, 12th Lord of Knockgraffon-5, Aodh O'Sullivan, 11th Lord of Knockgraffon-4, Baudhach O'Sullivan, 10th Lord of Knockgraffon-3, Lorcan MacSullivan, 9th Lord of Knockgraffon-2, Eochaid Súilleabháinn, 8th Lord of Knockgraffon-1)

Owen O'Sullivan Mór, of Dunkerron Castle had the following known son:

i Dermod O'Sullivan Mór [11].

38 **Donal O'Sullivan Mór, Lord of Dunkerron Castle** [11].

(Owen O'Sullivan Mór Lord of Dunkerron Castle-16, Donal O'Sullivan Mór, Lord of Dunkerron O'Sullivan-15, Donal na Sgreadaidhe O'Sullivan Mór-14, Owen O'Sullivan Mór-13, Giolla Mohud O'Sullivan Mór-12, Anaduff O'Sullivan-11, Philip O'Sullivan-10, Giolla na Bhflainn O'Sullivan Mór-9, Donal O'Sullivan Mór, 15th Lord of Knockgraffon-8, MacCraith O'Sullivan Mór, 14th Lord of Knockgraffon-7, Baudhach O'Sullivan, 13th Lord of Knockgraffon-6, Cathal O'Sullivan, 12th Lord of Knockgraffon-5, Aodh O'Sullivan, 11th Lord of Knockgraffon-4, Baudhach O'Sullivan, 10th Lord of Knockgraffon-3, Lorcan MacSullivan, 9th Lord of Knockgraffon-2, Eochaid Súilleabháinn, 8th Lord of Knockgraffon-1)

(John O'Hart's *Irish Pedigrees* does not have this generation.)

He married **Honora FitzGibbon,** daughter of Edmond FitzGibbon [11]. They had no known children.

He married **Jane FitzMaurice,** daughter of Patrick FitzMaurice [11]. They had the following known children:

i Owen O'Sullivan Mór, Lord of Dunkerron Castle [11]. Owen was *The O'Sullivan Mór* (clan chief) Lord of Dunkerron Castle. During the Cromwellian Wars of 1641, his property was forfeited to the English.

46 ii **Donal O'Sullivan Mór** [11]. He died in 1699 [11].

iii Philip O'Sullivan Mór [11].

iv Dominick O'Sullivan Mór [11].

v Ellen O'Sullivan Mór [11].

vi Mary O'Sullivan Mór [11].

vii Dermod O'Sullivan Mór [11].

viii Julia O'Sullivan Mór [11].

39 **Eoghan O'Sullivan MacCragh** [9, 10, 225] was born in 1474 [9, 10].

(Conor O'Sullivan MacCragh-16, Donal O'Sullivan MacCragh-15, Cragh O'Sullivan Mór-14, Dunlong O'Sullivan Mór-13, Bernard O'Sullivan Mór-12, Murtagh O'Sullivan-11, Dunlong O'Sullivan-10, Giolla na Bhflainn O'Sullivan Mór-9, Donal O'Sullivan Mór, 15th Lord of Knockgraffon-8, MacCraith O'Sullivan Mór, 14th Lord of Knockgraffon-7, Baudhach O'Sullivan, 13th Lord of Knockgraffon-6, Cathal O'Sullivan, 12th Lord of Knockgraffon-5, Aodh O'Sullivan, 11th Lord of Knockgraffon-4, Baudhach O'Sullivan, 10th Lord of Knockgraffon-3, Lorcan MacSullivan, 9th Lord of Knockgraffon-2, Eochaid Súilleabháinn, 8th Lord of Knockgraffon-1)

Dermod (aka Dermond) Lord of Dunkerron Castle, *The O'Sullivan Mór*, died and his younger brother Donal na Sgreadaidhe was elected O'Sullivan Mór. There are few records on Eoghan because as a young member of the O'Sullivan MacCragh sept, he and his mother were forced to leave Cappanucuss Castle. This family became fragmented and dispersed to seek their fortune elsewhere. With the loss of property and status, this senior O'Sullivan sept was rarely recorded in history.

Eoghan was *The O'Sullivan MacCragh* (chief of the O'Sullivan MacCragh sept).

Eoghan O'Sullivan MacCragh had the following known son:

47 i **Buadach O'Sullivan MacCragh**[9, 10] was born in 1504[9, 10].

Generation 18

40 **Sir John William O'Sullivan Beare, Baronet** [33, 34].

(Dermod (aka Dermond) O'Sullivan Beare-17, Dermod O'Sullivan Beare, 11th Lord of Beare and Bantry-16, Donal O'Sullivan Beare, the Swarthy, 8th Lord of Beare and Bantry-15, Dermod (aka Dermond) Balluf O'Sullivan Beare-14, Teige O'Sullivan Beare-13, Amhiaffe O'Sullivan Beare-12, Annaidh O'Sullivan, 1st Lord of Beare and Bantry-11, Philip O'Sullivan-10, Giolla na Bhflainn

O'Sullivan Mór-9, Donal O'Sullivan Mór, 15th Lord of Knockgraffon-8, MacCraith O'Sullivan Mór, 14th Lord of Knockgraffon-7, Baudhach O'Sullivan, 13th Lord of Knockgraffon-6, Cathal O'Sullivan, 12th Lord of Knockgraffon-5, Aodh O'Sullivan, 11th Lord of Knockgraffon-4, Baudhach O'Sullivan, 10th Lord of Knockgraffon-3, Lorcan MacSullivan, 9th Lord of Knockgraffon-2, Eochaid Súilleabháinn, 8th Lord of Knockgraffon-1)

John O'Sullivan was with Bonnie Prince Charles of Scotland (Charles Edward Stuart) when he was defeated at the Battle of Culloden, ending his Jacobite revolution. John was made a Baronet by King James III. The title of Baronet was invented by King James I, who sold the title for £1,000 to finance the troops required for his occupation of Ireland. A baronet ranked below a baron and above a knight, except for the Knight of the Garter and in Scotland the Knight of the Thistle which both outranked a baronet.

He married **Louisa FitzGerald** [33, 34]. They had the following known son:

48 i **Thomas Herbert O'Sullivan** [33, 34].

41 **Donal Cam O'Sullivan Beare, 15th Lord of Beare and Bantry, Prince of Eóganachta** [3, 6, 17, 18, 19, 21, 25, 40, 41, 42, 43, 44].

Born in 1561 in Dunboy Castle, County Cork, Munster, Ireland [3, 19].
Died on the 16th of July 1618 in Madrid, Spain [3, 19].

(Donal O'Sullivan Beare, 13th Lord of Beare and Bantry-17, Dermod O'Sullivan Beare, 11th Lord of Beare and Bantry-16, Donal O'Sullivan Beare, the Swarthy, 8th Lord of Beare and Bantry-15, Dermod (aka Dermond) Balluf O'Sullivan Beare-14, Teige O'Sullivan Beare-13, Amhiaffe O'Sullivan Beare-12, Annaidh O'Sullivan, 1st Lord of Beare and Bantry-11, Philip O'Sullivan-10, Giolla na Bhflainn O'Sullivan Mór-9, Donal O'Sullivan Mór, 15th Lord of Knockgraffon-8, MacCraith O'Sullivan Mór, 14th Lord of Knockgraffon-7, Baudhach O'Sullivan, 13th Lord of Knockgraffon-6, Cathal O'Sullivan, 12th Lord of Knockgraffon-5, Aodh O'Sullivan, 11th Lord of Knockgraffon-4, Baudhach O'Sullivan, 10th Lord of Knockgraffon-3, Lorcan MacSullivan, 9th Lord of Knockgraffon-2, Eochaid Súilleabháinn, 8th Lord of Knockgraffon-1)

In 1581, Captain Zouch (*Siuitsi*) came to plunder Beare. Donal Cam O'Sullivan, with his small army of less than fifty men, defeated Captain Zouch and killed circa 300 of his men. *The Annals of The Four Masters* said:

> " ... *The son of O'Sullivan Beare* [Donal Cam] *gave a defeat to the people of Carberry in the month of December. It was thus effected: Captain Siuitsi set out from Cork, through Carberry, for the monastery of Bantry. He sent the sons of Turlough, son of Mulmurry, son of Donough MacSweeny, Dermot, son of O'Donovan Donnell, the son of Teige, son of Dermot, and some others of the heads of tribes and gentlemen of Carberry, to plunder the son of O'Sullivan. These parties sent by the Captain seized great preys* [hostages] *and much booty. Donnell thought it shameful to suffer his property to be carried away, he himself being alive; and he attacked the Irish bands around the booty, and proved on that day that it is not by the numbers of men that battle is gained, for Donnell slew nearly three hundred of the Carberry-men, though his own forces in that engagement scarcely exceeded fifty men able to bear arms*.... "

Under Irish law, Donal Cam would have been elected clan chief and Lord of Beare and Bantry, but he was only two years old when his father died, therefore his uncle Owen was elected. When Donal Cam came of age, he believed that by law he should be clan chief. He seized Carriganass Castle. His uncle Owen surrendered his property, including the part in the hands of his nephew Donal Cam, to the English Crown under the condition he would be made a knight, and his property would be re-granted to him. Then he evicted his nephew Donal Cam from Carriganass Castle.

Donal Cam O'Sullivan appealed to Queen Elizabeth I under the English primogeniture law, which does not recognize age as a factor in inheritance. Sir Owen was displaced and Donal Cam O'Sullivan became clan chief and 15th Lord of Beare and Bantry. As the new clan chief, Donal Cam claimed Carriganass Castle and made it his main base. In 1593, Sir Owen appealed the decision. The English divided the estate, giving Beare to Donal Cam and Bantry to Sir Owen. Sir Owen's son Owen succeeded him as Lord of Bantry and Donal Cam remained Lord of Beare.

When the O'Neill clan chief Hugh O'Neill revolted against the English, Donal Cam O'Sullivan, Lord of Beare, sided with him, hoping to gain complete independence from the English Crown. Believing the odds were against his cousin, Owen, Lord of Bantry, sided with the English and put himself forward as the Queen's O'Sullivan.

England was already at war with Spain, so Spain supported the Irish rebellion with troops and equipment. After the fall of Kinsale, Lord Donal Cam O'Sullivan Beare permitted a Spanish garrison of 100 infantrymen, ten artillery pieces, and munitions into Dunboy (Dunbuidhe) Castle. The Spanish also garrisoned other castles.

After his defeat in County Cork, Donal Cam led an epic march from Glengarriff to Leitrim Castle in the north. Of the 1,000 who set out for Leitrim Castle only thirty-five reached their destination: Eighteen fighting men, sixteen servants and one woman. For detailed information about Donal Cam O'Sullivan during Sir George Carew's Siege of Dunboy Castle, its aftermath and Donal Cam's epic march from County Cork to Brian O'Rourke's Leitrim Castle, see: *Part I The siege of Dunboy Castle.*

On the 2nd of January 1602, Donal Cam was declared an outlaw by the English. In 1604, he sailed to Spain with his uncle Dermod (aka Dermond) and Dermod's wife Joan McSweeney, where they joined their children who were already there. They were warmly welcomed by King Philip of Spain, who gave Donal Cam a pension of 300 gold pieces per month and made him a grandee of the Kingdom of Spain. This was an enormous sum of money at that time. He was made Knight of Saint Jago and Earl of Beare Haven. Donal Cam was assassinated in Madrid on the 16th of July 1618 at the age of 57 by an Anglo-Irishman named Bath.

As an English supporter, Donal Cam's cousin Owen was rewarded with Donal Cam's property on the Beara Peninsula and Bantry, but it was actually ruled by the English Sir George Carew, Lord President of Munster.

Donal Cam O'Sullivan married **Honora O'Sullivan Mór,** daughter of Owen O'Sullivan Mór, 7th Lord of Dunkerron [19, 25] and they had the following known sons:

i Donal O'Sullivan, Prince of Beare, 2nd Earl of Beare Haven [3, 19, 35] was born in 1600. He was killled between 1615-1621 in Belgrade, Serbia [19]. Donal was four years old when his father fled to Spain. He was living with Philip O'Sullivan when Philip wrote his book in 1621. He was page to King Philip IV of Spain and later a knight of Saint Lege. He was known to be alive in 1615, but was not mentioned in Philip O'Sullivan's book published in 1621. Donal entered the Spanish army and was killed in Belgrade fighting the Turks.

ii Dermod (aka Dermond) O'Sullivan, Count of Dunboy [1, 3, 19] was born in 1604 [19]. He died after 1621.

Donal Cam O'Sullivan, 15th Lord of Beare and Bantry, Prince of Eóganachta married Ellen O'Sullivan Mór, daughter of Donal O'Sullivan Mór. [3]. They had no known children.

42 **Dermod (aka Dermond) O'Sullivan** [3].
Born in Coruña, Spain.

(Donal O'Sullivan Beare, 13th Lord of Beare and Bantry-17, Dermod O'Sullivan Beare, 11th Lord of Beare and Bantry-16, Donal O'Sullivan Beare, the Swarthy, 8th Lord of Beare and Bantry-15, Dermod (aka Dermond) Balluf O'Sullivan Beare-14, Teige O'Sullivan Beare-13, Amhiaffe O'Sullivan Beare-12, Annaidh O'Sullivan, 1st Lord of Beare and Bantry-11, Philip O'Sullivan-10, Giolla na Bhflainn O'Sullivan Mór-9, Donal O'Sullivan Mór, 15th Lord of Knockgraffon-8, MacCraith O'Sullivan Mór, 14th Lord of Knockgraffon-7, Baudhach O'Sullivan, 13th Lord of Knockgraffon-6, Cathal O'Sullivan, 12th Lord of Knockgraffon-5, Aodh O'Sullivan, 11th Lord of Knockgraffon-4, Baudhach O'Sullivan, 10th Lord of Knockgraffon-3, Lorcan MacSullivan, 9th Lord of Knockgraffon-2, Eochaid Súilleabháinn, 8th Lord of Knockgraffon-1)

Dermod died at the age of 100 years in Coruña, Spain. His wife died soon after. They had the following known son:

i Philip O'Sullivan [3, 19].

43 **Owen O'Sullivan Beare, 16th Lord of Beare and Bantry** [19, 23, 27, 35, 41, 45].
Born in circa 1570 in Dunboy Castle, County Cork, Munster, Ireland.
Died on the 31st of August 1616.

(Sir Owen O'Sullivan Beare, 14th Lord of Beare and Bantry-17, Dermod O'Sullivan Beare, 11th Lord of Beare and Bantry-16, Donal O'Sullivan Beare, the Swarthy, 8th Lord of Beare and Bantry-15, Dermod (aka Dermond) Balluf O'Sullivan Beare-14, Teige O'Sullivan Beare-13, Amhiaffe O'Sullivan Beare-12, Annaidh O'Sullivan, 1st Lord of Beare and Bantry-11, Philip O'Sullivan-10, Giolla na Bhflainn O'Sullivan Mór-9, Donal O'Sullivan Mór, 15th Lord of Knockgraffon-8, MacCraith O'Sullivan Mór, 14th Lord of Knockgraffon-7, Baudhach O'Sullivan, 13th Lord of Knockgraffon-6, Cathal O'Sullivan, 12th Lord of Knockgraffon-5, Aodh O'Sullivan, 11th Lord of Knockgraffon-4, Baudhach O'Sullivan, 10th Lord of Knockgraffon-3, Lorcan MacSullivan, 9th Lord of Knockgraffon-2, Eochaid Súilleabháinn, 8th Lord of Knockgraffon-1)

When Hugh O'Neill, chief of the O'Neill clan, revolted to gain complete independence from England, Owen O'Sullivan Beare, Lord of Bantry, son of Sir Owen O'Sullivan Beare,

14th Lord of Beare and Bantry, supported the English. He decided the English would be the winning side and put himself forward as the Queen's O'Sullivan. Owen provided the English with Irish troop strength and disposition.

After Donal Cam was defeated and fled to Spain, Queen Elizabeth I rewarded Owen with his cousin Donal Cam O'Sullivan's property and he became the 16th Lord Beare and Bantry. In fact the real rulers were the English. Owen was bitterly despised by the other O'Sullivans for his treachery and called his line the O'Sullivan Gilda (foreigners). Owen abandoned Carriganass Castle and moved to Reenadisert Castle in County Cork between Bantry and Glengarriff.

He married **Helena Butler,** daughter of Pierce Butler, [6, 27, 35] born in circa 1575 in Ireland. She died after 1616 [27]. The Butlers were Hiberno-Normans, Norman lords who settled in Ireland on confiscated Irish property, adopted Irish customs, spoke the Irish language and married into Irish families.

Owen O'Sullivan Beare, 16th Lord of Beare and Bantry, and Helena Butler had the following known children:

	i	Dermod (aka Dermond) O'Sullivan Beare [1, 19, 45, 46] was born in 1595 in Dunboy Castle, County Cork, Munster, Ireland.
49	ii	**Owen Donal O'Sullivan Beare** [19, 27, 45, 47, 48] was born after 1599 in Dunboy Castle, County Cork, Munster, Ireland.
	iii	Connor O'Sullivan Beare [45] was born after1600 in Dunboy Castle, County Cork, Munster, Ireland.
	iv	Helena O'Sullivan Beare [45] was born after 1600 in Dunboy Castle, County Cork, Munster, Ireland.
	v	Julia O'Sullivan Beare [19, 45] was born after 1600 in Dunboy Castle, County Cork, Munster, Ireland.
	vi	Catherine O'Sullivan Beare [19].
	vii	Honora O'Sullivan Beare [19, 45].
50	viii	**Philip O'Sullivan Beare** [19, 25, 45] was born after 1600 in Dunboy Castle, County Cork, Munster, Ireland. He died after 1674.
	ix	Donal O'Sullivan Beare [1, 19].

44 **Gillycuddy O'Sullivan Beare** [1, 19].
Born in Dunboy Castle, County Cork, Munster, Ireland.

(Sir Owen O'Sullivan Beare, 14th Lord of Beare and Bantry-17, Dermod O'Sullivan Beare, 11th Lord of Beare and Bantry-16, Donal O'Sullivan Beare, the Swarthy, 8th Lord of Beare and Bantry-15, Dermod (aka Dermond) Balluf O'Sullivan Beare-14, Teige O'Sullivan Beare-13, Amhiaffe O'Sullivan Beare-12, Annaidh O'Sullivan, 1st Lord of Beare and Bantry-11, Philip O'Sullivan-10, Giolla na Bhflainn O'Sullivan Mór-9, Donal O'Sullivan Mór, 15th Lord of Knockgraffon-8, MacCraith O'Sullivan Mór, 14th Lord of Knockgraffon-7, Baudhach O'Sullivan, 13th Lord of Knockgraffon-6, Cathal O'Sullivan, 12th Lord of Knockgraffon-5, Aodh O'Sullivan, 11th Lord of Knockgraffon-4, Baudhach O'Sullivan, 10th Lord of Knockgraffon-3, Lorcan MacSullivan, 9th Lord of Knockgraffon-2, Eochaid Súilleabháinn, 8th Lord of Knockgraffon-1)

Gillycuddy O'Sullivan Beare had the following known son:

51 i **Conor O'Sullivan Beare** [1, 19].

45 **Donal O'Sullivan Beare, Lord of Ardea Castle** [11, 13, 18, 19, 21, 26].

(Sir Philip O'Sullivan Beare Lord of Ardea Castle-17, Dermod O'Sullivan Beare, 11th Lord of Beare and Bantry-16, Donal O'Sullivan Beare, the Swarthy, 8th Lord of Beare and Bantry-15, Dermod (aka Dermond) Balluf O'Sullivan Beare-14, Teige O'Sullivan Beare-13, Amhiaffe O'Sullivan Beare-12, Annaidh O'Sullivan, 1st Lord of Beare and Bantry-11, Philip O'Sullivan Mór-10, Giolla na Bhflainn O'Sullivan Mór-9, Donal O'Sullivan Mór, 15th Lord of Knockgraffon-8, MacCraith O'Sullivan Mór, 14th Lord of Knockgraffon-7, Baudhach O'Sullivan, 13th Lord of Knockgraffon-6, Cathal O'Sullivan, 12th Lord of Knockgraffon-5, Aodh O'Sullivan, 11th Lord of Knockgraffon-4, Baudhach O'Sullivan, 10th Lord of Knockgraffon-3, Lorcan MacSullivan, 9th Lord of Knockgraffon-2, Eochaid Súilleabháinn, 8th Lord of Knockgraffon-1)

He married **Ellen O'Sullivan Mór** (30) daughter of Donal O'Sullivan Mór, Lord of Dunkerron Castle, and Mary Oge [11, 13, 18, 19, 21].

Donal O'Sullivan Beare, Lord of Ardea Castle and **Ellen O'Sullivan Mór** had the following known son:

52 i Philip O'Sullivan Beare, Lord of Ardea Castle [18, 19, 26, 28].

46 **Donal O'Sullivan Mór** [11].
Died in 1699 [11].

(Donal O'Sullivan, Lord of Dunkerron Castle-17 Owen O'Sullivan Mór, Lord of Dunkerron Castle-16, Donal O'Sullivan Mór, Lord of Dunkerron O'Sullivan-15, Donal na Sgreadaidhe O'Sullivan Mór-14, Owen O'Sullivan Mór-13, Giolla Mohud O'Sullivan Mór-12, Anaduff O'Sullivan-11, Philip O'Sullivan-10, Giolla na Bhflainn O'Sullivan Mór-9, Donal O'Sullivan Mór, 15th Lord of Knockgraffon-8, MacCraith O'Sullivan Mór, 14th Lord of Knockgraffon-7, Baudhach O'Sullivan, 13th Lord of Knockgraffon-6, Cathal O'Sullivan, 12th Lord of Knockgraffon-5, Aodh O'Sullivan, 11th Lord of Knockgraffon-4, Baudhach O'Sullivan, 10th Lord of Knockgraffon-3, Lorcan MacSullivan, 9th Lord of Knockgraffon-2, Eochaid Súilleabháinn, 8th Lord of Knockgraffon-1)

Donal O'Sullivan Mór had the following known son:

53 i **Rory-Rambar O'Sullivan Mór** [11].

47 **Buadach O'Sullivan MacCragh** [9, 10, 226].
Born in 1504 [9, 10].

(Eoghan O'Sullivan MacCragh-17, Conor O'Sullivan MacCragh-16, Donal O'Sullivan MacCragh-15, Cragh O'Sullivan Mór-14, Dunlong O'Sullivan Mór-13, Bernard O'Sullivan Mór-12, Murtagh O'Sullivan-11, Dunlong O'Sullivan-10, Giolla na Bhflainn O'Sullivan Mór-9, Donal O'Sullivan Mór, 15th Lord of Knockgraffon-8, MacCraith O'Sullivan Mór, 14th Lord of Knockgraffon-7, Baudhach O'Sullivan, 13th Lord of Knockgraffon-6, Cathal O'Sullivan, 12th Lord of Knockgraffon-5, Aodh O'Sullivan, 11th Lord of Knockgraffon-4, Baudhach O'Sullivan, 10th Lord of Knockgraffon-3, Lorcan MacSullivan, 9th Lord of Knockgraffon-2, Eochaid Súilleabháinn, 8th Lord of Knockgraffon-

1)

Buadach was *The O'Sullivan MacCragh* (chief of the O'Sullivan MacCragh sept).

Buadach O'Sullivan MacCragh had the following known son:

54 i **Donogh O'Sullivan MacCragh** [9, 10] was born in 1534 [9, 10].

Generation 19

48 **Thomas Herbert O'Sullivan** [33, 34].

(Sir John William O'Sullivan Beare, Baronet-18, Dermod (aka Dermond) O'Sullivan Beare-17, Dermod O'Sullivan Beare, 11th Lord of Beare and Bantry-16, Donal O'Sullivan Beare, the Swarthy, 8th Lord of Beare and Bantry-15, Dermod (aka Dermond) Balluf O'Sullivan Beare-14, Teige O'Sullivan Beare-13, Amhiaffe O'Sullivan Beare-12, Annaidh O'Sullivan, 1st Lord of Beare and Bantry-11, Philip O'Sullivan-10, Giolla na Bhflainn O'Sullivan Mór-9, Donal O'Sullivan Mór, 15th Lord of Knockgraffon-8, MacCraith O'Sullivan Mór, 14th Lord of Knockgraffon-7, Baudhach O'Sullivan, 13th Lord of Knockgraffon-6, Cathal O'Sullivan, 12th Lord of Knockgraffon-5, Aodh O'Sullivan, 11th Lord of Knockgraffon-4, Baudhach O'Sullivan, 10th Lord of Knockgraffon-3, Lorcan MacSullivan, 9th Lord of Knockgraffon-2, Eochaid Súilleabháinn, 8th Lord of Knockgraffon-1)

He married **Mary McReady** [33, 34] and they had the following known son:

55 i **John Thomas FitzGerald O'Sullivan** [33, 34].

49 **Owen Donal O'Sullivan Beare** [19, 27, 45, 47, 48]
Born after 1599 in Dunboy Castle, County Cork, Munster, Ireland.

(Owen O'Sullivan Beare Lord of Beare and Bantry-18, Sir Owen O'Sullivan Beare, 14th Lord of Beare and Bantry-17, Dermod O'Sullivan Beare, 11th Lord of Beare and Bantry-16, Donal O'Sullivan Beare, the Swarthy, 8th Lord of Beare and Bantry-15, Dermod (aka Dermond) Balluf O'Sullivan Beare-14, Teige O'Sullivan Beare-13, Amhiaffe O'Sullivan Beare-12, Annaidh O'Sullivan, 1st Lord of Beare and Bantry-11, Philip O'Sullivan-10, Giolla na Bhflainn O'Sullivan Mór-9, Donal O'Sullivan Mór, 15th Lord of Knockgraffon-8, MacCraith O'Sullivan Mór, 14th Lord of Knockgraffon-7, Baudhach O'Sullivan, 13th Lord of Knockgraffon-6, Cathal O'Sullivan, 12th Lord of Knockgraffon-5, Aodh O'Sullivan, 11th Lord of Knockgraffon-4, Baudhach O'Sullivan, 10th Lord of Knockgraffon-3, Lorcan MacSullivan, 9th Lord of Knockgraffon-2, Eochaid Súilleabháinn, 8th Lord of Knockgraffon-1)

Owen Donal's father, Owen, supported the English against his own family in the battles of Kinsale and Dunboy in 1602. But 39 years later, in 1641, the younger Owen was involved in a rebellion against the English in support of the Stuarts. Owen Donal O'Sullivan was condemned and fled Ireland. His family scattered among relatives and friends, and some immigrated to America. He was attained in 1660 and forfeited his property.

He married **Joanne Elisabeth Browne,** daughter of William Browne and Margaret Wilson and granddaughter of John Browne [27]. They had the following known children:

56 i **John Thomas O'Sullivan Beare** [27, 45, 49, 50, 51, 52, 53, 54] was born in 1637. He died on the 7th of September 1698 in Princess Ann County, Virginia.

ii Dermod (aka Dermond) O'Sullivan Beare [45] immigrated to America in 1656 and died in the same year. He left a will.

iii Elisabeth O'Sullivan Beare [45] was born in Ireland.

iv Anne O'Sullivan Beare [45] was born in Ireland.

50 **Philip O'Sullivan Beare** [19, 25, 45].
Born in circa1600 in Dunboy Castle, County Cork, Munster, Ireland.
Died after 1674.

(Owen O'Sullivan Beare Lord of Beare and Bantry-18, Sir Owen O'Sullivan Beare, 14th Lord of Beare and Bantry-17, Dermod O'Sullivan Beare, 11th Lord of Beare and Bantry-16, Donal O'Sullivan Beare, the Swarthy, 8th Lord of Beare and Bantry-15, Dermod (aka Dermond) Balluf O'Sullivan Beare-14, Teige O'Sullivan Beare-13, Amhiaffe O'Sullivan Beare-12, Annaidh O'Sullivan, 1st Lord of Beare and Bantry-11, Philip O'Sullivan-10, Giolla na Bhflainn O'Sullivan Mór-9, Donal O'Sullivan Mór, 15th Lord of Knockgraffon-8, MacCraith O'Sullivan Mór, 14th Lord of Knockgraffon-7, Baudhach O'Sullivan, 13th Lord of Knockgraffon-6, Cathal O'Sullivan, 12th Lord of Knockgraffon-5, Aodh O'Sullivan, 11th Lord of Knockgraffon-4, Baudhach O'Sullivan, 10th Lord of Knockgraffon-3, Lorcan MacSullivan, 9th Lord of Knockgraffon-2, Eochaid Súilleabháinn, 8th Lord of Knockgraffon-1)

He married **Ellen MacTeige MacCarthy,** daughter of MacTeige MacCarthy [1, 19]. They had the following son.

57 i **Daniel O'Sullivan Beare, Lord of Ardea Castle** [21, 25, 26, 28].

51 **Conor O'Sullivan Beare** [1, 19].

(Gillycuddy O'Sullivan Beare-18, Sir Owen O'Sullivan Beare, 14th Lord of Beare and Bantry-17, Dermod O'Sullivan Beare, 11th Lord of Beare and Bantry-16, Donal O'Sullivan Beare, the Swarthy, 8th Lord of Beare and Bantry-15, Dermod (aka Dermond) Balluf O'Sullivan Beare-14, Teige O'Sullivan Beare-13, Amhiaffe O'Sullivan Beare-12, Annaidh O'Sullivan, 1st Lord of Beare and Bantry-11, Philip O'Sullivan-10, Giolla na Bhflainn O'Sullivan Mór-9, Donal O'Sullivan Mór, 15th Lord of Knockgraffon-8, MacCraith O'Sullivan Mór, 14th Lord of Knockgraffon-7, Baudhach O'Sullivan, 13th Lord of Knockgraffon-6, Cathal O'Sullivan, 12th Lord of Knockgraffon-5, Aodh O'Sullivan, 11th Lord of Knockgraffon-4, Baudhach O'Sullivan, 10th Lord of Knockgraffon-3, Lorcan MacSullivan, 9th Lord of Knockgraffon-2, Eochaid Súilleabháinn, 8th Lord of Knockgraffon-1)

He was attained by the English in 1641 and lost his property.

Conor O'Sullivan Beare had the following known son:

i Philip O'Sullivan [1, 19] owned Ardea Castle, but was attained in 1641 and lost his property. It appears that he, his father and a number of other relatives all supported the Stuarts and as a result their property was confiscated by the English crown.

52 **Philip O'Sullivan Beare, Lord of Ardea Castle** [18, 19, 26, 28].

(Donal O'Sullivan Beare, Lord of Ardea Castle-18, Sir Philip O'Sullivan Beare, Lord of Ardea Castle-17, Dermod O'Sullivan Beare, 11th Lord of Beare and Bantry-16, Donal O'Sullivan Beare, the Swarthy, 8th Lord of Beare and Bantry-15, Dermod (aka Dermond) Balluf O'Sullivan Beare-14, Teige O'Sullivan Beare-13, Amhiaffe O'Sullivan Beare-12, Annaidh O'Sullivan, 1st Lord of Beare and Bantry-11, Philip O'Sullivan-10, Giolla na Bhflainn O'Sullivan Mór-9, Donal O'Sullivan Mór, 15th Lord of Knockgraffon-8, MacCraith O'Sullivan Mór, 14th Lord of Knockgraffon-7, Baudhach O'Sullivan, 13th Lord of Knockgraffon-6, Cathal O'Sullivan, 12th Lord of Knockgraffon-5, Aodh O'Sullivan, 11th Lord of Knockgraffon-4, Baudhach O'Sullivan, 10th Lord of Knockgraffon-3, Lorcan MacSullivan, 9th Lord of Knockgraffon-2, Eochaid Súilleabháinn, 8th Lord of Knockgraffon-1)

Philip was attained in 1641 and his property was confiscated.

Philip O'Sullivan Beare, Lord of Ardea Castle had the following son:

57 i Daniel O'Sullivan, Lord of Ardea Castle

53 **Rory-Rambar O'Sullivan Mór** [11].

(Donal O'Sullivan Mór-18, Donal O'Sullivanl, Lord of Dunkerron Castle-17 Owen O'Sullivan Mór. Lord of Dunkerron Castle-16, Donal O'Sullivan Mór, Lord of Dunkerron O'Sullivan-15, Donal na Sgreadaidhe O'Sullivan Mór-14, Owen O'Sullivan Mór-13, Giolla Mohud O'Sullivan Mór-12, Anaduff O'Sullivan-11, Philip O'Sullivan-10, Giolla na Bhflainn O'Sullivan Mór-9, Donal O'Sullivan Mór, 15th Lord of Knockgraffon-8, MacCraith O'Sullivan Mór, 14th Lord of Knockgraffon-7, Baudhach O'Sullivan, 13th Lord of Knockgraffon-6, Cathal O'Sullivan, 12th Lord of Knockgraffon-5, Aodh O'Sullivan, 11th Lord of Knockgraffon-4, Baudhach O'Sullivan, 10th Lord of Knockgraffon-3, Lorcan MacSullivan, 9th Lord of Knockgraffon-2, Eochaid Súilleabháinn, 8th Lord of Knockgraffon-1)

He married **Juliana O'Sullivan Beare** [11].

Rory-Rambar O'Sullivan Mór and Juliana O'Sullivan Beare had the following known son:

i Donal O'Sullivan Mór [11]. He died on the 16th of April 1754 [11]. Donal was the hereditary Prince of Dunkerron. He was the last male representative of the House of O'Sullivan Mór.

54 **Donogh O'Sullivan MacCragh** [9, 10, 226].
Born in 1534 [9, 10].

(Buadach O'Sullivan MacCragh-18, Eoghan O'Sullivan MacCragh-17, Conor O'Sullivan MacCragh-16, Donal O'Sullivan MacCragh-15, Cragh O'Sullivan Mór-14, Dunlong O'Sullivan Mór-13, Bernard O'Sullivan Mór-12, Murtagh O'Sullivan-11, Dunlong O'Sullivan-10, Giolla na Bhflainn O'Sullivan Mór-9, Donal O'Sullivan Mór, 15th Lord of Knockgraffon-8, MacCraith O'Sullivan Mór, 14th Lord of Knockgraffon-7, Baudhach O'Sullivan, 13th Lord of Knockgraffon-6, Cathal O'Sullivan, 12th Lord of Knockgraffon-5, Aodh O'Sullivan, 11th Lord of Knockgraffon-4, Baudhach O'Sullivan, 10th Lord of Knockgraffon-3, Lorcan MacSullivan, 9th Lord of Knockgraffon-2, Eochaid Súilleabháinn, 8th Lord of Knockgraffon-1)

Donogh was *The O'Sullivan MacCragh* (chief of the O'Sullivan MacCragh sept).

Donogh O'Sullivan MacCragh had the following known son:

58 i **Conor O'Sullivan MacCragh** [9, 10] was born in 1564 [9, 10].

Generation 20

55 **John Thomas FitzGerald O'Sullivan Beare** [33, 34].

(Thomas Herbert O'Sullivan Beare-19, Sir John William O'Sullivan Beare, Baronet-18, Dermod (aka Dermond) O'Sullivan Beare-17, Dermod O'Sullivan Beare, 11th Lord of Beare and Bantry-16, Donal O'Sullivan Beare, the Swarthy, 8th Lord of Beare and Bantry-15, Dermod (aka Dermond) Balluf O'Sullivan Beare-14, Teige O'Sullivan Beare-13, Amhiaffe O'Sullivan Beare-12, Annaidh O'Sullivan, 1st Lord of Beare and Bantry-11, Philip O'Sullivan-10, Giolla na Bhflainn O'Sullivan Mór-9, Donal O'Sullivan Mór, 15th Lord of Knockgraffon-8, MacCraith O'Sullivan Mór, 14th Lord of Knockgraffon-7, Baudhach O'Sullivan, 13th Lord of Knockgraffon-6, Cathal O'Sullivan, 12th Lord of Knockgraffon-5, Aodh O'Sullivan, 11th Lord of Knockgraffon-4, Baudhach O'Sullivan, 10th Lord of Knockgraffon-3, Lorcan MacSullivan, 9th Lord of Knockgraffon-2, Eochaid Súilleabháinn, 8th Lord of Knockgraffon-1)

He married **Mary Rowley** [33] born in Bower End, Staffordshire, England. They had the following known son:

i John Louis O'Sullivan [33, 34].

56 **John Thomas O'Sullivan Beare** [27, 45, 49, 50, 51].
Born in 1637.
Died on the 7th of September 1698 in Princess Ann County, Virginia.

(Owen Donal O'Sullivan-19, Owen O'Sullivan Beare Lord of Beare and Bantry-18, Sir Owen O'Sullivan Beare, 14th Lord of Beare and Bantry-17, Dermod O'Sullivan Beare, 11th Lord of Beare and Bantry-16, Donal O'Sullivan Beare, the Swarthy, 8th Lord of Beare and Bantry-15, Dermod (aka Dermond) Balluf O'Sullivan Beare-14, Teige O'Sullivan Beare-13, Amhiaffe O'Sullivan Beare-12, Annaidh O'Sullivan, 1st Lord of Beare and Bantry-11, Philip O'Sullivan-10, Giolla na Bhflainn O'Sullivan Mór-9, Donal O'Sullivan Mór, 15th Lord of Knockgraffon-8, MacCraith O'Sullivan Mór, 14th Lord of Knockgraffon-7, Baudhach O'Sullivan, 13th Lord of Knockgraffon-6, Cathal O'Sullivan, 12th Lord of Knockgraffon-5, Aodh O'Sullivan, 11th Lord of Knockgraffon-4, Baudhach O'Sullivan, 10th Lord of Knockgraffon-3, Lorcan MacSullivan, 9th Lord of Knockgraffon-2, Eochaid Súilleabháinn, 8th Lord of Knockgraffon-1)

John Thomas O'Sullivan Beare was named for two maternal ancestors. His father was condemned for his participation in an unsuccessful rebellion against the English in 1641 and fled the country. His family scattered to friends and relatives and some immigrated to America. Therefore, it is not clear where John Thomas was born or where he was for fourteen years before he immigrated to Virginia in 1655. John Thomas O'Sullivan Beare immigrated to America on the 24th of October 1655 at the age of 18 with his mother, or his sister, both of whom were named Elisabeth. He appears in "*A List of Lower Norfolk People*" in 1673 as 36 years old. His first wife was Mary Hayes of Lynhaven Parish. His second wife was Sarah Gore and his third wife was Hester née unknown. In the early Virginia records, the name is spelled: Sehullevan, Siliman, O'Swellivant, O'Sullivan, and Sullivan. The will of John O'Sullivan is recorded in Lynhaven Parish, Princess Anne County, Virginia, dated the 12th of May 1698, proved on the 7th of September 1698. Virginia Lands owned by him are mentioned in the will of Matthew Brinson, dated the 12th of June 1681.

He married **Mary Hayes,** daughter of Owen Hayes [27] in Lynhaven Parish. They had the following known children:

	i	Morris Sullivan [55, 56] was born in Lynhaven Parish, Princess Anne County, Virginia. He died in Charlotte County, Virginia.
	ii	Mary Sullivan was born in Lynhaven Parish, Princess Anne County, Virginia.
	iii	Amie Sullivan was born in Lynhaven Parish, Princess Anne County, Virginia.
59	iv	**Owen Sullivan** [27, 45, 48, 55, 57, 58, 59, 60] was born in circa1673 in Lynhaven Parish, Princess Anne County, Virginia. He died before the 6th of February 1769 in Charlotte County, Virginia.
	v	John Sullivan [53]. He died before the 16th of December 1694 [53].

John Thomas O'Sullivan Beare married **Hester** née unknown. They had the following known son:

i	John Sullivan was born on the 7th of September 1698.

57 **Daniel O'Sullivan Beare, Lord of Ardea Castle** [21, 25, 26, 28].

(Philip O'Sullivan Beare-19, Donal O'Sullivan Beare, Lord of Ardea Castle-18, Sir Philip O'Sullivan Beare, Lord of Ardea Castle-17, Dermod O'Sullivan Beare, 11th Lord of Beare and Bantry-16, Donal O'Sullivan Beare, the Swarthy, 8th Lord of Beare and Bantry-15, Dermod (aka Dermond) Balluf O'Sullivan Beare-14, Teige O'Sullivan Beare-13, Amhiaffe O'Sullivan Beare-12, Annaidh O'Sullivan, 1st Lord of Beare and Bantry-11, Philip O'Sullivan-10, Giolla na Bhflainn O'Sullivan Mór-9, Donal O'Sullivan Mór, 15th Lord of Knockgraffon-8, MacCraith O'Sullivan Mór, 14th Lord of Knockgraffon-7, Baudhach O'Sullivan, 13th Lord of Knockgraffon-6, Cathal O'Sullivan, 12th Lord of Knockgraffon-5, Aodh O'Sullivan, 11th Lord of Knockgraffon-4, Baudhach O'Sullivan, 10th Lord of Knockgraffon-3, Lorcan MacSullivan, 9th Lord of Knockgraffon-2, Eochaid Súilleabháinn, 8th Lord of Knockgraffon-1)

He was killed in battle fighting for Spain against the Turks.

He married **Sarah O'Brian,** daughter of Conor O'Brian, 2nd Viscount of Clare and Honora O'Brian of Dough [21, 25, 26, 61]. They had the following known son:

60	i	**Owen O'Sullivan Beare, Lord of Ardea** [26, 28].

58 **Conor O'Sullivan MacCragh** [9, 10, 226].
Born in 1564 [9, 10].

(Donogh O'Sullivan MacCragh-19, Buadach O'Suillivan MacCragh-18, Eoghan O'Sullivan MacCragh-17, Conor O'Sullivan MacCragh-16, Donal O'Sullivan MacCragh-15, Cragh O'Sullivan Mór-14, Dunlong O'Sullivan Mór-13, Bernard O'Sullivan Mór-12, Murtagh O'Sullivan-11, Dunlong O'Sullivan-10, Giolla na Bhflainn O'Sullivan Mór-9, Donal O'Sullivan Mór, 15th Lord of Knockgraffon-8, MacCraith O'Sullivan Mór, 14th Lord of Knockgraffon-7, Baudhach O'Sullivan, 13th Lord of Knockgraffon-6, Cathal O'Sullivan, 12th Lord of Knockgraffon-5, Aodh O'Sullivan, 11th Lord of Knockgraffon-4, Baudhach O'Sullivan, 10th Lord of Knockgraffon-3, Lorcan MacSullivan, 9th Lord of Knockgraffon-2, Eochaid Súilleabháinn, 8th Lord of Knockgraffon-1)

Conor was *The O'Sullivan MacCragh* (chief of the O'Sullivan MacCragh sept). Conor O'Sullivan MacCragh had the following known son:

62 i **Owen O'Sullivan MacCragh** [9, 10] was born in 1594 [9, 10].

Generation 21

59 **Owen Sullivan** [27, 45, 48, 55, 57, 58, 59, 60, 227, 228, 229].
Born in circa 1673 in Lynhaven Parish, Princess Anne County, Virginia.
Died before the 6th of February 1769 in Charlotte County, Virginia.

(John Thomas O'Sullivan Beare-20, Owen Donal O'Sullivan-19, Owen O'Sullivan Beare Lord of Beare and Bantry-18, Sir Owen O'Sullivan Beare, 14th Lord of Beare and Bantry-17, Dermod O'Sullivan Beare, 11th Lord of Beare and Bantry-16, Donal O'Sullivan Beare, the Swarthy, 8th Lord of Beare and Bantry-15, Dermod (aka Dermond) Balluf O'Sullivan Beare-14, Teige O'Sullivan Beare-13, Amhiaffe O'Sullivan Beare-12, Annaidh O'Sullivan, 1st Lord of Beare and Bantry-11, Philip O'Sullivan-10, Giolla na Bhflainn O'Sullivan Mór-9, Donal O'Sullivan Mór, 15th Lord of Knockgraffon-8, MacCraith O'Sullivan Mór, 14th Lord of Knockgraffon-7, Baudhach O'Sullivan, 13th Lord of Knockgraffon-6, Cathal O'Sullivan, 12th Lord of Knockgraffon-5, Aodh O'Sullivan, 11th Lord of Knockgraffon-4, Baudhach O'Sullivan, 10th Lord of Knockgraffon-3, Lorcan MacSullivan, 9th Lord of Knockgraffon-2, Eochaid Súilleabháinn, 8th Lord of Knockgraffon-1)

John Thomas O'Sullivan Beare must have come to Virginia with considerable money. Governor Francis Nicholson granted his son Owen 254 acres for transporting five settlers to the colony (Mary Doyle, Thomas Morse, James Davgement, Thomas Stoones and Thomas Bristow). Owen Sullivan land grants were:

- Governor Nicholson granted 254 acres at Dam Neck, near Owen Hayes at Fish Pond, Princess Anne County, Virginia, on the 7th of November 1700.
- 862 acres in Lunenburg County on the 10th of September 1755.
- King George II granted 162 acres on Twitty's Creek for payment of forty shillings, on the 10th of September 1755.
- 255 acres Bell's Free State, on the 15th of July 1760.

The tithable list of William Caldwell, taken in 1749 for Lunenburg shows Owen Sullivan. Owen's will was dated the 12th of October 1768 and proved on the 6th of February 1769 in Charlotte County, which separated from Lunenburg in 1764. He married several times, first to Elisabeth Claiborne in 1693. Owen Sullivan's last wife appears to have been Mary Ruth Pleasant. The names Owen, Claiborne, John, Pleasant, Hewlett, Elisabeth, and others were repeated for many generations.

He married **Elisabeth Claiborne,** daughter of Lieutenant Colonel Thomas Claiborne and Sarah Fenn [27], born between 1678 and 1679 [27]. They had the following known children:

63 i **Owen Sullivan** [27, 45, 48, 60, 65, 66, 67, 68, 69] was born in 1699 in Lunenburg County, Virginia [27]. He died in 1790 in Charlotte County, Virginia.
ii Charles Sullivan [45, 48, 60, 70] was born in Virginia.
iii William Sullivan [45] was born in Virginia.
64 iv **John Sullivan** [45, 48, 71] was born in Virginia.
v Pleasant Sullivan [45, 60, 70].
vi Mary Sullivan [45].
vii Temperance Sullivan [45].
viii Esther Sullivan [45].
ix Madeline Sullivan [45, 48]. She married Samuel Wharton in 1771 in South Carolina [48].
x Frances Sullivan [45].
xi Elisabeth Sullivan [45].
xii Margaret Sullivan [60].

He married **Mary Ruth Pleasant,** daughter of John Pleasant and Lane Larcome Tucker, [27, 55] born between 1671 and 1674 in Virginia [27]. She died on the 6th of February 1769 in Charlotte or Lunenburg County, Virginia. They had the following known children:

i Pleasant Sullivan was born in Virginia.
ii Mary Sullivan was born in Virginia.
iii Temperance Sullivan was born in Virginia.
iv Esther Sullivan was born in Virginia.
v Madeline Sullivan was born in Virginia.
vi Margaret Sullivan was born in Virginia.
vii Frances Sullivan was born in Virginia.
viii Patience Sullivan was born in Virginia.
ix Elisabeth Sullivan was born in Virginia.

60 **Owen O'Sullivan Beare, Lord of Ardea Castle** [26, 28].

(Daniel O'Sullivan. Lord of Ardea Castle-20, Philip O'Sullivan Beare-19, Donal O'Sullivan Beare, Lord of Ardea Castle-18, Sir Philip O'Sullivan Beare, Lord of Ardea Castle-17, Dermod O'Sullivan Beare, 11th Lord of Beare and Bantry-16, Donal O'Sullivan Beare, the Swarthy, 8th Lord of Beare and Bantry-15, Dermod (aka Dermond) Balluf O'Sullivan Beare-14, Teige O'Sullivan Beare-13, Amhiaffe O'Sullivan Beare-12, Annaidh O'Sullivan, 1st Lord of Beare and Bantry-11, Philip O'Sullivan-10, Giolla na Bhflainn O'Sullivan Mór-9, Donal O'Sullivan Mór, 15th Lord of Knockgraffon-8, MacCraith O'Sullivan Mór, 14th Lord of Knockgraffon-7, Baudhach O'Sullivan, 13th Lord of Knockgraffon-6, Cathal O'Sullivan, 12th Lord of Knockgraffon-5, Aodh O'Sullivan, 11th Lord of Knockgraffon-4, Baudhach O'Sullivan, 10th Lord of Knockgraffon-3, Lorcan

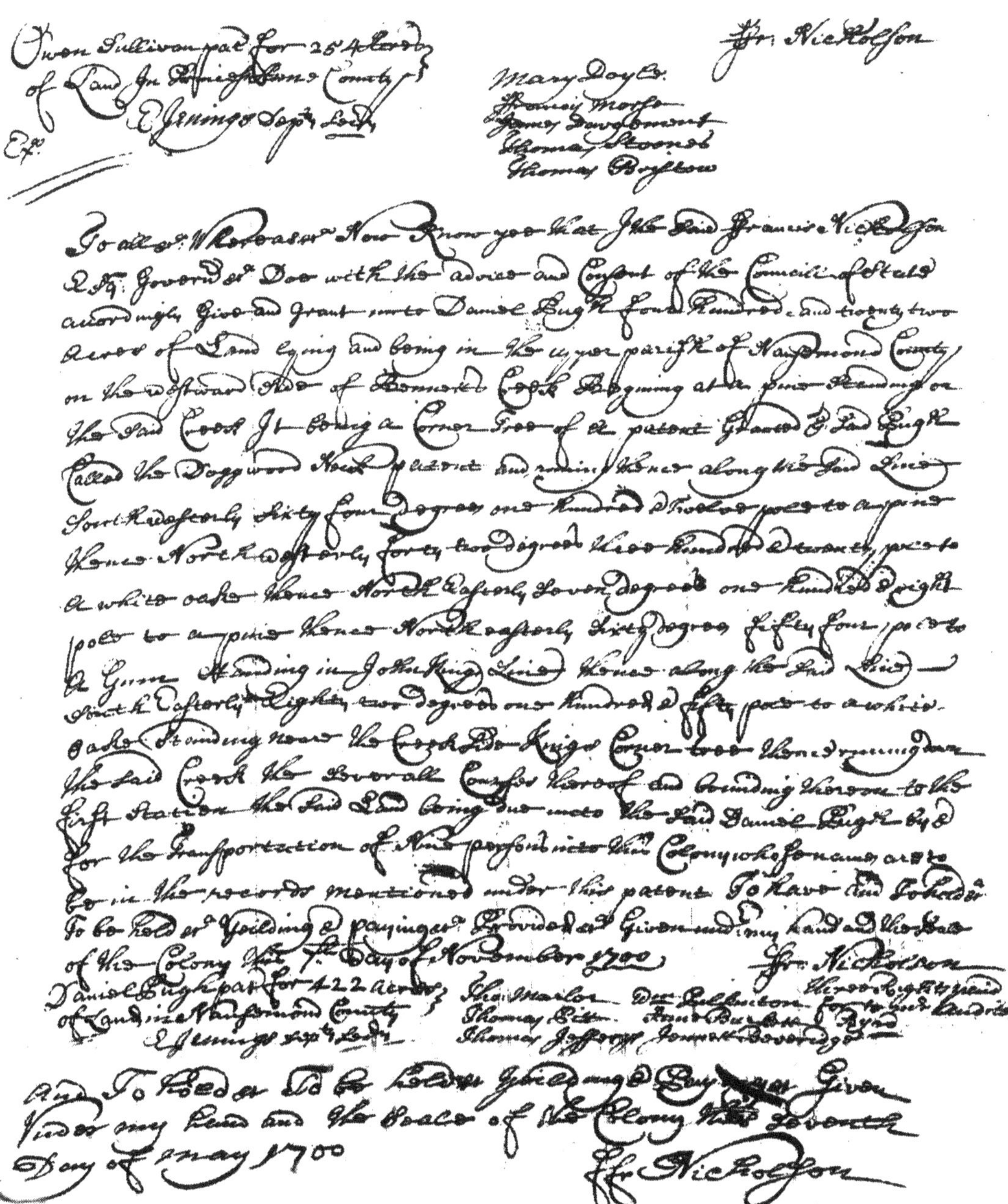

Owen Sullivan pat for 254 Acres of Land In Princess Anne County
E Jennings Dep Secy

Fr: Nicholson

Mary Doyle
Thomas Morse
James Davgement
Thomas Stoones
Thomas Bristow

To all &c Whereas &c Now Know yee that I the said Francis Nicholson Esq Governor &c Doe with the advice and Consent of the Councill of State accordingly Give and grant unto Daniel Pugh four hundred and twenty two Acres of Land lying and being in the upper parish of Nansemond County on the westward side of [illegible] Creek Beginning at a pine standing on the said Creek It being a Corner Tree of a patent Granted the said Pugh Called the Doggwood Neck [illegible] thence along the said Line Southwesterly sixty four degrees one hundred & twelve poles to a pine thence Northwesterly forty two degrees three hundred & twenty poles to a white oake thence North Easterly seven degrees one hundred & eight poles to a pine thence Northeasterly sixty degrees fifty four poles to a Gum standing in the Kings Line thence along the said Line South Easterly eighty two degrees one hundred & fifty poles to a white Oake standing near the Creekside Kings Corner tree thence running down the said Creek the severall Courses thereof and bounding thereon to the first Station the said Land being due unto the said Daniel Pugh by & for the transportation of Nine persons into this Colony whose names are to be in the records mentioned under this patent To have and To hold &c To be held &c Yielding & paying &c Provided &c Given under my hand and the Seale of this Colony this 7th Day of November 1700

Fr: Nicholson

Daniel Pugh pat for 422 acres of Land in Nansemond County
E Jennings Dep Secy

[illegible]

And To hold &c To be held &c Yielding & paying &c Given Under my hand and the Seale of the Colony this Seventh Day of May 1700

Fr Nicholson

Owen Sullivan 254 acre land grant. On the 7th of November 1700, Francis Nicholson, Governor of Virginia, granted Owen 254 acres of land at Dam Neck, Princess Ann County, Virginia for transporting five settlers to the colony. Their names were: Mary Doyle, Thomas Morse, James Davgement, Thomas Stoones and Thomas Bristow. Virginia Land Office Grants and Patents, Library of Virginia, number 9, 1678-1706, volume 1 & 2, 1-742, page 271, reel 9.

Owen Sullavant's
Pat 862 Acres
Form Page 3

George the Second &c. To all &c. Know ye that for divers good causes and considerations but more especially for and in consideration of the Sum of Forty Shillings of good and lawful money for our use paid to our Receiver General of our Revenues in this our colony and Dominion of Virginia We have Given Granted and confirmed and by these Presents for us our Heirs and Successors Do Give Grant and confirm unto Owen Sullivant one certain Tract or Parcel of Land containing eight Hundred and sixty two Acres Lying and being in the County of Lunenburgh on both sides of Twitty's Creek and bounded as followeth, to wit, Beginning at Jones's corner Hickory on the said Creek, thence along his Lines North seventy two degrees West one hundred & twenty two Poles to a small spanish Oak North eighty five degrees West one hundred & fifty Poles to a Red Oak thence off but still along the Patent lines South nineteen degrees West one hundred and ninety Poles to a Hickory South five degrees East one hundred and six Poles to a red Oak South fourteen degrees West eighty Poles to Randolph's line thence along his lines South eighty one degrees East thirty eight Poles to a Pine South four degrees West two hundred and eighteen Poles to a Hiccory thence a new Lines North fifty four degrees east four hundred and thirty eight Poles to Jones's Corner white Oak thence along his Lines North fifteen degrees West two hundred and eight Poles to a white oak North sixty five degrees West thirty eight Poles to a Hiccory on the Creek aforesaid and thence up the same as it Meanders to the first Station (four hundred and sixty two Acres part thereof being formerly granted unto John Hardin by our Letters Patent bearing date the twentieth day of August One thousand seven Hundred & forty three eight and Title of which is since become vested in the said Owen Sullavant and four hundred Acres the Residue never before granted) With all &c. To have hold &c. To be held &c. Yielding and Paying &c. Provided &c. In Witness &c. Witness our Trusty and Welbeloved Robert Dinwiddie Esq. our Lieut. Governor & Commander in chief of our said Colony and Dominion at Williamsburgh Under the Seal of our said Colony the Tenth day of September One thousand seven hundred & fifty five In the

Owen Sullivan 862 acre land grant. On the 10th of September 1755, King George II granted Owen Sullivan 862 acres of Land on both sides of Twitty's Creek in Lunenburg County, Virginia in consideration of 40 shillings. Virginia Land Office Grants and Patents, Library of Virginia, number 32, 1752-1756, volume 1 & 2, 1-715, page 311, reel 30.

The will of Owen Sullivan, page 1 of 2, dated the 12th of October 1768 and proved on the 6th of February 1769 in Charlotte County.

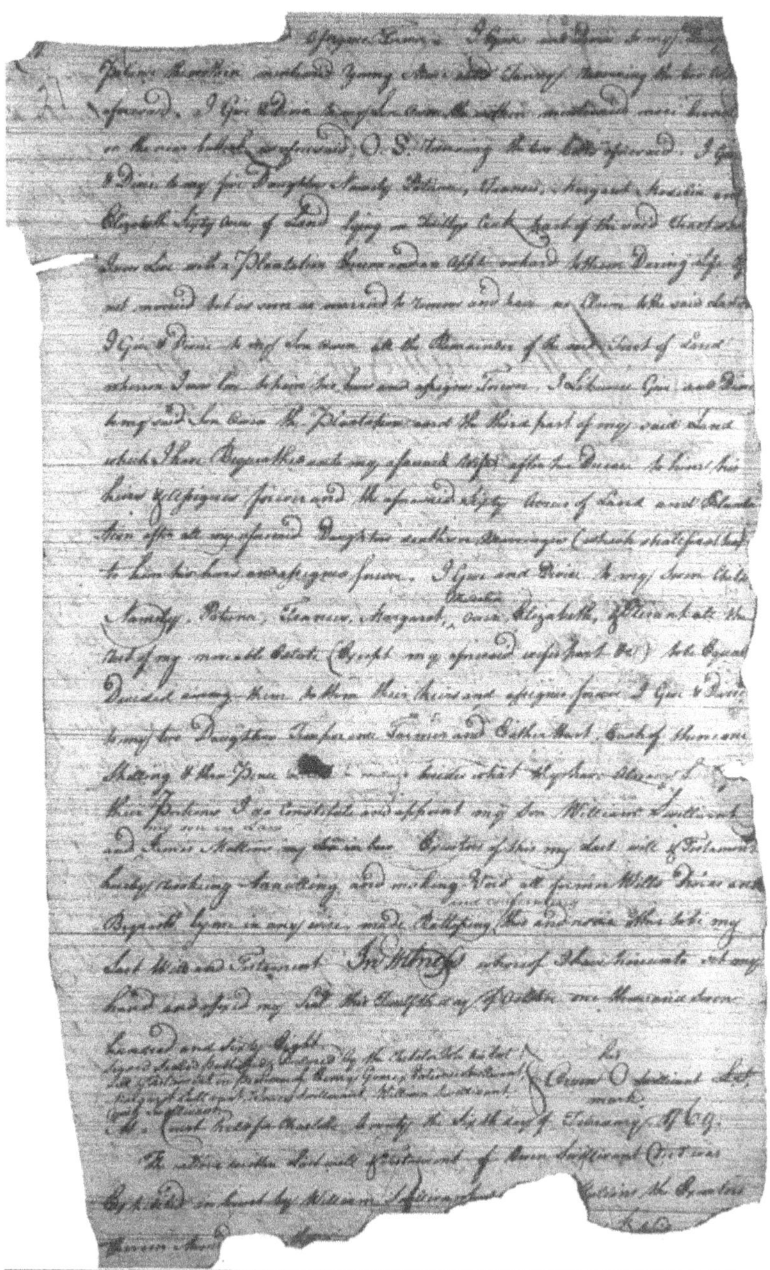

The will of Owen Sullivan, page 2 of 2, dated the 12th of October 1768 and proved on the 6th of February 1769 in Charlotte County.

MacSullivan, 9th Lord of Knockgraffon-2, Eochaid Súilleabháinn, 8th, Lord of Knockgraffon-1)

He married his foster sister **Mary MacSweeny,** daughter of Colonel Owen MacSweeny [13, 21, 26, 62, 63, 73]. They had the following known son:

61 i **Major Philip O'Sullivan Beare, Lord of Ardea Castle** [13, 21, 26, 28, 33, 35, 62, 63, 64, 65].

62 **Owen O'Sullivan MacCragh** [9, 10, 226].
Born in 1594 [9, 10].

(Conor O'Sullivan MacCragh-20, Donogh O'Sullivan MacCragh-19, Buadach O'Suillivan MacCragh-18, Eoghan O'Sullivan MacCragh-17, Conor O'Sullivan MacCragh-16, Donal O'Sullivan MacCragh-15, Cragh O'Sullivan Mór-14, Dunlong O'Sullivan Mór-13, Bernard O'Sullivan Mór-12, Murtagh O'Sullivan-11, Dunlong O'Sullivan-10, Giolla na Bhflainn O'Sullivan Mór-9, Donal O'Sullivan Mór, 15th Lord of Knockgraffon-8, MacCraith O'Sullivan Mór, 14th Lord of Knockgraffon-7, Baudhach O'Sullivan, 13th Lord of Knockgraffon-6, Cathal O'Sullivan, 12th Lord of Knockgraffon-5, Aodh O'Sullivan, 11th Lord of Knockgraffon-4, Baudhach O'Sullivan, 10th Lord of Knockgraffon-3, Lorcan MacSullivan, 9th Lord of Knockgraffon-2, Eochaid Súilleabháinn, 8th Lord of Knockgraffon-1)

In 1609, under the *Articles of Plantation,* the land of many Irish lords was confiscated and given to Englishmen called *undertakers* because they undertook to import and settle English and Scottish tenant farmers on the land. Many Irish lords were reduced to peasants. Many of the Irish nobles went to France, Spain and America. This period in Irish history is called *the flight of the earls.*

Owen was *The O'Sullivan MacCragh* (chief of the O'Sullivan MacCragh sept).

Owen O'Sullivan MacCragh had the following known son:

67 i **Dermot O'Sullivan MacCragh** [9, 10] was born in 1624 [9, 10].

Law suit for debt: William Evins versus Owen, John and Charles Sullivan. On the 13th of July 1774, plantiff William Evins brought a debt law suit against Owen, Jno [John] and Charles Sullivent [Sullivan]. The jury decided for the plantiff in the amount of 662 pounds of tobacco. Carolina County, Virginia order book 1731-1746

Generation 22

61 **Major Philip O'Sullivan Beare, Lord of Ardea Castle** [13, 21, 26, 28, 33, 35, 62, 63, 64, 65].

(Owen O'Sullivan Beare, Lord of Ardea Castle-21, Daniel O'Sullivan. Lord of Ardea Castle-20, Philip O'Sullivan Beare-19, Donal O'Sullivan Beare, Lord of Ardea Castle-18, Sir Philip O'Sullivan Beare, Lord of Ardea Castle-17, Dermod O'Sullivan Beare, 11th Lord of Beare and Bantry-16, Donal O'Sullivan Beare, the Swarthy, 8th Lord of Beare and Bantry-15, Dermod (aka Dermond) Balluf O'Sullivan Beare-14, Teige O'Sullivan Beare-13, Amhiaffe O'Sullivan Beare-12, Annaidh O'Sullivan, 1st Lord of Beare and Bantry-11, Philip O'Sullivan-10, Giolla na Bhflainn O'Sullivan Mór-9, Donal O'Sullivan Mór, 15th Lord of Knockgraffon-8, MacCraith O'Sullivan Mór, 14th Lord of Knockgraffon-7, Baudhach O'Sullivan, 13th Lord of Knockgraffon-6, Cathal O'Sullivan, 12th Lord of Knockgraffon-5, Aodh O'Sullivan, 11th Lord of Knockgraffon-4, Baudhach O'Sullivan, 10th Lord of Knockgraffon-3, Lorcan MacSullivan, 9th Lord of Knockgraffon-2, Eochaid Súilleabháinn, 8th Lord of Knockgraffon-1)

He married **Johanna MacCarthy,** daughter of Dermod (aka Dermond) MacCarthy and MacCarthy Reagh [13, 21, 26, 33, 35, 62, 63, 65, 72, 73]. They had the following known children:

65 i **Owen O'Sullivan Beare** [13, 21, 26, 28, 62, 65, 72, 74] was born between the 17th of June 1690 and the 20th of June 1695 in Limerick, Ireland [13, 28, 74]. He died on the 20th of June 1795 in Berwick, Maine [13, 74].

66 ii **Patrick O'Sullivan Beare** [13, 26, 62, 65, 75].

iii John Sullivan, of Berwick Maine [35, 63, 64, 73, 76].

63 **Owen Sullivan** [27, 45, 48, 60, 65, 66, 67, 68, 69]
Born in 1699 in Lunenburg County, Virginia [27].
Died in 1790 in Charlotte County, Virginia.

(Owen Sullivan-21, John Thomas O'Sullivan-20, Owen Donal O'Sullivan-19, Owen O'Sullivan Beare Lord of Beare and Bantry-18, Sir Owen O'Sullivan Beare, 14th Lord of Beare and Bantry-17, Dermod O'Sullivan Beare, 11th Lord of Beare and Bantry-16, Donal O'Sullivan Beare, the Swarthy, 8th Lord of Beare and Bantry-15, Dermod (aka Dermond) Balluf O'Sullivan Beare-14, Teige O'Sullivan Beare-13, Amhiaffe O'Sullivan Beare-12, Annaidh O'Sullivan, 1st Lord of Beare and Bantry-11, Philip O'Sullivan-10, Giolla na Bhflainn O'Sullivan Mór-9, Donal O'Sullivan Mór, 15th Lord of Knockgraffon-8, MacCraith O'Sullivan Mór, 14th Lord of Knockgraffon-7, Baudhach O'Sullivan, 13th Lord of Knockgraffon-6, Cathal O'Sullivan, 12th Lord of Knockgraffon-5, Aodh O'Sullivan, 11th Lord of Knockgraffon-4, Baudhach O'Sullivan, 10th Lord of Knockgraffon-3, Lorcan MacSullivan, 9th Lord of Knockgraffon-2, Eochaid Súilleabháinn, 8th Lord of Knockgraffon-1)

Owen Jr. is named in his father's will. By deed dated the 1st of October 1781, Owen Sullivan conveyed 151 acres of land to Charles Crenshaw, including the dwelling house of the late Owen Sullivan he inherited from his father. It is reported that Owen and Margaret had 5 children and move from Virginia to South Carolina, but they do not appear in the South Carolina census in either Laurens or Greenville Counties where their son Charles and grandson Hewlett settled.

History of South Carolina, Volume 3, by Yates Snowden, Harry Gardner Cutler Lewis

Publishing Company, 1920, pages 137-138, says Owen was a native of Ireland and met his wife Margaret Hewlett, of English descent, on shipboard underway to Charleston. They went to Georgia, then to Virginia before returning to South Carolina. In fact, Owen was born in Virginia. His grandfather John Thomas O'Sullivan was the immigrant from Ireland in 1655, forty-four years before Owen was born. The author probably confused Owen with his son Charles and his grandson Hewlett. They did go to Georgia, where they were troubled by Cherokee attacks and finally settled in Laurens County, South Carolina.

Owen married **Mary Margaret Hewlett,** daughter of William Hewlett and Mary Fearne [27, 67, 68] in May 1721. She was born on the 4th of March 1707 in Virginia. She died in Virginia.

They had the following known children:

68 i **Charles B. Sullivan** [27, 45, 67, 69, 77, 78, 79, 80, 81, 82] as born on the 2nd of April 1728 in Twitty's Creek, Charlotte County, Virginia [27, 45, 67]. He died on the 3rd of November 1808 in Greenville County, South Carolina [45, 67].

ii James Sullivan [45, 67, 68, 70]. In 1785, he received two land grants in South Carolina for 200 and 440 acres.

iii Owen Sullivan [45, 67, 68]. He died in 1797 in Newberry District, South Carolina [45].

iv Margaret Sullivan [45, 67, 68] was born in Caroline County, Virginia.

v Pleasant Sullivan [45, 67, 68, 77] was born on the 25th of August 1759 in Anderson, South Carolina [67].

64 **John Sullivan** [45, 48, 71].
Born in Virginia.

(Owen Sullivan-21, John Thomas O'Sullivan-20, Owen Donal O'Sullivan-19, Owen O'Sullivan Beare Lord of Beare and Bantry-18, Sir Owen O'Sullivan Beare, 14th Lord of Beare and Bantry-17, Dermod O'Sullivan Beare, 11th Lord of Beare and Bantry-16, Donal O'Sullivan Beare, the Swarthy, 8th Lord of Beare and Bantry-15, Dermod (aka Dermond) Balluf O'Sullivan Beare-14, Teige O'Sullivan Beare-13, Amhiaffe O'Sullivan Beare-12, Annaidh O'Sullivan, 1st Lord of Beare and Bantry-11, Philip O'Sullivan-10, Giolla na Bhflainn O'Sullivan Mór-9, Donal O'Sullivan Mór, 15th Lord of Knockgraffon-8, MacCraith O'Sullivan Mór, 14th Lord of Knockgraffon-7, Baudhach O'Sullivan, 13th Lord of Knockgraffon-6, Cathal O'Sullivan, 12th Lord of Knockgraffon-5, Aodh O'Sullivan, 11th Lord of Knockgraffon-4, Baudhach O'Sullivan, 10th Lord of Knockgraffon-3, Lorcan MacSullivan, 9th Lord of Knockgraffon-2, Eochaid Súilleabháinn, 8th Lord of Knockgraffon-1)

John Sullivan had the following known children:

69 i **James Sullivan** [48, 71, 83, 84, 85] was born in Twitty's Creek, Charlotte County, Virginia. He died on the 29th of July 1809 [85].

70 ii **Manoah Sullivan** [77, 78, 86].

67 **Dermot O'Sullivan MacCragh** [9, 10, 226].
Born in 1624 [9, 10].

(Owen O'Sullivan MacCragh-21, Conor O'Sullivan MacCragh-20, Donogh O'Sullivan MacCragh-19, Buadach O'Suillivan MacCragh-18, Eoghan O'Sullivan MacCragh-17, Conor O'Sullivan MacCragh-16, Donal O'Sullivan MacCragh-15, Cragh O'Sullivan Mór-14, Dunlong O'Sullivan Mór-13, Bernard O'Sullivan Mór-12, Murtagh O'Sullivan-11, Dunlong O'Sullivan-10, Giolla na Bhflainn O'Sullivan Mór-9, Donal O'Sullivan Mór, 15th Lord of Knockgraffon-8, MacCraith O'Sullivan Mór, 14th Lord of Knockgraffon-7, Baudhach O'Sullivan, 13th Lord of Knockgraffon-6, Cathal O'Sullivan, 12th Lord of Knockgraffon-5, Aodh O'Sullivan, 11th Lord of Knockgraffon-4, Baudhach O'Sullivan, 10th Lord of Knockgraffon-3, Lorcan MacSullivan, 9th Lord of Knockgraffon-2, Eochaid Súilleabháinn, 8th Lord of Knockgraffon-1)

Dermot was *The O'Sullivan MacCragh* (chief of the O'Sullivan MacCragh sept). The primogeniture bloodline recorded in the *Book of Munster* ends with him.

Dermot O'Sullivan MacCragh had the following known son:

76 i **Owen O'Sullivan MacCragh** [9, 10] was born in 1654 [9, 10].

Generation 23

65 **Owen O'Sullivan Beare** [13, 21, 26, 28, 62, 65, 72, 74].
Born in 1692 in Limerick, Ireland [13, 28, 74].
Died on the 20th of June 1796 in Berwick, Maine [13, 74].

(Major Philip O'Sullivan of Ardea O'Sullivan-22, Owen O'Sullivan Beare, Lord of Ardea Castle-21, Daniel O'Sullivan. Lord of Ardea Castle-20, Philip O'Sullivan Beare-19, Donal O'Sullivan Beare, Lord of Ardea Castle-18, Sir Philip O'Sullivan Beare, Lord of Ardea Castle-17, Dermod O'Sullivan Beare, 11th Lord of Beare and Bantry-16, Donal O'Sullivan Beare, the Swarthy, 8th Lord of Beare and Bantry-15, Dermod (aka Dermond) Balluf O'Sullivan Beare-14, Teige O'Sullivan Beare-13, Amhiaffe O'Sullivan Beare-12, Annaidh O'Sullivan, 1st Lord of Beare and Bantry-11, Philip O'Sullivan-10, Giolla na Bhflainn O'Sullivan Mór-9, Donal O'Sullivan Mór, 15th Lord of Knockgraffon-8, MacCraith O'Sullivan Mór, 14th Lord of Knockgraffon-7, Baudhach O'Sullivan, 13th Lord of Knockgraffon-6, Cathal O'Sullivan, 12th Lord of Knockgraffon-5, Aodh O'Sullivan, 11th Lord of Knockgraffon-4, Baudhach O'Sullivan, 10th Lord of Knockgraffon-3, Lorcan MacSullivan, 9th Lord of Knockgraffon-2, Eochaid Súilleabháinn, 8th Lord of Knockgraffon-1)

Owen went to America and landed at York, Maine. He settled in Berwick, Maine, where he was known as John. He was a farmer, wrote deeds, and was a schoolmaster.

He married **Margery Browne** [13, 21, 26, 28, 62, 65, 74] in 1736 [62, 74]. She was born in 1714 in County Cork, Ireland [62, 74]. Margery went to America in 1723 when she was nine years old. She died in Berwick, Maine [28, 62, 74]. They had the following known children:

i Benjamin Sullivan [26, 65, 74] was born circa 1736 [74]. He died before 1776. Benjamin served in the Royal Navy and was lost at sea before the American Revolution.

71 ii **Daniel Sullivan** [26, 74, 87] was born circa 1738 in Berwick, Maine [74, 87]. He died in 1781.[74, 87].

72 iii **Major General John Sullivan** [26, 62, 65, 74, 87, 88, 89, 90] was born on the 17th of February 1740 in Berwick, Maine [26, 74, 87, 89]. He died on the 23rd of

January 1795 in Durham, New Hampshire [26, 89].

73 iv **James Sullivan** [26, 28, 62, 65, 74, 91] was born on the 22nd of April 1744 in Berwick, Maine [26, 62, 91]. He died on the 10th of December 1808 in Boston, Massachusetts [62, 74, 91].

v Mary Sullivan [26, 65, 74, 92] was born in 1752 in Berwick, Maine [26, 74, 92]. She married Theophilus Hardy on the 4th of May 1768 [26, 74]. She died in 1827 in Strafford, New Hampshire, [26, 74, 92]. Mary lived in Durham, New Hampshire near her brother Major General John Sullivan.

74 vi **Ebenezer Sullivan** [26, 65, 74, 93] was born on the 8th of October 1753 in Berwick, Maine [26, 74, 93]. He died on the 3rd of June 1799 in Charleston, South Carolina [26, 74, 93].

66 **Patrick O'Sullivan Beare** [13, 26, 62, 65, 75].

(Owen O'Sullivan of Ardea O'Sullivan-23, Major Philip O'Sullivan of Ardea O'Sullivan-22, Owen O'Sullivan Beare, Lord of Ardea Castle-21, Daniel O'Sullivan. Lord of Ardea Castle-20, Philip O'Sullivan Beare-19, Donal O'Sullivan Beare, Lord of Ardea Castle-18, Sir Philip O'Sullivan Beare, Lord of Ardea Castle-17, Dermod O'Sullivan Beare, 11th Lord of Beare and Bantry-16, Donal O'Sullivan Beare, the Swarthy, 8th Lord of Beare and Bantry-15, Dermod (aka Dermond) Balluf O'Sullivan Beare-14, Teige O'Sullivan Beare-13, Amhiaffe O'Sullivan Beare-12, Annaidh O'Sullivan, 1st Lord of Beare and Bantry-11, Philip O'Sullivan-10, Giolla na Bhflainn O'Sullivan Mór-9, Donal O'Sullivan Mór, 15th Lord of Knockgraffon-8, MacCraith O'Sullivan Mór, 14th Lord of Knockgraffon-7, Baudhach O'Sullivan, 13th Lord of Knockgraffon-6, Cathal O'Sullivan, 12th Lord of Knockgraffon-5, Aodh O'Sullivan, 11th Lord of Knockgraffon-4, Baudhach O'Sullivan, 10th Lord of Knockgraffon-3, Lorcan MacSullivan, 9th Lord of Knockgraffon-2, Eochaid Súilleabháinn, 8th Lord of Knockgraffon-1)

Patrick settled in Berwick, Maine.

He married **Margaret FitzGerald,** daughter of John FitzGerald. [13, 62] They had the following son.

71 i **Daniel O'Sullivan** [13, 62].

68 **Charles B. Sullivan** [27, 45, 67, 69, 77, 78, 79, 80, 81, 82].
Born on the 2nd of April 1728 in Twitty's Creek, Charlotte County, Virginia [27, 45, 67].
Died on the 3rd of November 1808 in Greenville County, South Carolina [45, 67].

(Owen Sullivan-22, Owen Sullivan-21, John Thomas O'Sullivan-20, Owen Donal O'Sullivan-19, Owen O'Sullivan Beare Lord of Beare and Bantry-18, Sir Owen O'Sullivan Beare, 14th Lord of Beare and Bantry-17, Dermod O'Sullivan Beare, 11th Lord of Beare and Bantry-16, Donal O'Sullivan Beare, the Swarthy, 8th Lord of Beare and Bantry-15, Dermod (aka Dermond) Balluf O'Sullivan Beare-14, Teige O'Sullivan Beare-13, Amhiaffe O'Sullivan Beare-12, Annaidh O'Sullivan, 1st Lord of Beare and Bantry-11, Philip O'Sullivan-10, Giolla na Bhflainn O'Sullivan Mór-9, Donal O'Sullivan Mór, 15th Lord of Knockgraffon-8, MacCraith O'Sullivan Mór, 14th Lord of Knockgraffon-7, Baudhach O'Sullivan, 13th Lord of Knockgraffon-6, Cathal O'Sullivan, 12th Lord of Knockgraffon-5, Aodh O'Sullivan, 11th Lord of Knockgraffon-4, Baudhach O'Sullivan, 10th Lord of Knockgraffon-3, Lorcan MacSullivan, 9th Lord of Knockgraffon-2, Eochaid Súilleabháinn, 8th Lord of Knockgraffon-1)

Charles Sullivan's gravestone inscription says he was a Revolutionary War soldier. He moved from Virginia, first to Georgia and later to South Carolina at the beginning of the Revolutionary War. Charles was granted:

- 170 acres of land on a branch of Horse Creek on the 4th of December1780.
- 400 acres on the 26th of May 1784. The district was not legible.
- 100 Acres on Horse Creek on the 4th of December 1785.
- 200 acres on Line Creek on the 11th of February 1788.

The amount of land in the grants found totalled 870 acres. Charles died on his plantation, called *The Grove*, on the 30th of November 1808. Another source, *History of South Carolina,* says he named his home Charlton Hall in honor of his wife.

He married **Mary Charlton** [27, 45, 67, 69] on the15th of June 1749 in Virginia [45]. She was born on the 1st of June 1722 in Goochland County, Virginia [45, 67]. She died at the age of 115 on the 20th of December 1837 in Greenville County, South Carolina, and was known as "*the Granny in the bed.*" [45, 67]. They had the following known children:

77 i **Hewlett Sullivan** [27, 45, 65, 67, 69, 77, 78, 94, 95, 96, 97, 98, 99, 100, 101] was born on the 28th of December 1763 in Charlotte County, Virginia [27, 67, 96]. He died on the 11th of July 1830 in Greenville County, South Carolina [27, 45, 67, 96].

78 ii **Moses Sullivan** [27, 45, 67, 77] was born in 1754 in Twitty's Creek, Charlotte County, Virginia [45]. He died in 1810 in Lebanon, South Carolina [45, 67].

iii Sarah Margaret Sullivan [27, 45, 67] was born in 1756 in Twitty's Creek, Charlotte, Virginia [45].

iv Claiborne Sullivan [27, 45, 67, 70] was born on the 1st of December 1772 in Twitty's Creek, Charlotte, Virginia [45, 67]. He died in September 1857 in Washington County, Missouri[45].

v Stephen Sullivan [27, 45, 67, 70, 77].

69 **James Sullivan** [48, 71, 83, 84, 85].
Born in Twitty's Creek, Charlotte County, Virginia.
Died on the 29th of July 1809 [85].

(John Sullivan-22, Owen Sullivan-21, John Thomas O'Sullivan-20, Owen Donal O'Sullivan-19, Owen O'Sullivan Beare Lord of Beare and Bantry-18, Sir Owen O'Sullivan Beare, 14th Lord of Beare and Bantry-17, Dermod O'Sullivan Beare, 11th Lord of Beare and Bantry-16, Donal O'Sullivan Beare, the Swarthy, 8th Lord of Beare and Bantry-15, Dermod (aka Dermond) Balluf O'Sullivan Beare-14, Teige O'Sullivan Beare-13, Amhiaffe O'Sullivan Beare-12, Annaidh O'Sullivan, 1st Lord of Beare and Bantry-11, Philip O'Sullivan-10, Giolla na Bhflainn O'Sullivan Mór-9, Donal O'Sullivan Mór, 15th Lord of Knockgraffon-8, MacCraith O'Sullivan Mór, 14th Lord of Knockgraffon-7, Baudhach O'Sullivan, 13th Lord of Knockgraffon-6, Cathal O'Sullivan, 12th Lord of Knockgraffon-5, Aodh O'Sullivan, 11th Lord of Knockgraffon-4, Baudhach O'Sullivan, 10th Lord of Knockgraffon-3, Lorcan MacSullivan, 9th Lord of Knockgraffon-2, Eochaid Súilleabháinn, 8th Lord of Knockgraffon-1)

James Sullivan was born in Twitty's Creek, Lunenburg County, Virginia. Several legal actions are recorded in the courthouse. Land deeds are on record in both Lunenburg and Charlotte Counties. The last recorded land transaction in Virginia was the sale of 500 acres

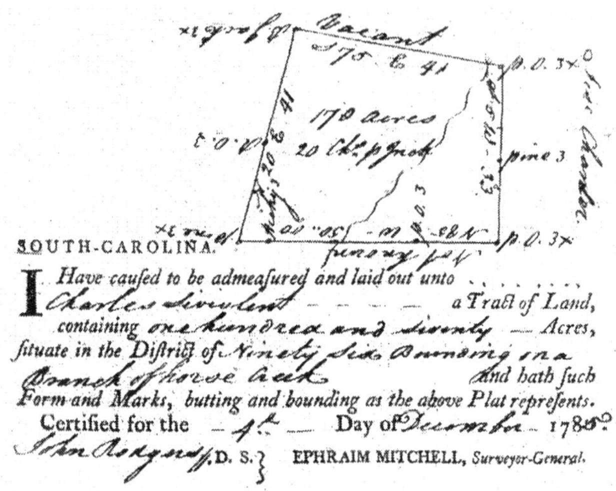

SOUTH-CAROLINA.

I Have caused to be admeasured and laid out unto Charles [illegible] a Tract of Land, containing one hundred and sixty Acres, situate in the District of Ninety Six [illegible] on a Branch of horse creek and hath such Form and Marks, butting and bounding as the above Plat represents.

Certified for the 4th Day of December 1780.

John Rodgers D. S. EPHRAIM MITCHELL, Surveyor-General.

Charles Sullivan's land grant of 170 acres issued on the 4th of December 1780

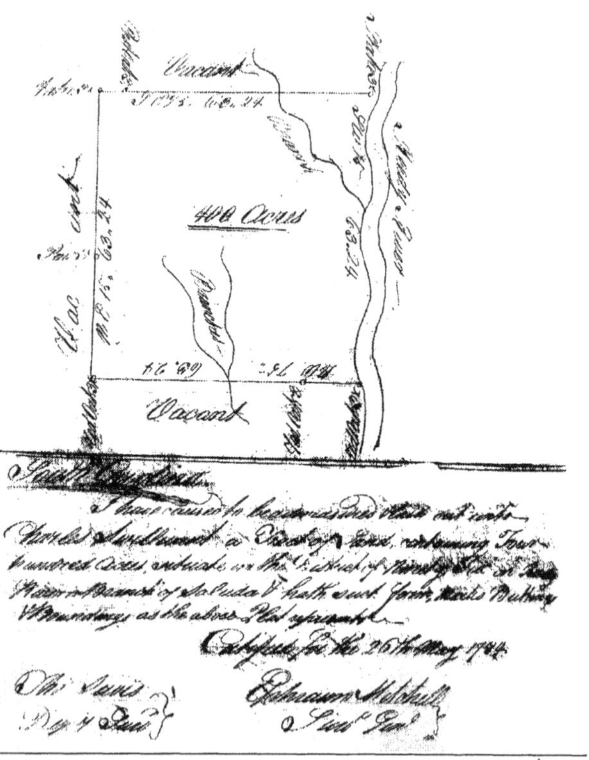

Charles Sullivan's land grant of 400 acres issued on the 26th of May 1784

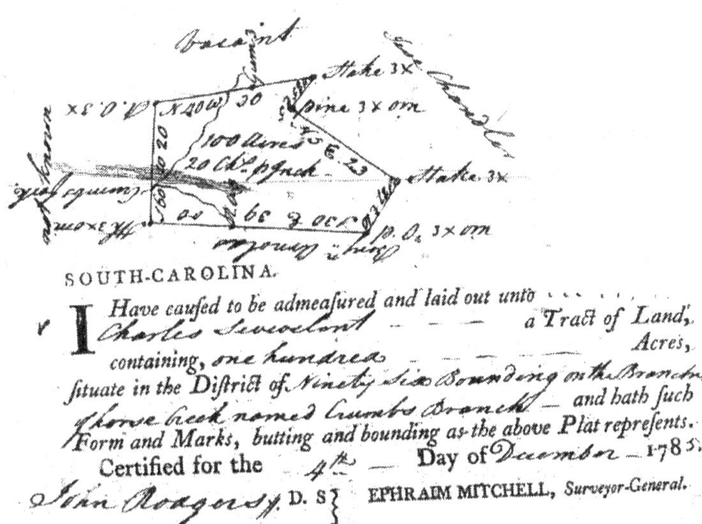

SOUTH-CAROLINA.

I Have caused to be admeasured and laid out unto Charles [illegible] a Tract of Land, containing, one hundred Acres, situate in the District of Ninety Six Bounding on the Branches of horse Creek named [illegible] Branch — and hath such Form and Marks, butting and bounding as the above Plat represents.

Certified for the 4th Day of December 1785.

John Rodgers D. S. EPHRAIM MITCHELL, Surveyor-General.

Charles Sullivan's land grant of 100 acres issued on the 4th of December 1785. Courtesy of the South Carolina State Archive

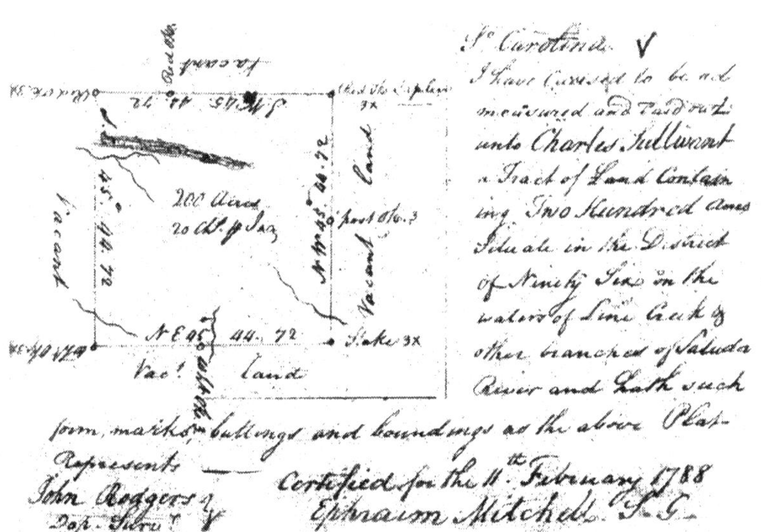

S. Carolina

I have Caused to be ad measured and laid out unto Charles Sullivant a Tract of Land Containing Two Hundred Acres Situate in the District of Ninety Six on the waters of Line Creek & other branches of Saluda River and hath such form, marks, buttings and boundings as the above Plat Represents

Certified for the 11th February 1788

John Rodgers Dep. Survr.

Ephraim Mitchell S. G.

Charles Sullivan's land grant of 200 acres issued on the 11th of February 1788. Courtesy of the South Carolina State Archive.

to Francis Barn in Charlotte County, on both sides of Twitty's Creek, on the 26th of April 1783. At some time before the 6th of November 1784, he moved to South Carolina where some of his cousins had already resettled. On that day, it was recorded that he bought 150 acres of land in District 96 of Craven County, South Carolina, on a branch of Little River. On the 28th of June 1785, he bought 200 acres of land in the same district on Wilson's Creek for 175 pounds in Virginia Money. At that time the states printed their own money. He spent the rest of his life on Little Creek as a tobacco planter and he died intestate on the 29th of July 1809. Only five of his twelve children outlived him and the court appointed guardians for the minor children. These children and grandchildren later brought a lawsuit against the guardians. These court records, including 139 loose papers, name all of his heirs, children, and grandchildren and are on file in the South Carolina Archives.

He married **Sarah Perrin,** daughter of Joseph Perrin [48, 83, 85, 102]. They had the following known children:

79 i **Elisabeth Sullivan** [48, 85] was born in 1798. She died on the 7th of August 1811[85].
ii Larkin Sullivan [48, 85]. He died after the 29th of July 1809 [85].
iii Delphi Sullivan [48, 85]. She died after the 29th of July 1809 [85].
iv Rebecca Sullivan [48, 85]. She died after the 29th of July 1809 [85].
v Sarah Sullivan [48, 85]. She died after the 29th of July 1809 [85].
vi Nancy Sullivan [48, 85]. She died before the 29th of July 1809[85].
vii Harrison Sullivan [48, 85]. He died before the 29th of July 1809 [85].
viii Pricilla Sullivan [48, 85]. She died before the 29th of July 1809 [85].
ix John Sullivan [48, 85]. He died before the 29th of July 1809 [85].
x Elisabeth Sullivan [48, 85]. She died before the 29th of July 1809 [85].
xi Matthew Sullivan [48, 85]. He died before the 29th of July 1809 [85].
xii James Sullivan [85]. He died before the 29th of July 1809 [85].

70 **Manoah Sullivan** [77, 78, 86].

(John Sullivan-22, Owen Sullivan-21, John Thomas O'Sullivan-20, Owen Donal O'Sullivan-19, Owen O'Sullivan Beare Lord of Beare and Bantry-18, Sir Owen O'Sullivan Beare, 14th Lord of Beare and Bantry-17, Dermod O'Sullivan Beare, 11th Lord of Beare and Bantry-16, Donal O'Sullivan Beare, the Swarthy, 8th Lord of Beare and Bantry-15, Dermod (aka Dermond) Balluf O'Sullivan Beare-14, Teige O'Sullivan Beare-13, Amhiaffe O'Sullivan Beare-12, Annaidh O'Sullivan, 1st Lord of Beare and Bantry-11, Philip O'Sullivan-10, Giolla na Bhflainn O'Sullivan Mór-9, Donal O'Sullivan Mór, 15th Lord of Knockgraffon-8, MacCraith O'Sullivan Mór, 14th Lord of Knockgraffon-7, Baudhach O'Sullivan, 13th Lord of Knockgraffon-6, Cathal O'Sullivan, 12th Lord of Knockgraffon-5, Aodh O'Sullivan, 11th Lord of Knockgraffon-4, Baudhach O'Sullivan, 10th Lord of Knockgraffon-3, Lorcan MacSullivan, 9th Lord of Knockgraffon-2, Eochaid Súilleabháinn, 8th Lord of Knockgraffon-1)

The book, *Carolinians in the Revolution*, published in 1949, by Sarah Sullivan Ervin says Manoah Sullivan was the son of John Sullivan. Parts of this book have been discredited in an article by Carolyn Copeland Bland in the *Magazine of Virginia Genealogy* Volume 25, November 1987, Number 4, pages 3-13. The reason concerned the doubtful validity of a non-notarized transcript from the James Sullivan Bible used as proof James Sullivan was the son of Owen Sullivan for qualification as a Daughter of the American Revolution.

Another reason was quotations from the book by John Dunklin Sullivan, which quoted no references and various parts were proven wrong. However, Manoah was mentioned in the United States census, Laurens County, South Carolina in 1800 and 1810. But the census does not specifically say he was the son of John Sullivan.

He married **Susannah Nance** [86]. They had the following known children:

- i Susannah Nancy Sullivan [78].
- ii Little Berry Sullivan [77].
- iii Frederick Sullivan [77].
- iv Manoah Sullivan [77, 78].

75 **Daniel O'Sullivan** [13, 62].
Died between the 11th of February 1769 and the 30th of April 1773 [62].

(Patrick O'Sullivan Beare-22, Major Philip O'Sullivan of Ardea O'Sullivan-22, Major Philip O'Sullivan of Ardea O'Sullivan-22, Owen O'Sullivan Beare, Lord of Ardea Castle-21, Daniel O'Sullivan. Lord of Ardea Castle-20, Philip O'Sullivan Beare-19, Donal O'Sullivan Beare, Lord of Ardea Castle-18, Sir Philip O'Sullivan Beare, Lord of Ardea Castle-17, Dermod O'Sullivan Beare, 11th Lord of Beare and Bantry-16, Donal O'Sullivan Beare, the Swarthy, 8th Lord of Beare and Bantry-15, Dermod (aka Dermond) Balluf O'Sullivan Beare-14, Teige O'Sullivan Beare-13, Amhiaffe O'Sullivan Beare-12, Annaidh O'Sullivan, 1st Lord of Beare and Bantry-11, Philip O'Sullivan-10, Giolla na Bhflainn O'Sullivan Mór-9, Donal O'Sullivan Mór, 15th Lord of Knockgraffon-8, MacCraith O'Sullivan Mór, 14th Lord of Knockgraffon-7, Baudhach O'Sullivan, 13th Lord of Knockgraffon-6, Cathal O'Sullivan, 12th Lord of Knockgraffon-5, Aodh O'Sullivan, 11th Lord of Knockgraffon-4, Baudhach O'Sullivan, 10th Lord of Knockgraffon-3, Lorcan MacSullivan, 9th Lord of Knockgraffon-2, Eochaid Súilleabháinn, 8th Lord of Knockgraffon-1)

Daniel was from Ardea, Ireland and held lands in Dromboughhilly in the parish of Tuosist. His will was dated the 11th of February 1769 and proved on the 30th of April 1773.

He married **Juliana O'Sullivan,** daughter of Daniel of Dromboughilly O'Sullivan [13, 62]. They had the following known children:

- i Philip O'Sullivan [13, 62, 73]. He died after the 16th of May 1796. On the 16th of May 1796 Philip wrote a letter to James Sullivan, Governor of the State of Massachusetts saying:

  "... A grand-uncle of mine having gone to America about sixty years ago, his relatives have suffered greatly from being without the means of finding out his fate, till now, by the great good fortune, I am informed that you are a son of his. If you find, by the account below, that I have not been misinformed, I shall be glad to hear from you. Mr. Owen O'Sullivan, son of Major Philip O'Sullivan, of Ardea in the County of Kerry, Ireland, by Joanna daughter of Dermon MacCarthy, of Killoween, Esq. in said county. They were connected with the most respectable families in the province of Munster, particularly the count of Beare Haven, MacCarthy Earl Clancare, McFinnen of Barrymore Earl of

O'Sullivan (*Ó Súillebháin) Genealogy*

Thomond, Earl of Clancasthy, McFinen of Glanarough O'Donough of Ross, O'Donough of Glynn, MacCarthy of Carberry, Lord Clancarthy and O'Donovan &c.

I am, Sir respectfully Philip O'Sullivan

Ardea, May 16th 1796 ...."

There are some errors in this letter.

ii John O'Sullivan [13, 62].
iii Margaret O'Sullivan [13, 62].
iv Julia O'Sullivan [13, 62].
v Mary O'Sullivan [13, 62].

76 **Owen O'Sullivan MacCragh** [9, 10, 226].
Born in 1654 [9, 10].

(Dermot O'Sullivan MacCragh-22, Owen O'Sullivan MacCragh-21, Conor O'Sullivan MacCragh-20, Donogh O'Sullivan MacCragh-19, Buadach O'Suillivan MacCragh-18, Eoghan O'Sullivan MacCragh-17, Conor O'Sullivan MacCragh-16, Donal O'Sullivan MacCragh-15, Cragh O'Sullivan Mór-14, Dunlong O'Sullivan Mór-13, Bernard O'Sullivan Mór-12, Murtagh O'Sullivan-11, Dunlong O'Sullivan-10, Giolla na Bhflainn O'Sullivan Mór-9, Donal O'Sullivan Mór, 15th Lord of Knockgraffon-8, MacCraith O'Sullivan Mór, 14th Lord of Knockgraffon-7, Baudhach O'Sullivan, 13th Lord of Knockgraffon-6, Cathal O'Sullivan, 12th Lord of Knockgraffon-5, Aodh O'Sullivan, 11th Lord of Knockgraffon-4, Baudhach O'Sullivan, 10th Lord of Knockgraffon-3, Lorcan MacSullivan, 9th Lord of Knockgraffon-2, Eochaid Súilleabháinn, 8th Lord of Knockgraffon-1)

Owen was *The O'Sullivan MacCragh* (chief of the O'Sullivan MacCragh sept). He was recorded in the *Book of Munster.*

Owen O'Sullivan MacCragh had the following known son:

86 i **Dermot O'Sullivan MacCragh** [9, 10] was born in 1684 [9, 10].

Generation 24

71 **Daniel Sullivan** [26, 74, 87].
Born in circa 1738 in Berwick, Maine [74, 87].
Died in 1781 [74, 87].

(Owen O'Sullivan-23, Major Philip O'Sullivan of Ardea O'Sullivan-22, Owen O'Sullivan Beare, Lord of Ardea Castle-21, Daniel O'Sullivan. Lord of Ardea Castle-20, Philip O'Sullivan Beare-19, Donal O'Sullivan Beare, Lord of Ardea Castle-18, Sir Philip O'Sullivan Beare, Lord of Ardea Castle-17, Dermod O'Sullivan Beare, 11th Lord of Beare and Bantry-16, Donal O'Sullivan Beare, the Swarthy, 8th Lord of Beare and Bantry-15, Dermod (aka Dermond) Balluf O'Sullivan Beare-14, Teige O'Sullivan Beare-13, Amhiaffe O'Sullivan Beare-12, Annaidh O'Sullivan, 1st Lord of Beare and Bantry-11, Philip O'Sullivan-10, Giolla na Bhflainn O'Sullivan Mór-9, Donal O'Sullivan Mór, 15th Lord of Knockgraffon-8, MacCraith O'Sullivan Mór, 14th Lord of Knockgraffon-7, Baudhach

O'Sullivan, 13th Lord of Knockgraffon-6, Cathal O'Sullivan, 12th Lord of Knockgraffon-5, Aodh O'Sullivan, 11th Lord of Knockgraffon-4, Baudhach O'Sullivan, 10th Lord of Knockgraffon-3, Lorcan MacSullivan, 9th Lord of Knockgraffon-2, Eochaid Súilleabháinn, 8th Lord of Knockgraffon-1)

He settled in New Bristol, Maine, now called Sullivan. Daniel was serving as a captain in the Revolutionary War when the British captured him and burned his house in Sullivan. He spent six months on a British prison ship and died after his release while on his way home.

He married **Anne Paul** [26, 74, 87] on the 24th of March 1758 in York, Maine [74, 87]. They had the following daughter. Anne and her child died soon after its birth.

i Anne Paul Sullivan was born on the 10th of December 1760.

He married **Abigail Bean,** daughter of John Bean and Hannah née unknown [26, 74, 87], on the 17th of June 1765 in Fort Penal, Waldo County, Maine (later called Prospect) [74]. They had the following known children:

i Rachel Sullivan [87] was born on the 10th of December 1766 [87]. She died on the 10th of August 1806. [87]

ii James Sullivan [87] was born in 1768. [87] He died on the 28th of August 1830. [87]

iii Hannah Sullivan [87] was born on the 4th of March 1770 [87]. She married Paul Simpson on the 11th of March 1804 [87]. She died on the 24th of July 1849. [87]

iv Mary Sullivan [87] was born in 1773. [87] She married Josiah Simpson in 1792. [87] She died on the 28th of April 1857. [87]

v Lydia Sullivan [87] was born in March 1775. [87] She died on the 2nd of December 1851 in Sullivan, Maine. [87]

vi Infant John Sullivan. [87] He died at birth, date unknown.

72.. **Major General John Sullivan** [26, 62, 65, 74, 87, 88, 89, 90].
Born on the 17th of February 1740 in Berwick, Maine. [26, 74, 87, 89]
Died on the 23rd of January 1795 in Durham, New Hampshire. [26, 89]

(Owen O'Sullivan-23, Major Philip O'Sullivan of Ardea O'Sullivan-22, Owen O'Sullivan Beare, Lord of Ardea Castle-21, Daniel O'Sullivan. Lord of Ardea Castle-20, Philip O'Sullivan Beare-19, Donal O'Sullivan Beare, Lord of Ardea Castle-18, Sir Philip O'Sullivan Beare, Lord of Ardea Castle-17, Dermod O'Sullivan Beare, 11th Lord of Beare and Bantry-16, Donal O'Sullivan Beare, the Swarthy, 8th Lord of Beare and Bantry-15, Dermod (aka Dermond) Balluf O'Sullivan Beare-14, Teige O'Sullivan Beare-13, Amhiaffe O'Sullivan Beare-12, Annaidh O'Sullivan, 1st Lord of Beare and Bantry-11, Philip O'Sullivan-10, Giolla na Bhflainn O'Sullivan Mór-9, Donal O'Sullivan Mór, 15th Lord of Knockgraffon-8, MacCraith O'Sullivan Mór, 14th Lord of Knockgraffon-7, Baudhach O'Sullivan, 13th Lord of Knockgraffon-6, Cathal O'Sullivan, 12th Lord of Knockgraffon-5, Aodh O'Sullivan, 11th Lord of Knockgraffon-4, Baudhach O'Sullivan, 10th Lord of Knockgraffon-3, Lorcan MacSullivan, 9th Lord of Knockgraffon-2, Eochaid Súilleabháinn, 8th Lord of Knockgraffon-1)

John Sullivan practiced law and according to *A Guide to Likenesses of New Hampshire Officials and Governors on Public Display at the Legislative Office Buildings*, he was born in Somersworth, New Hampshire, not Berwick, Maine, as other sources state. It also says he was the first president (1786-1788) and Governor (1789-1790) of the state of New Hampshire. He attended the 1774 Continental Congress in Philadelphia and was a Major General in the American Revolutionary War. He wrote a letter to Thomas Jefferson threatening to resign his commission from the Continental Army after General Horatio Gates was appointed as his superior officer. His opinion of Gates was proven valid when General Gates fled the field with his army in a panic at the first shots in the Battle of Camden. General Johann de Kalb (aka DeKalb) did not know Gates had left the field and charged the British as planned. General de Kalb suffered seven sabre and bullet wounds. He was taken by the British to Camden where he was treated by Dr. Isaac Alexander, but died of his wounds. General Gates died in disgrace.

John Sullivan's letter to Thomas Jefferson was printed in *The Papers of Thomas Jefferson*, Princeton University Press, 1950, volume 1, pages 447 to 448, edited by Julian Parks Boyd. It is among the Lee family papers 1638-1867 at the Virginia Historical Society record, number 185961.

On orders from George Washington, General John Sullivan led an expedition from the 18th of June to the 3rd of October 1779 with an army of 3,200 continental soldiers. He defeated British loyalists supported by circa 1,000 Iroquois Indians. He destroyed forty Iroquois villages and ended the Indian support of the British. This was regarded as one of the most important strategic efforts of the Revolutionary War. A monument was erected at Lodi, New York, to commemorate the expedition.

For details of the life of General of Duhollow John Sullivan see the book:

> *Military Service and Public Life of Major General John Sullivan* originally published in 1868, by Thomas Coffin Amory, republished by Applewood Books in Bedford, Massachusetts.

He married **Lydia Worcester** [26, 74, 89] born on the 14th of October 1738. [74, 89] She died on the 22nd of March 1820 [74, 89]. They had the following known children:

i Margery Sullivan [89] was born on the 2nd of February 1761. [89] She died on the 10th of April 1764. [89]

ii Lydia Sullivan [89] was born on the 17th of March 1763. [89] She married

Jonathan Steele in January 1788. [89] She died on the 9th of April 1842. [89]

iii John Sullivan [89] was born on the 29th of October 1767. [89] He died in 1819 in Baton Rouge, Louisiana. [89]

80 iv **James Sullivan** [89] was born on the 1st of September 1769. [89] He died in July 1796 in Georgetown, South Carolina. [89]

81 v **George Sullivan** [89] was born on the 29th of August 1771. [89] He died on the 14th of June 1838. [89]

vi Margery Sullivan [89] was born in 1775. [89] She died in 1777. [89]

73 **James Sullivan** [26, 28, 62, 65, 74, 91].
Born on the 22nd of April 1744 in Berwick, Maine [26, 62, 91].
Died on the 10th of December 1808 in Boston, Massachusetts [62, 74, 91].

(Owen O'Sullivan-23, Major Philip O'Sullivan of Ardea O'Sullivan-22, Owen O'Sullivan Beare, Lord of Ardea Castle-21, Daniel O'Sullivan. Lord of Ardea Castle-20, Philip O'Sullivan Beare-19, Donal O'Sullivan Beare, Lord of Ardea Castle-18, Sir Philip O'Sullivan Beare, Lord of Ardea Castle-17, Dermod O'Sullivan Beare, 11th Lord of Beare and Bantry-16, Donal O'Sullivan Beare, the Swarthy, 8th Lord of Beare and Bantry-15, Dermod (aka Dermond) Balluf O'Sullivan Beare-14, Teige O'Sullivan Beare-13, Amhiaffe O'Sullivan Beare-12, Annaidh O'Sullivan, 1st Lord of Beare and Bantry-11, Philip O'Sullivan-10, Giolla na Bhflainn O'Sullivan Mór-9, Donal O'Sullivan Mór, 15th Lord of Knockgraffon-8, MacCraith O'Sullivan Mór, 14th Lord of Knockgraffon-7, Baudhach O'Sullivan, 13th Lord of Knockgraffon-6, Cathal O'Sullivan, 12th Lord of Knockgraffon-5, Aodh O'Sullivan, 11th Lord of Knockgraffon-4, Baudhach O'Sullivan, 10th Lord of Knockgraffon-3, Lorcan MacSullivan, 9th Lord of Knockgraffon-2, Eochaid Súilleabháinn, 8th Lord of Knockgraffon-1)

James Sullivan lived in Saco, Maine; Groton, Massachusetts; and Boston, Massachusetts. He studied law at Harvard University and received his LLD (Doctor of Jurisprudence) degree. He was:

- Member of the Provincial Council 1775,
- Judge of the Superior Court 1776-1783,
- Attorney General 1790-1807,
- Governor of the state of Massachusetts 1807-1880.

On the 16th of May 1796, he received a letter from Philip Sullivan which said:

> *"... A grand-uncle of mine having gone to America about sixty years ago, his relatives have suffered greatly from being without the means of finding out his fate, till now, by the great good fortune, I am informed that you are a son of his. If you find, by the account below, that I have not been misinformed, I shall be glad to hear from you Mr. Owen O'Sullivan, son of Major Philip O'Sullivan, of Ardea in the County of Kerry, Ireland, by Joanna daughter of Dermon MacCarthy, of Killoween, Esq. in said county. They were connected with the most respectable families in the province of Munster, particularly the count of Beare Haven, MacCarthy Earl Clancare, McFinnen of Barrymore Earl of Thomond, Earl of Clancasthy, McFinen of Glanarough O'Donough of Ross, O'Donough of Glynn, MacCarthy of Carberry, Lord Clancarthy and O'Donovan &c.*

I am, Sir respectfully Philip O'Sullivan

Ardea, May 15th 1896 ...."

This letter contains some errors.

He married **Mehetable Odiorne,** daughter of William Odiorne [26, 62, 74, 91] on the 22nd of February 1768. [91] She was born on the 26th of June 1748 in Durham, New Hampshire. [74, 91] She died on the 26th of January 1786 in Boston, Massachusetts. [74, 91] They had the following known children:

	i	James Sullivan [26, 91] was born on the 4th of January 1769 in Saco, Maine. [26] He died on the 29th of June 1787 in Boston, Massachusetts. [26]
	ii	Jonathan Amory Sullivan [26, 91, 93] was born on the 7th of July 1770 in Boston, Massachusetts. [91] He married Nancy Weir in 1794. [91] He died on the 24th of August 1828 in Boston, Massachusetts. [91]
	iii	Avis Sullivan [26, 91] was born on the 6th of October 1771 in Biddeford, (now Saco), Maine. [26, 91] He died on the 16th of October 1771. [91]
	iv	Memetable Sullivan [26, 91] was born on the 29th of July 1772 in Saco, Maine. [26, 91] She married James Cutler on the 5th of February 1793 in Boston, Massachusetts. [26, 91] She died on the 24th of March 1847 in Boston, Massachusetts. [26, 91]
82	v	**Brigadier General William Sullivan** [26, 91] was born on the 30th of November 1774 in Saco, Maine. [26, 91] He died on the 8th of September 1839 in Boston, Massachusetts. [26, 91]
94	vi	**Dr. John Landon Sullivan** [26, 28, 91] was born on the 9th of April 1777 in Saco, Maine. [26, 28, 91] He died on the 10th of February 1865 in Boston, Massachusetts. [26, 28, 91]
83	vii	**Richard Sullivan** [26, 62, 91] was born on the 17th of June 1779 in Groton, Massachusetts. [26, 62, 91] He died on the 11th of December 1861. [26, 91]
	viii	William Bant Sullivan [26, 91] was born on the 16th of March 1781 in Groton, Massachusetts. [26, 91] He died on the 4th of December 1806 in Boston, Massachusetts. [26, 91]
84	ix	**George Sullivan** [26, 91] was born on the 21st of February 1783 in Boston, Massachusetts. [26, 91] He died on the 14th of December 1866 in Pau, France. [26, 91]
	x	Nancy Sullivan[26, 91] was born on the 24th of April 1784 in Boston, Massachusetts. [26, 91] She died on the 22nd of July 1785 in Boston, Massachusetts. [91]

He married **Martha Langdon.** [62, 74, 91] She died on the 26th of August 1812. [74, 91] They had no known children.

74 **Ebenezer Sullivan.** [26, 65, 74, 93]
Born on the 8th of October 1753 in Berwick, Maine. [26, 74, 93]
Died on the 3rd of June 1799 in Charleston, South Carolina. [26, 74, 93]

(Owen O'Sullivan-23, Major Philip O'Sullivan of Ardea O'Sullivan-22, Owen O'Sullivan Beare, Lord of Ardea Castle-21, Daniel O'Sullivan. Lord of Ardea Castle-20, Philip O'Sullivan Beare-19, Donal O'Sullivan Beare, Lord of Ardea Castle-18, Sir Philip O'Sullivan Beare, Lord of Ardea Castle-17, Dermod O'Sullivan Beare, 11th Lord of Beare and Bantry-16, Donal O'Sullivan Beare, the Swarthy, 8th Lord of Beare and Bantry-15, Dermod (aka Dermond) Balluf O'Sullivan Beare-14, Teige O'Sullivan Beare-13, Amhiaffe O'Sullivan Beare-12, Annaidh O'Sullivan, 1st Lord of Beare and Bantry-11, Philip O'Sullivan-10, Giolla na Bhflainn O'Sullivan Mór-9, Donal O'Sullivan Mór, 15th Lord of Knockgraffon-8, MacCraith O'Sullivan Mór, 14th Lord of Knockgraffon-7, Baudhach O'Sullivan, 13th Lord of Knockgraffon-6, Cathal O'Sullivan, 12th Lord of Knockgraffon-5, Aodh O'Sullivan, 11th Lord of Knockgraffon-4, Baudhach O'Sullivan, 10th Lord of Knockgraffon-3, Lorcan MacSullivan, 9th Lord of Knockgraffon-2, Eochaid Súilleabháinn, 8th Lord of Knockgraffon-1)

He served as a captain in the Revolutionary War and practiced law in South Berwick, Maine.

He married **Abigail Cotton** [26, 74, 93] from Portsmouth, New Hampshire. They had the following known children:

85 i **John Sullivan** [93] was born on the 1st of April 1773. He died on the 18th of July 1818 in Norfolk, Virginia.

ii Margery Sullivan [93] was born on the 16th of November 1774.

iii Moses Sullivan [93] was born in 1776. He died in Sullivan, Maine.

iv Sarah Sullivan [93] was born in 1778. She died in Berwick, Maine.

v Lydia Sullivan [93] was born in 1779 in Berwick, Maine. She died in Shapleigh, Maine.

77 **Moses O'Sullivan.** [27, 45, 67, 77]
Born in 1754 in Twitty's Creek, Charlotte, Virginia. [45]
Died in 1810 in Lebanon, South Carolina. [45, 67]

(Charles B. Sullivan-23, Owen Sullivan-22, Owen Sullivan-21, John Thomas O'Sullivan-20, Owen Donal O'Sullivan-19, Owen O'Sullivan Beare Lord of Beare and Bantry-18, Sir Owen O'Sullivan Beare, 14th Lord of Beare and Bantry-17, Dermod O'Sullivan Beare, 11th Lord of Beare and Bantry-16, Donal O'Sullivan Beare, the Swarthy, 8th Lord of Beare and Bantry-15, Dermod (aka Dermond) Balluf O'Sullivan Beare-14, Teige O'Sullivan Beare-13, Amhiaffe O'Sullivan Beare-12, Annaidh O'Sullivan, 1st Lord of Beare and Bantry-11, Philip O'Sullivan-10, Giolla na Bhflainn O'Sullivan Mór-9, Donal O'Sullivan Mór, 15th Lord of Knockgraffon-8, MacCraith O'Sullivan Mór, 14th Lord of Knockgraffon-7, Baudhach O'Sullivan, 13th Lord of Knockgraffon-6, Cathal O'Sullivan, 12th Lord of Knockgraffon-5, Aodh O'Sullivan, 11th Lord of Knockgraffon-4, Baudhach O'Sullivan, 10th Lord of Knockgraffon-3, Lorcan MacSullivan, 9th Lord of Knockgraffon-2, Eochaid Súilleabháinn, 8th Lord of Knockgraffon-1)

His gravestone says he was born in 1762 and died in 1806. Source documents say 1754 and 1810.

He married **Millandra (Millie) Chandler** [27] in 1780 and they had the following known daughter:

i **Mary O'Sullivan** [67] was born on the 15th of December 1785. [67]

78 **Hewlett Sullivan.** [27, 45, 65, 67, 69, 77, 78, 94, 95, 96, 97, 98, 99, 100, 101]
Born on 28th of December 1763 in Charlotte County, Virginia. [27, 67, 96]
Died on 11th of July 1830 in Greenville County, South Carolina. [27, 45, 67, 96]

(Charles B. Sullivan-23, Owen Sullivan-22, Owen Sullivan-21, John Thomas O'Sullivan-20, Owen Donal O'Sullivan-19, Owen O'Sullivan Beare Lord of Beare and Bantry-18, Sir Owen O'Sullivan Beare, 14th Lord of Beare and Bantry-17, Dermod O'Sullivan Beare, 11th Lord of Beare and Bantry-16, Donal O'Sullivan Beare, the Swarthy, 8th Lord of Beare and Bantry-15, Dermod (aka Dermond) Balluf O'Sullivan Beare-14, Teige O'Sullivan Beare-13, Amhiaffe O'Sullivan Beare-12, Annaidh O'Sullivan, 1st Lord of Beare and Bantry-11, Philip O'Sullivan-10, Giolla na Bhflainn O'Sullivan Mór-9, Donal O'Sullivan Mór, 15th Lord of Knockgraffon-8, MacCraith O'Sullivan Mór, 14th Lord of Knockgraffon-7, Baudhach O'Sullivan, 13th Lord of Knockgraffon-6, Cathal O'Sullivan, 12th Lord of Knockgraffon-5, Aodh O'Sullivan, 11th Lord of Knockgraffon-4, Baudhach O'Sullivan, 10th Lord of Knockgraffon-3, Lorcan MacSullivan, 9th Lord of Knockgraffon-2, Eochaid Súilleabháinn, 8th Lord of Knockgraffon-1)

A monument placed by the Daughters of the American Revolution in the Lebanon Church Yard cemetery in Greenville, South Carolina, says Hewlett Sullivan and his father Charles were Revolutionary War patriots.

Hewlett Sullivan was born in Virginia, the son of Charles Sullivan and Mary Charlton. When he was a 16 year old boy, he served in the army during the Revolutionary War under Captain Game Harvey for 6 months near Louisville, Georgia. He then did service as a private in the Revolutionary War under Captain Joseph Hays in Laurens County, South Carolina. When "Bloody Bill" Cunningham captured Fort Hays and hanged many in the garrison, he was on detached duty and escaped. He was captured twice in the battle of Musgroves Hill, but managed to escape both times. At the close of the war, he belonged to a company of Rangers who *"cleared South Carolina of Tories."* Both sides in the revolutionary war had para-military commando groups, who were actually vigilantes that harassed, and often killed civilians who sympathized with their opponents.

James C. Heaney published an article regarding Sullivans serving during the Revolutionary War. The reference reads as follows:

> *"... Hewlett Born Dec. 28, 1763 Virginia Died July 11, 1830 South Carolina m. Mary Dunklin. Private South Carolina ..."*

According to an entry in Thomas Jefferson Sullivan's Bible, Hewlett was a captain in the South Carolina militia. His obituary also says he was an officer and a monument in Greenville County, South Carolina, says he was a captain.

Hewlett moved to Greenville County, with his father, in 1784 and settled near Lebanon. He married Mary Dunklin on the 18th of December 1787 after her family moved from Four Hole Swamp in Berkley County, South Carolina, to Greenville County. He, his father and brothers stayed with the Dunklin family in Four Hole Swamp when they made their trading trips to Charleston, South Carolina and told the Dunklin's about their new purchase of rich and healthy lands in Greenville County.

- Hewlett was granted 200 acres of land in district 96 on the 11th of June 1784.
- He was granted 510 acres of land in Greenville District on the 9th of November1808.

Hewlett served two terms in the South Carolina legislature and twice in the Senate representing Greenville County. He was one of the first to advocate a free school system for South Carolina. He served as magistrate until his death. He accumulated a considerable property in land and slaves. Hewlett Sullivan was buried at Lebanon Church Cemetery where the tombstones give the dates and histories of the Sullivan and Arnold families.

In the 1790 census, Hewlett was a part of his father's household. Hewlett and his family appeared in the 1800, 1810 and 1820 census, Greenville County, South Carolina:

- In the 1800 census, Hewlett's household consisted of 6 males, 3 females and 10 slaves for a total of 19 people.
- In the 1810 census, his household consisted of 8 males, 5 females and 25 slaves for a total of 38 people.
- In the 1820 census, his household consisted of 22 men and 35 women for a total of 57 people. This presumable included about 45 slaves.

It was reported that he appeared in the 1830 census, but Hewlett died on the 11th of July 1830 and did not appear in the 1830 census. There was a Hewlett Sullivan in the 1830 census, but it could not be this Hewlett, and may have been his son Hewlett, because his entire household consisted of one male person. Ten years earlier, the census recorded Hewlett's household as consisting of 57 people and his obituary said he left a large family.

Hewlett's will did not specify how many acres of land and slaves he owned. In his will, Hewlett gave six of his children land and slaves valued at $21,273. For the other six children, he specified four tracts of land valued at an average of $3.65 per acre and slaves to be distributed equally. He specified that the value of his estate be divided equally and this implies that the land and slaves willed to the other six children were also worth about $21,273. In addition, he willed an unspecified amount of land originally granted to his father Charles, plus five slaves to his wife Mary. Charles had four land grants totaling 870 acres. This implies Hewlett's net worth was about $46,000 plus the value of his slaves, building, equipment, and livestock. This was a considerable amount of money at that time.

Obituary of Hewlett Sullivan

" ... 6 [June] 1830 Issue

At his residence in this dist. Hewlett Sullivan Sq., 67 yr. died July 11th, left a large family. In his youth he saw the difficulties of the Revolutionary War-in time of when his father moved from Virginia to Georgia, but the Cherokee Indians were so troublesome he moved to Laurens, where he met with a species of foe little better than the savages. His father, brother and himself were constantly in the field and bore a conspicuous part in that kind of warfare then carried on in the state. He was a militia officer. His parents were reduced after the fall of Charleston from a state of affluence to extreme poverty, being robbed of

S. Carolina

I do hereby Certify for Hewlet Sullivant a tract of Land Containing five hundred & ten acres Surveyed for him 9 July 1808 Situate in the District of Greenville on the Rocky fork of ... Creek & Branches of Saluda River and hath such shape form and marks buttings and boundings as the above plat represents Given under my hand this 28th Nov.r 1808

John H Harrison D.S.

Hewlett Sullivans land grant of 510 acres on the 28th of November 1808. Courtesy of the South Carolina State Archive

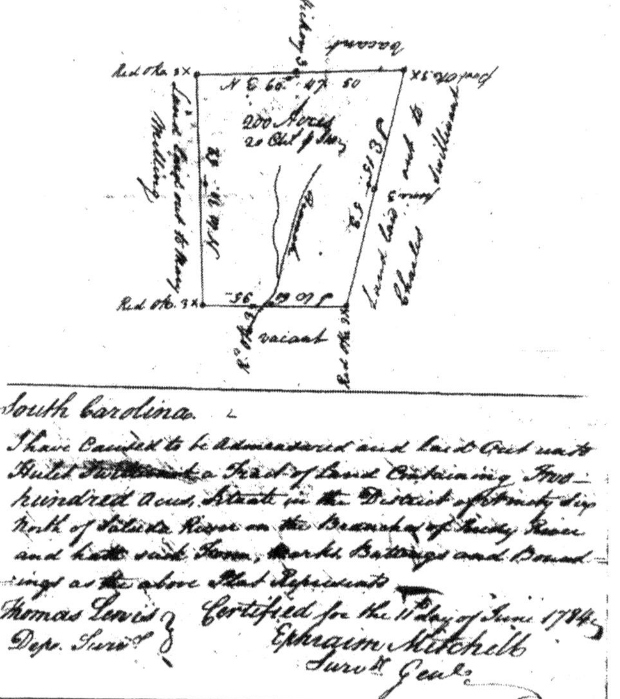

South Carolina

I have Caused to be Admeasured and laid Out unto Hulet Sullivant a Tract of Land Containing Two hundred Acres, Situate in the District of Ninety Six North of Saluda River on the Branches of Reedy River and hath such Form, Marks, Buttings and Boundings as the above Plat Represents

Thomas Lewis Dep. Surv.r — Certified for the 11th day of June 1784

Ephraim Mitchell Surv.r Genl.

Hewlett Sullivans land grant of 200 acres on the 11th of June 1784. Courtesy of the South Carolina State Archive

THE STATE OF SOUTH-CAROLINA.

To all to whom these Presents shall come, *Greeting:*

Know Ye, *That in pursuance of an act of the legislature, entitled, "An Act for establishing the mode of granting the "lands now vacant in this state, and for allowing a commutation to be "received for some lands that have been granted," passed the 19th day of February, 1791; We have granted, and by these presents do grant unto* Hewlett Sullivan his *heirs and assigns, a plantation or tract of land, containing* Five hundred and ten Surveyed for him the 4 July 1808 Situate in the [illegible] of Greenville on the [illegible] fork of Grove Creek a branch of Saluda River Bounded by lines running [illegible] [illegible] [illegible] [illegible] [illegible] and Maxwell's land [illegible] on the Old line [illegible]

having such shape, form and marks, as are represented by a plat hereunto annexed, together with all woods, trees, waters, water-courses, profits, commodities, appurtenances and hereditaments whatsoever, thereunto belonging, TO HAVE AND TO HOLD *the said tract of* Five hundred and ten *acres of land, and all and singular other the premises hereby granted unto the said* Hewlett Sullivan his *heirs and assigns forever, in free and common soccage.*

Given under the Great Seal of the State.

WITNESS, *his Excellency* Charles Pinckney *Esquire, Governor and Commander in Chief in and over the said State, at Columbia, this* fifth *Day of* December *Anno Domini one thousand eight hundred* & Eight *and of the Independence of the United States of America the thirty* third

Charles (L. M. S.) Pinckney

And hath thereunto a plat thereof annexed, representing the same, certified by John Du Bose *Surveyor General.*

28th Nov. 1808

Hewlett Sullivans land grant of 510 acres on the 28th of November 1808. Courtesy of the South Carolina State Archive

> *all their slaves, horses, cattle and everything else of any value. After the war he moved and has been a citizen of this district for at least 50 years, He served twice in the [state] legislature ..."*

Hewlett Sullivan and **Mary Dunklin**, daughter of Joseph Dunklin [25, 43, 63, 92, 94, 97, 101, 102] and Mary Jean Caroline Warthan, were married by the Reverend Solomon on the 19th of December 1787 in Greenville County, South Carolina. [25, 43, 65, 94] Their address was listed as "*Horse Cr. Br. Reedy River*". Hewlett and Mary lived in Greenville County at Lickville, near Dunklin's Bridge. Later they lived on Reedy River, Dunklin Township. She was born on the 17th of February 1771 in Four Hole Swamp, near Monk's Corner near Bonneau, Berkley County, South Carolina.[43, 65] She died on the 12th of June 1850 in Greenville County, South Carolina. [43, 65, 94]

A monument placed by the Daughters of the American Revolution in the Lebanon Church Yard cemetery in Greenville, South Carolina says Mary Dunklin was a Revolutionary War patriot. This is also stated in Supplement to *Index of the 1800 Census of NC*, Elisabeth Petty Bently and Sarah Sullivan, Genealogical Publishing Company, 1965, page 186d, reprinted from *South Carolinians in the Revolutionary War*, Clearfield Publishing, 1947, which says Mary Dunklin, daughter of Joseph Dunklin, was a revolutionary patriot. If this is true, either it was not this Mary Dunklin, or her birth date is wrong, because she was only five years old in 1776. It could have been her mother Mary Jean Caroline Dunklin née Warthan.

Her parents emigrated from Ireland and settled in Four Hole Swamp in Berkley County, South Carolina. She and her entire family moved to Dunklin Township, Greenville County, South Carolina, on the Reedy River in 1785. Mary Dunklin married Hewlett Sullivan on the 19th of December 1787 when she was 16 years old. She said when the Sullivans were stopping with her people in Berkley County; she never thought she would marry one of those big rough Sullivans from up country!

Mary had eight sons and four daughters. Her gravestone says she died in on the 12th of June 1850 at the age of 79 and her obituary said she died at the home of her son-in-law, Captain James M. Latimer, near her own residence in the Greenville District. She was buried on the old homestead. Her obituary in the Laurens County newspaper states that after the death of her husband, Hewlett Sullivan, a native of Virginia, the bereaved widow joined the Methodist Church and was a devoted and consistent member up until her death.

There are several conflicts in some of these dates; her obituary and gravestone do not mention her birth date. Various undocumented sources say she was born:

- In December 1763 in Ireland.
- In circa 1752 in Charleston, South Carolina.
- The 17th of February 1772 in Dunklin, Greenville County, South Carolina.

If Mary died in 1850, at the age of 79 as her gravestone states, she would have been born in 1771, not 1763, 1775, or 1772. If she married at the age of sixteen in 1787, she would have been born in 1771. Therefore, her most likely year of birth was 1771 or 1772 depending on the months in which she was born and died. If she were born on the 17th of February 1772, she would have been 26 days, 9 months and 78 years old at her death. This is close enough to assume this is her correct birth date. Mary Dunklin's obituary from the Laurens County newspaper:

> *"... Died June 12, 1850, after a short illness, at the house of Capt. James M. Latimer, her son-in-law, near her own residence, in Greenville District, Mrs. Mary Sullivan, widow of Hewlet Sullivan, Sr. The deceased was born on her native parish in the state. Her parents were Joseph Dunklin, an immigrant from Ireland, and her mother, Mary Warthan of England, both of whom sailed from London in the same vessel, and shortly after their arrival in Charleston married and finally settled in the parish above mentioned. Mary, the subject of this obituary, was the fourth child. Her eldest brothers, Joseph and John, served with Marion and Horry through the greater part of the War of the Revolution. Her father died about the close of the war and her mother some two years afterwards. The balance of the family in 1785 removed to Greenville County on Reedy River, where Mary intermarried with Hewlett Sullivan, a native of Virginia, on 19 Dec 1787. Twelve children, eight sons and four daughters were the fruits of her marriage, and she had the rare fortune to bring them up and see them all comfortably settled in life. She, however, by the death of her husband, on 11 July 1830, became a bereaved widow and shortly after that calamity, attached herself to the Methodist Church, which she continued a zealous and consistent member up to her death. She also survived two of her sons and two of her daughters. The deceased was distinguished through life for her devotion to the honor and prosperity of her family and her amiable and generous deportment in society. All the branches of a most numerous family concentrated their affection upon her and have rendered their debt of gratitude. But she is no more! And her family and social circle, now filled with grief and humiliation by this dispensation of Providence, deeply deplore the loss of one so dear to them...."*

Hewlett Sullivan and Mary Dunklin had the following known children:

i Dunklin Sullivan [27, 45, 67, 99] was born on the 27th of February 1791 in Greenville County, South Carolina. [45, 67] He died in 1837 in Alabama [67]. Dunklin Sullivan moved to Alabama. He was a judge.

87 ii **Dr. John Creasy Sullivan** [27, 45, 67, 96, 97, 98, 99, 105, 106, 107] was born on the 8th of November 1793 in Greenville County, South Carolina. [45, 67] He died on the 14th of February 1864.

88 iii **Joseph Pickney Sullivan** [27, 45, 67, 96, 99, 108, 109, 110, 111, 112] was born on the 17th of June 1796 in Greenville County, South Carolina. [45, 67, 96] He died on the 24th of October 1849 in Charleston, Berkeley County, South Carolina of yellow fever. [45, 67, 96]

iv Jane Caroline Sullivan [27, 45, 67, 96, 99] was born on the 21st of September 1798 in Licksville, Greenville County, South Carolina. [45, 67]

v Hewlett Sullivan[27, 45, 67, 99] was born on the 28th of April 1801 in Dunklin Township, Greenville County, South Carolina. [45, 67]

vi Frances W. Sullivan [27, 45, 67, 96, 99] was born on 28th of December 1803 in Greenville County, South Carolina. [45, 67] She died on the 8th of May 1837. [67]

vii Elisabeth Sullivan [27, 45, 67, 96, 99] was born on the 28th of October 1805 in

Greenville County, South Carolina. [45]

89 viii **Thomas Jefferson Sullivan** [27, 45, 67, 96, 99, 113] was born on the 28th of September 1807 in Greenville County, South Carolina. [45, 67] He died on the 13th of January 1866 in his home in Mount Bethel, South Carolina. [67]

90.. ix **George Washington Sullivan** [45, 67, 69, 96, 99, 110, 114, 115, 116, 117] was born on the 27th of September 1809 in Dunklin Township, Greenville County, South Carolina. [45, 67] He died on the 19th of December 1887 in Charleston Hall, Laurens County, South Carolina. [67]

91 x **Charles Pickney Sullivan** [45, 67, 96, 99, 110, 118, 119, 120, 121, 122, 123] was born on the 3rd of October 1811 in Greenville County, South Carolina. [45, 67]

xi Mary Dunklin Sullivan [27, 45, 67, 96, 99] was born on the 30th of October 1813 in Greenville County, South Carolina. [45, 67] She died on the 10th of February 1883.[67]

92 xii **Dr. James Madison Sullivan** [27, 45, 67, 96, 99, 124, 125] was born on the 11th of March 1816 in Greenville County, South Carolina. [45, 67] He died on the 9th of April 1875 at home in Warthen, South Carolina. [67]

79 **Elisabeth Sullivan** [48, 85].
Died in 1798 two weeks after her son's birth.

(James Sullivan-23, John Sullivan-22, Owen Sullivan-21, John Thomas O'Sullivan-20, Owen Donal O'Sullivan-19, Owen O'Sullivan Beare Lord of Beare and Bantry-18, Sir Owen O'Sullivan Beare, 14th Lord of Beare and Bantry-17, Dermod O'Sullivan Beare, 11th Lord of Beare and Bantry-16, Donal O'Sullivan Beare, the Swarthy, 8th Lord of Beare and Bantry-15, Dermod (aka Dermond) Balluf O'Sullivan Beare-14, Teige O'Sullivan Beare-13, Amhiaffe O'Sullivan Beare-12, Annaidh O'Sullivan, 1st Lord of Beare and Bantry-11, Philip O'Sullivan-10, Giolla na Bhflainn O'Sullivan Mór-9, Donal O'Sullivan Mór, 15th Lord of Knockgraffon-8, MacCraith O'Sullivan Mór, 14th Lord of Knockgraffon-7, Baudhach O'Sullivan, 13th Lord of Knockgraffon-6, Cathal O'Sullivan, 12th Lord of Knockgraffon-5, Aodh O'Sullivan, 11th Lord of Knockgraffon-4, Baudhach O'Sullivan, 10th Lord of Knockgraffon-3, Lorcan MacSullivan, 9th Lord of Knockgraffon-2, Eochaid Súilleabháinn, 8th Lord of Knockgraffon-1)

She married **Benjamin Burton,** son of Thomas Burton and Ann Perrin, [48] born in Laurens District, South Carolina [48] and died on the 7th of August 1811.[48] They had the following known son:

i Robert Perrin Burton [48] was born in 1798 in Laurens County, South Carolina. Robert Perrin Burton's son wrote that his mother died about two weeks after his birth and he lived with his Sullivan grandmother until he was twelve years old. His two grandmothers were sisters.

86 **Dermot O'Sullivan MacCragh** [9, 10, 226].
Born in 1684 [9, 10].

(Owen O'Sullivan MacCragh-23, Dermot O'Sullivan MacCragh-22, Owen O'Sullivan MacCragh-21, Conor O'Sullivan MacCragh-20, Donogh O'Sullivan MacCragh-19, Buadach O'Suillivan MacCragh-18, Eoghan O'Sullivan MacCragh-17, Conor O'Sullivan MacCragh-16, Donal O'Sullivan MacCragh-15, Cragh O'Sullivan Mór-14, Dunlong O'Sullivan Mór-13, Bernard O'Sullivan Mór-12, Murtagh

O'Sullivan-11, Dunlong O'Sullivan-10, Giolla na Bhflainn O'Sullivan Mór-9, Donal O'Sullivan Mór, 15th Lord of Knockgraffon-8, MacCraith O'Sullivan Mór, 14th Lord of Knockgraffon -7, Baudhach O'Sullivan, 13th Lord of Knockgraffon-6, Cathal O'Sullivan, 12th Lord of Knockgraffon-5, Aodh O'Sullivan, 11th Lord of Knockgraffon-4, Baudhach O'Sullivan, 10th Lord of Knockgraffon-3, Lorcan MacSullivan, 9th Lord of Knockgraffon-2, Eochaid Súilleabháinn, 8th Lord of Knockgraffon-1)

Dermot was *The O'Sullivan MacCragh* (chief of the O'Sullivan MacCragh sept). The primogeniture bloodline recorded in the O'Donovan Ordinance Survey ends with him. He was the last O'Sullivan MacCragh recorded in the *Book of Munster* and it is not known where the next three generations lived. They refused to convert to the English Protestant religion and the English treated the oldest Irish royal bloodline as common peasants. They probably lived the life of tenant farmers on small plots of land.

Dermot O'Sullivan MacCragh had the following known son:

97 i **Sean O'Sullivan MacCragh** [10] was born in 1714. [10]

Generation 25

80 **James Sullivan** [89].
Born on the 1st of September 1769. [89]
Died in July 1796 in Georgetown, South Carolina. [89]

(Major General John Sullivan-23, Owen O'Sullivan-22, Major Philip O'Sullivan of Ardea O'Sullivan-22, Major Philip O'Sullivan of Ardea O'Sullivan-22, Owen O'Sullivan Beare, Lord of Ardea Castle-21, Daniel O'Sullivan. Lord of Ardea Castle-20, Philip O'Sullivan Beare-19, Donal O'Sullivan Beare, Lord of Ardea Castle-18, Sir Philip O'Sullivan Beare, Lord of Ardea Castle-17, Dermod O'Sullivan Beare, 11th Lord of Beare and Bantry-16, Donal O'Sullivan Beare, the Swarthy, 8th Lord of Beare and Bantry-15, Dermod (aka Dermond) Balluf O'Sullivan Beare-14, Teige O'Sullivan Beare-13, Amhiaffe O'Sullivan Beare-12, Annaidh O'Sullivan, 1st Lord of Beare and Bantry-11, Philip O'Sullivan-10, Giolla na Bhflainn O'Sullivan Mór-9, Donal O'Sullivan Mór, 15th Lord of Knockgraffon-8, MacCraith O'Sullivan Mór, 14th Lord of Knockgraffon-7, Baudhach O'Sullivan, 13th Lord of Knockgraffon-6, Cathal O'Sullivan, 12th Lord of Knockgraffon-5, Aodh O'Sullivan, 11th Lord of Knockgraffon-4, Baudhach O'Sullivan, 10th Lord of Knockgraffon-3, Lorcan MacSullivan, 9th Lord of Knockgraffon-2, Eochaid Súilleabháinn, 8th Lord of Knockgraffon-1)

James Sullivan had no known children:

81 **George Sullivan** [89] was born on the 29th of August 1771. [89]
Died on the 14th of June 1838. [89]

(Major General John Sullivan-23, Owen O'Sullivan-22, Major Philip O'Sullivan of Ardea O'Sullivan-22, Major Philip O'Sullivan of Ardea O'Sullivan-22, Owen O'Sullivan Beare, Lord of Ardea Castle-21, Daniel O'Sullivan. Lord of Ardea Castle-20, Philip O'Sullivan Beare-19, Donal O'Sullivan Beare, Lord of Ardea Castle-18, Sir Philip O'Sullivan Beare, Lord of Ardea Castle-17, Dermod O'Sullivan Beare, 11th Lord of Beare and Bantry-16, Donal O'Sullivan Beare, the Swarthy, 8th Lord of Beare and Bantry-15, Dermod (aka Dermond) Balluf O'Sullivan Beare-14, Teige O'Sullivan Beare-13, Amhiaffe O'Sullivan Beare-12, Annaidh O'Sullivan, 1st Lord of Beare and Bantry-11, Philip O'Sullivan-10, Giolla na Bhflainn O'Sullivan Mór-9, Donal O'Sullivan Mór, 15th Lord of

Knockgraffon-8, MacCraith O'Sullivan Mór, 14th Lord of Knockgraffon-7, Baudhach O'Sullivan, 13th Lord of Knockgraffon-6, Cathal O'Sullivan, 12th Lord of Knockgraffon-5, Aodh O'Sullivan, 11th Lord of Knockgraffon-4, Baudhach O'Sullivan, 10th Lord of Knockgraffon-3, Lorcan MacSullivan, 9th Lord of Knockgraffon-2, Eochaid Súilleabháinn, 8th Lord of Knockgraffon-1)

He was Attorney General of New Hampshire.

George Sullivan married **Clarissa Lamson** [89] and they had the following known children:

i John Sullivan [89] was born on the 23rd of March 1800. [89] He married Olivia Rowe on the 8th of September 1832. [89] He died on the 7th of January 1875 in Boston, Massachusetts. [89]

ii Martha Lamson Sullivan [89] was born on the 11th of January 1802. [89] She died on the 22nd of January 1831. [89]

iii Clarissa Lamson Sullivan [89] was born on the 9th of August 1804. [89] She died on the 18th of September 1809. [89]

iv Lydia Sullivan [89] was born on the 4th of October 1806. [89] She married David A. Gregg in March 1844. [89] She died on the 2nd of June 1849. [89]

v George Sullivan [89] was born on the 18th of October 1808 [89]. He died on the 11th of January 1830. [89]

vi James Sullivan was born on the 6th of December 1811.[89] He married Nancy Morrison in 1842. [89] James lived in Michigan.

vii William Sullivan [89] was born on the 28th of January 1814. [89] He married Mary S. Neal in 1845. [89] He died in 1864 in Michigan. [89]

viii Clarissa Lamson Sullivan [89] was born on the 31st of December 1815 [89]. She died in 1870. [89]

ix Margaret Wood Sullivan [89] was born on the 19th of July 1818. [89]

x Edward Sullivan [89] was born on the 23rd of August 1820. [89] He died on the 13th of May 1843. [89]

xi Mary Frances Sullivan [89] was born on the 23rd of August 1822. [89] She died on the 30th of August 1825. [89]

George Sullivan married **Philippa Call.** [89, 93] They had no known children.

82 **Brigadier General William Sullivan** [91].
Born on the 30th of November 1774 in Saco, Maine [26, 91].
Died on the 8th of September 1839 in Boston, Massachusetts [26, 91].

(James Sullivan-24, Owen O'Sullivan-23, Major Philip O'Sullivan of Ardea O'Sullivan-22, Major Philip O'Sullivan of Ardea O'Sullivan-22, Owen O'Sullivan Beare, Lord of Ardea Castle-21, Daniel O'Sullivan. Lord of Ardea Castle-20, Philip O'Sullivan Beare-19, Donal O'Sullivan Beare, Lord of Ardea Castle-18, Sir Philip O'Sullivan Beare, Lord of Ardea Castle-17, Dermod O'Sullivan Beare, 11th Lord of Beare and Bantry-16, Donal O'Sullivan Beare, the Swarthy, 8th Lord of Beare and Bantry-15, Dermod (aka Dermond) Balluf O'Sullivan Beare-14, Teige O'Sullivan Beare-13, Amhiaffe O'Sullivan Beare-12, Annaidh O'Sullivan, 1st Lord of Beare and Bantry-11, Philip O'Sullivan-10, Giolla na Bhflainn O'Sullivan Mór-9, Donal O'Sullivan Mór, 15th Lord of Knockgraffon-8, MacCraith O'Sullivan Mór, 14th Lord of Knockgraffon-7, Baudhach O'Sullivan, 13th Lord of Knockgraffon-6, Cathal O'Sullivan, 12th Lord of Knockgraffon-5, Aodh O'Sullivan, 11th Lord of Knockgraffon-4, Baudhach O'Sullivan, 10th Lord of Knockgraffon-3, Lorcan MacSullivan, 9th Lord of Knockgraffon-2, Eochaid Súilleabháinn, 8th Lord of Knockgraffon-1)

William studied law at Harvard University and was awarded an LLD (Doctor of Jurisprudence) degree. He was a member of the Massachusetts State Legislature and council for many years. He was a Brigadier General in the Militia.

William Sullivan married **Sarah Web Swan** [91] was born on the 10th of May 1782. [91] They had the following known children:

i James Sullivan [91] was born on the 5th of July 1803. [91] He died in August 1829. [91]
ii Christiana Sullivan [91] was born on the 6th of September 1805. [91] She died on the 18th of October 1806 [91].
iii William Amory Sullivan [91] was born on the 19th of April 1807 [91]. He died in 1849 [91].
iv James Swan Sullivan [91] was born on the 18th of February 1809 [91]. He married Jane Valentine in 1839 [91]. He died in 1874 in Savannah, Georgia [91].
v Sarah Williams Sullivan [91] was born on the 10th of October 1810 [91]. She married Gilbert Stuart Newton on the 22nd of August 1832 [91]. She died on the 11th of March 1892 in Saratoga, New York [91].
vi John Turner Sargent Sullivan [91] was born on the 24th of September 1813 in Boston, Massachusetts [91]. He died on the 31st of December 1849 in Boston, Massachusetts [91].
vii Meredith Amory Sullivan was born on the 5th of January 1817 [91]. He married Catherine Wilcocks on the 25th of December 1833. He died on the 3rd of January 1886 in Philadelphia, Pennsylvania [91]. According to these dates in the source he married at age 16 years, 11 months, and 20 days.
viii Olivia Buckminster Sullivan [91] was born on the 1st of April 1819 [91]. She married John Elliot Ward on the 15th of August 1839 [91]. She died in 1890 in Morristown, New Jersey [91].
ix Hepzibah Swan Sullivan [91] was born on the 7th of June 1820 [91].

83 **Richard Sullivan.** [26, 62, 91]
Born on the 17th of June 1779 in Groton, Massachusetts. [26, 62, 91]
Died on the 11th of December 1861. [26, 91]

(James Sullivan-24, Owen O'Sullivan-23, Major Philip O'Sullivan of Ardea O'Sullivan-22, Owen O'Sullivan Beare, Lord of Ardea Castle-21, Daniel O'Sullivan. Lord of Ardea Castle-20, Philip O'Sullivan Beare-19, Donal O'Sullivan Beare, Lord of Ardea Castle-18, Sir Philip O'Sullivan Beare, Lord of Ardea Castle-17, Dermod O'Sullivan Beare, 11th Lord of Beare and Bantry-16, Donal O'Sullivan Beare, the Swarthy, 8th Lord of Beare and Bantry-15, Dermod (aka Dermond) Balluf O'Sullivan Beare-14, Teige O'Sullivan Beare-13, Amhiaffe O'Sullivan Beare-12, Annaidh O'Sullivan, 1st Lord of Beare and Bantry-11, Philip O'Sullivan-10, Giolla na Bhflainn O'Sullivan Mór-9, Donal O'Sullivan Mór, 15th Lord of Knockgraffon-8, MacCraith O'Sullivan Mór, 14th Lord of Knockgraffon-7, Baudhach O'Sullivan, 13th Lord of Knockgraffon-6, Cathal O'Sullivan, 12th Lord of Knockgraffon-5, Aodh O'Sullivan, 11th Lord of Knockgraffon-4, Baudhach O'Sullivan, 10th Lord of Knockgraffon-3, Lorcan MacSullivan, 9th Lord of Knockgraffon-2, Eochaid Súilleabháinn, 8th

Lord of Knockgraffon-1)

He married **Sarah Russell** [26, 62, 91] on the 22nd of May 1804. [26, 91] She was born on the 1st of December 1786 [91] and died on the 8th of June 1881. [91] They had the following known children:

i Elisabeth Lowell Sullivan [91] was born on the 22nd of August 1805 in Brookline, Massachusetts. [91] She died on the 18th of April 1833 in Boston, Massachusetts. [91]

ii Susan Server Sullivan [91] was born on the 30th of March 1808 in Paris, France. [91] She married Stephen H. Perkins on the 22nd of November 1831. [91] She died on the 14th of March 1839 in Boston, Massachusetts. [91]

iii Anna Cabot Lowell Sullivan [91] was born on the 17th of December 1810. [91] She married Francis Cunningham on the 8th of October 1834. [91] She died on the 6th of September 1840. [91]

iv Mary Russell Sullivan [91] was born on the 28th of January 1816 in Brookline, Massachusetts. [91] She died on the 17th of April 1828 in Brookline, Massachusetts. [91]

v Richard Sullivan [62, 91] was born on the 19th of March 1820 in Brookline, Massachusetts. [62, 91] He married Henrietta Gardner on the 10th of September 1846. [91]

vi Francis William Sullivan [91] was born on the 1st of November 1821. [91] He died on the 2nd of December 1824 in Brookline, Massachusetts. [91]

vii James Sullivan [91] was born on the 27th of June 1829. [91] He died on the 28th of March 1866 in Brookline, Massachusetts. [91]

84 **George Sullivan** [26, 91].
Born on the 14th of December 1783 in Boston, Massachusetts. [26, 91]
Died on the 4th of December 1866 in Pau, France. [26, 91]

(James Sullivan-24, Owen O'Sullivan-23, Major Philip O'Sullivan of Ardea O'Sullivan-22, Owen O'Sullivan Beare, Lord of Ardea Castle-21, Daniel O'Sullivan. Lord of Ardea Castle-20, Philip O'Sullivan Beare-19, Donal O'Sullivan Beare, Lord of Ardea Castle-18, Sir Philip O'Sullivan Beare, Lord of Ardea Castle-17, Dermod O'Sullivan Beare, 11th Lord of Beare and Bantry-16, Donal O'Sullivan Beare, the Swarthy, 8th Lord of Beare and Bantry-15, Dermod (aka Dermond) Balluf O'Sullivan Beare-14, Teige O'Sullivan Beare-13, Amhiaffe O'Sullivan Beare-12, Annaidh O'Sullivan, 1st Lord of Beare and Bantry-11, Philip O'Sullivan-10, Giolla na Bhflainn O'Sullivan Mór-9, Donal O'Sullivan Mór, 15th Lord of Knockgraffon-8, MacCraith O'Sullivan Mór, 14th Lord of Knockgraffon-7, Baudhach O'Sullivan, 13th Lord of Knockgraffon-6, Cathal O'Sullivan, 12th Lord of Knockgraffon-5, Aodh O'Sullivan, 11th Lord of Knockgraffon-4, Baudhach O'Sullivan, 10th Lord of Knockgraffon-3, Lorcan MacSullivan, 9th Lord of Knockgraffon-2, Eochaid Súilleabháinn, 8th Lord of Knockgraffon-1)

He married **Sarah Bowdoin Winthrop** [26, 91] on the 26th of January 1809. She was born on the 7th of June 1788.[91] She died in February 1864 in Pau, France. [91] They had the following known children:

i George Richard Sullivan [91] was born on the 14th of November 1809.

[91] He married Fanny Hamilton on the 23rd of October 1832. [91] He died on the 14th of March 1870. [91] Both brothers changed their name from Sullivan to Bowdoin because that was the condition for inheriting property.

ii James Bowdoin Sullivan [91] was born on the 16th of May 1811. [91] He married Charlotte Kate Costabadie in May 1867. [91]

85 **John Sullivan** [93].
Born on the 1st of April 1773.
Died on the 18th of July 1818 in Norfolk, Virginia.

(Ebenezer Sullivan-23, Owen O'Sullivan-22, Major Philip O'Sullivan of Ardea O'Sullivan-22, Major Philip O'Sullivan of Ardea O'Sullivan-22, Owen O'Sullivan Beare, Lord of Ardea Castle-21, Daniel O'Sullivan. Lord of Ardea Castle-20, Philip O'Sullivan Beare-19, Donal O'Sullivan Beare, Lord of Ardea Castle-18, Sir Philip O'Sullivan Beare, Lord of Ardea Castle-17, Dermod O'Sullivan Beare, 11th Lord of Beare and Bantry-16, Donal O'Sullivan Beare, the Swarthy, 8th Lord of Beare and Bantry-15, Dermod (aka Dermond) Balluf O'Sullivan Beare-14, Teige O'Sullivan Beare-13, Amhiaffe O'Sullivan Beare-12, Annaidh O'Sullivan, 1st Lord of Beare and Bantry-11, Philip O'Sullivan-10, Giolla na Bhflainn O'Sullivan Mór-9, Donal O'Sullivan Mór, 15th Lord of Knockgraffon-8, MacCraith O'Sullivan Mór, 14th Lord of Knockgraffon-7, Baudhach O'Sullivan, 13th Lord of Knockgraffon-6, Cathal O'Sullivan, 12th Lord of Knockgraffon-5, Aodh O'Sullivan, 11th Lord of Knockgraffon-4, Baudhach O'Sullivan, 10th Lord of Knockgraffon-3, Lorcan MacSullivan, 9th Lord of Knockgraffon-2, Eochaid Súilleabháinn, 8th Lord of Knockgraffon-1)

John was adopted by his uncle Major General John Sullivan. He studied law, but decided to go to sea. He almost lost all of his property in the War of 1812.

He married **Mary Snow** [93] daughter of Samuel Snow and Margaret née unknown, born in 1779. She died in September 1813. They had the following known children:

i Eliza Sullivan was born on the 30th of March 1805 in Portsmouth, New Hampshire. She married Orlando Yeaton in June 1828. She died on the 2nd of November 1870 [93].

ii Mary Sullivan was born on the 2nd of July 1806. She married Dominic Peduzzi in October 1827. She died on the 22nd of August 1880 [93].

iii Elmira Sullivan was born on the 26th of August 1808 in Portsmouth, New Hampshire. She married Ammi R. H. Fernald on the 23rd of December 1832. She died on the 13th of June 1877 [93].

iv James Sullivan was born on the 23rd of January 1810 in Portsmouth, New Hampshire. He married Ann Matilda Shaw in August 1842. He died on the 18th of March 1871 in Portland, Maine [93].

v Sarah Sullivan was born on the 6th of May 1812 in Portsmouth, New Hampshire. She died on the 28th of November 1887 [93].

87 **Dr. John Creasy Sullivan** [27, 45, 67, 96, 97, 98, 99, 105, 106, 107].
Born on the 8th of November 1793 in Greenville County, South Carolina [45, 67].
Died on the 14th of February 1864.

(Hewlett Sullivan -24, Charles B. Sullivan -23, Owen Sullivan -22, Owen Sullivan -21, John Thomas

O'Sullivan-20, Owen Donal O'Sullivan-19, Owen O'Sullivan Beare Lord of Beare and Bantry -18, Sir Owen O'Sullivan Beare, 14th Lord of Beare and Bantry-17, Dermod O'Sullivan Beare, 11th Lord of Beare and Bantry -16, Donal O'Sullivan Beare, the Swarthy, 8th Lord of Beare and Bantry -15, Dermod (aka Dermond) Balluf O'Sullivan Beare-14, Teige O'Sullivan Beare-13, Amhiaffe O'Sullivan Beare-12, Annaidh O'Sullivan, 1st Lord of Beare and Bantry-11, Philip O'Sullivan-10, Giolla na Bhflainn O'Sullivan Mór-9, Donal O'Sullivan Mór, 15th Lord of Knockgraffon-8, MacCraith O'Sullivan Mór, 14th Lord of Knockgraffon-7, Baudhach O'Sullivan, 13th Lord of Knockgraffon-6, Cathal O'Sullivan, 12th Lord of Knockgraffon-5, Aodh O'Sullivan, 11th Lord of Knockgraffon-4, Baudhach O'Sullivan, 10th Lord of Knockgraffon-3, Lorcan MacSullivan, 9th Lord of Knockgraffon-2, Eochaid Súilleabháinn, 8th Lord of Knockgraffon-1)

John Sullivan was granted 155 acres of land on the 24th of November 1842, and another 271 acres on the 3rd of March 1845.

He married **Anna Hendricks Arnold** [27, 45, 105] in 1820 [67]. She was born in 1797 [105]. They had the following known children:

i	Elisabeth Sullivan [105] was born in 1827. [105]
ii	Clare Sullivan [105] was born in 1830. [105]
iii	Emma Sullivan [105] was born in 1832. [105]
iv	Martha Sullivan [105] was born in 1834. [105]

88 **Joseph Pickney Sullivan.** [27, 45, 67, 96, 99, 108, 109, 110, 111, 112]
Born on the 17th of June 1796 in Greenville County, South Carolina. [45, 67, 96]
Died on the 24th of October 1849 in Charleston, Berkeley County, South Carolina of yellow fever. [45, 67, 96]

(Hewlett Sullivan-24, Charles B. Sullivan-23, Owen Sullivan-22, Owen Sullivan-21, John Thomas O'Sullivan-20, Owen Donal O'Sullivan-19, Owen O'Sullivan Beare Lord of Beare and Bantry-18, Sir Owen O'Sullivan Beare, 14th Lord of Beare and Bantry-17, Dermod O'Sullivan Beare, 11th Lord of Beare and Bantry-16, Donal O'Sullivan Beare, the Swarthy, 8th Lord of Beare and Bantry-15, Dermod (aka Dermond) Balluf O'Sullivan Beare-14, Teige O'Sullivan Beare-13, Amhiaffe O'Sullivan Beare-12, Annaidh O'Sullivan, 1st Lord of Beare and Bantry-11, Philip O'Sullivan-10, Giolla na Bhflainn O'Sullivan Mór-9, Donal O'Sullivan Mór, 15th Lord of Knockgraffon-8, MacCraith O'Sullivan Mór, 14th Lord of Knockgraffon-7, Baudhach O'Sullivan, 13th Lord of Knockgraffon-6, Cathal O'Sullivan, 12th Lord of Knockgraffon-5, Aodh O'Sullivan, 11th Lord of Knockgraffon-4, Baudhach O'Sullivan, 10th Lord of Knockgraffon-3, Lorcan MacSullivan, 9th Lord of Knockgraffon-2, Eochaid Súilleabháinn, 8th Lord of Knockgraffon-1)

Joseph and his wife, Temperance Hamilton Arnold, were wealthy landowners in Laurens County, South Carolina. Joseph died before the 1850 Laurens census was taken. Temperance's net worth was stated as $5,000 and she owned 40-50 slaves. This was a considerable amount of money at that time.

Joseph P. Sullivan went to Charleston, South Carolina in October 1849 to purchase goods. He caught yellow fever and died ten days later. He is buried in Lebanon Church, Greenville County, South Carolina.

He corresponded with his cousin, Daniel Dunklin, of Missouri, sending news of family members in South Carolina. This correspondence is among the Daniel Dunklin Papers in the *Western Historical Manuscript Collection* of Ellis Library, University of Missouri, Columbia, Missouri. In one of these letters to Daniel Dunklin, dated August 13, 1834, from Tumbling Shoals, South Carolina, he wrote that he had visited his mother Mary Dunklin Sullivant [Sullivan], grandmother Mary Charlton Sullivan, and his brothers and sister in South Carolina. Dunklin Sullivan was not in South Carolina at the time. [He had been living in Alabama since 1816]. He wrote news of his brothers, Charles and James, and that Cousin Polly Gregory asked for financial assistance. He mentioned Hewlett Gregory, Dunklin Gregory, and David W. Gregory. He asked for news of his relations: Uncle John Dunklin and family; Uncle Claybourn Sullivan and family; Daniel's brothers, and Sister Jane. He wrote that he expected to go to Kentucky for two months and regretted that he had no time to visit Daniel and his Missouri relatives.

He wrote:

> *"... I have been living at this place five years and should like to move but I can't get more than half the value of my real estate. Consequently I fear I am settled for life. We make plenty to subsist on and can live as free from want here as anywhere, but we don't have a great surplus to pocket. My family is large and I have a good many small ones to provide for which renders good economy for to rub along....."*

Obituary of Joseph Pickney Sullivan

> *"... Amidst the shock and gloom of a numerous family and large circle of relatives and friends, it is with feeling of unutterable grief that I announce the death of Mr. Joseph Sullivan of this district, which occurred on the 20th inst. [October, 1849] in the city of Charleston, in the 54th year of his age, after ten days of intense suffering from the ravages of a destructive fever. He had visited the city on business and was actively engaged in its transaction for three days after his arrival, before he was confined to bed of sickness from which he was destined never to arise again. Being slightly indisposed before he reached there, no doubt a strong disposition to fever existed, and which the exciting causes prevalent in the city May have, unfortunately, developed into that disease which baffled the best medical skill, and set at naught the kind attention of his friends. The subject of this brief tribute was a successful merchant and planter, distinguished as well for his strong sense, sound judgment and practical views on all subjects to which he directed his attention, as for his kindness of heart, purity of character and exemplary deportment in the discharge of his duties in all the relations of life. As a husband and father he was devoted, as a master, indulgent, a good neighbor and excellent citizen in whom the poor found a valuable friend But alas! His earthly career so fully characterized by honorable deportment, moral excellence and great usefulness is closed. God the Creator, whose economy and providence in government of the world are regulated by infinite wisdom, has decreed it, and to His judgment let all bow with reverence, though it be with that sorrow and bleeding of heart inseparable from our nature. The remains of the deceased have been committed to their mother earth, in Greenville District on Reedy River, just above the Laurens line, surrounded by the tombs of his ancestors, who were*

amongst the first settlers of that portion of Carolina. [Both his and his wife's remains later were removed to Lebanon Church Cemetery]. In this melancholy event is painfully realized the solemn trust of the declaration: "Man that is born of woman hath but a short time to live, and full of misery. He cometh up and is cut down like a flower! He fleeth as it were a shadow, and never continueth in one stay...."

His gravestone inscription says: *Who departed this life in the city of Charleston in the 51st year of his life.* Neither this age at death, nor the age in the obituary are correct. He was 53 years, 4 months and 7 days old at death. Joseph's will has been repaired with tape making parts of it illegible, but it clearly says after two settlements, he leaves the balance of his estates to his brother Thomas to be held in trust. It further states his wife is to be permitted to live on the land and benefit from the revenues from the plantation, mills, and the labor of his Negros. A separate document of the settlement of his estate shows one settlement was to Charles Pleasant with a value of $14,057.70 and the other to William Dunklin Sullivan with a value of $14,089.04. In 1850, both William Dunklin and Charles Pleasant were still living in the household of Joseph's widow Temperance, as were some of her other children: Milton, Malinda, and Temperance. A separate trust document shows that the part of the estate being held in trust by Thomas was for Joseph's eldest son John Hewlett Sullivan.

He married **Temperance Hamilton Arnold** daughter of Benjamin Arnold and Temperance Hamilton Arnold [27, 45, 67, 96, 109, 111, 112, 116] on the 30th of April 1820 in either Laurens or Greenville County, South Carolina. [45, 96] She was born on the 8th of March 1801 in Laurens or Greenville County, South Carolina. [45, 96] She died on the 25th of September 1857 in Laurens County, South Carolina. [45, 67, 96, 111]

Joseph Pickney Sullivan and Temperance Hamilton Arnold had the following known children:

98 i **John Hewlett Sullivan** [67, 96, 110, 126, 127, 128, 129, 130, 131, 132, 133] was born on the 8th of March 1821 in Tumbling Shoals, Laurens County, South Carolina. [67, 96] He died on the 28th of June 1899 in Hickory Tavern, Laurens County, South Carolina. [96]

ii Keziah Sullivan [67] was born on the 29th of May 1824 in Tumbling Shoals, Laurens County, South Carolina. [67]

iii Mary Ann Sullivan [67] was born on the 7th of April 1826 in Tumbling Shoals, Laurens County, South Carolina. [67]

iv Clarissa Sullivan [67] was born on the 8th of March 1828. [67] She died on the 29th of April 1828.

v Captain Milton Arnold Sullivan [67, 116] was born on the 5th of June 1829 in Tumbling Shoals, Laurens County, South Carolina [67]. He died on the 19th of February 1865 in Columbia, South Carolina. [67] Milton Sullivan was a captain in the Confederate army. He died in a hospital in Columbia South Carolina.

vi Joseph Sullivan [67] was born on the 20th of May 1831 in Tumbling Shoals, Laurens County, South Carolina. [67]

vii Malinda Catherine Sullivan [67, 116] was born on the 3rd of October 1833 in Tumbling Shoals, Laurens County, South Carolina. [67] She died on the

14th of June 1911 in Lowndesville, Abbeville, South Carolina.

viii Temperance Clara Sullivan [67, 116] was born on the 6th of November 1835 in Tumbling Shoals, Laurens County, South Carolina. [67] She died on the 6th of April 1900.

ix Captain William Dunklin Sullivan [48, 67, 109, 112, 116, 117] was born on the 19th of April 1838 in Tumbling Shoals, Laurens County, South Carolina. [67] He died on the 2nd of September 1931 in Sullivan Township, Laurens County, South Carolina of heart-valve disease. [109, 112] He married Mary Elisabeth Quarles and their pictures are shown in the group photograph of his 50th wedding anniversary, taken in 1919, in this section. William Dunklin Sullivan wrote a book called *The History of the Sullivan Family* in 1882 that was republished in 1913. According to an article in the *Magazine of Virginia Genealogy,* Volume 25, November 1987, Number 4, pages 3-13, by Carolyn Copeland Bland, he wrote the book, without quoting any references, probably from his own knowledge. She also wrote that he was uninformed about the Virginia Sullivans and it has been demonstrated that he made a number of mistakes that have been perpetuated by genealogists who quoted him as a reference.

x Charles Pleasant Sullivan [67] was born on the 20th of February 1841 in Tumbling Shoals, Laurens County, South Carolina. [67]

According to the 1850 United States census Temperance was head of household and was living with five of her children.

89 **Thomas Jefferson Sullivan.** [27, 45, 67, 96, 99, 113]
Born on the 28th of September 1807 in Greenville County, South Carolina. [45, 67]
Died on the 13th of January 1866 in his home in Mount Bethel, South Carolina. [67].

(Hewlett Sullivan-24, Charles B. Sullivan-23, Owen Sullivan-22, Owen Sullivan-21, John Thomas O'Sullivan-20, Owen Donal O'Sullivan-19, Owen O'Sullivan Beare Lord of Beare and Bantry-18, Sir Owen O'Sullivan Beare, 14th Lord of Beare and Bantry-17, Dermod O'Sullivan Beare, 11th Lord of Beare and Bantry-16, Donal O'Sullivan Beare, the Swarthy, 8th Lord of Beare and Bantry-15, Dermod (aka Dermond) Balluf O'Sullivan Beare-14, Teige O'Sullivan Beare-13, Amhiaffe O'Sullivan Beare-12, Annaidh O'Sullivan, 1st Lord of Beare and Bantry-11, Philip O'Sullivan-10, Giolla na Bhflainn O'Sullivan Mór-9, Donal O'Sullivan Mór, 15th Lord of Knockgraffon-8, MacCraith O'Sullivan Mór, 14th Lord of Knockgraffon-7, Baudhach O'Sullivan, 13th Lord of Knockgraffon-6, Cathal O'Sullivan, 12th Lord of Knockgraffon-5, Aodh O'Sullivan, 11th Lord of Knockgraffon-4, Baudhach O'Sullivan, 10th Lord of Knockgraffon-3, Lorcan MacSullivan, 9th Lord of Knockgraffon-2, Eochaid Súilleabháinn, 8th Lord of Knockgraffon-1)

He married **Sarah Rutlege Cureton,** [67] who died on the 17th December 1882. [67] They had no known children. He married **Sarah Moon Cureton** [27, 45, 67, 113] on the 12th of September 1835. [67] They had the following known children:

99 i **Thomas Jefferson Sullivan** [67, 113, 136, 137, 138, 139, 140, 141, 142, 143, 144] was born on the 24th of December 1853 in Tumbling Shoals, Laurens County, South Carolina. [67, 113] He died on the 5th of November 1923 in Mount Bethel, South Carolina of chronic nephritis with contributing factors of arteriosclerosis arterial hemorrhagic coma. [67, 113]

Golden wedding anniversary of William Dunklin Sullivan and Mary Elisabeth Quarles at Tumbling Shoals Township, Laurens County, South Carolina, the 25th of November 1919.

Front Row (children)

Marion West
Dunk Culberson
Jennie Margie Culberson
Mary West
Dunk Sullivan
Cecil Sullivan
Billy McKelvey Jr.

Second Row
sitting on the ground

Joe Sullivan (Fee's son)
Milton Arnold Sullivan
Margie Sullivan Culberson
Annie Sullivan (colored)
Niza Sullivan McKelvey
Marie Sullivan
Richard Owen Sullivan
Thomas Quarles Sullivan
Name not known

Third Row
Sitting in chairs

Joe Sullivan
Mary Elisabeth Sullivan
William Dunklin Sullivan
Lee Meares
Captain George Washington Sullivan

Fourth Row
Standing

The preacher
Joseph Giroud Sullivan
Lidie Sullivan
Agnes Sullivan West
Thomas Jefferson Sullivan (Felicia's husband)
Felicia Arnold (Fee) Sullivan
Zelena (Beanie) Sullivan Wells
Nannie Brooks Sullivan (Wife of Benjamin Arnold Sullivan)
Mrs. McKelvey (Alvin's mother)
Lizzy Chiles Sullivan (wife of Captain George Washington Sullivan)
Dr. Caspar Q. West (Agnes' husband)
William Dunklin Sullivan Jr.

Fifth Row

Two colored family servants
Alvin McKelvey (Niza's husband)
Benjamin Arnold Sullivan

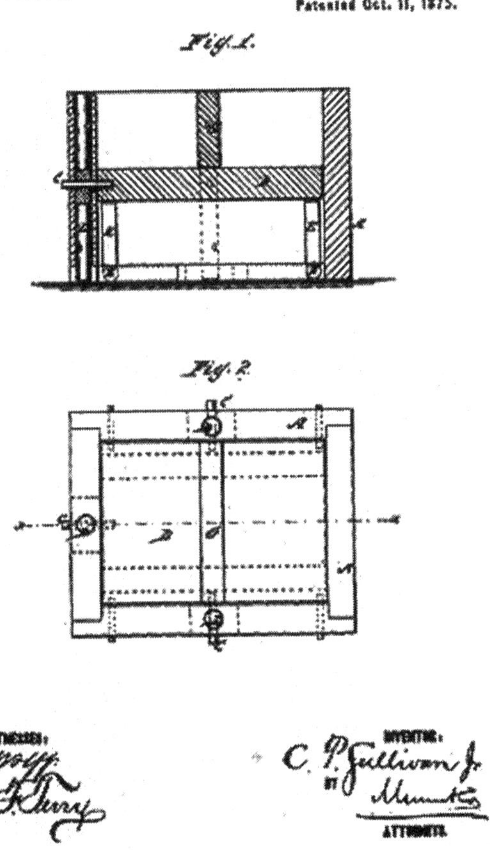

Charles Pleasant Sullivan's patent number 168,679, dated the 11th of October 1875for an improvement in variable measures. The improvement consists of a bottom capable of shifting up and down and pins fastened to different positions. The pins pass through the sides of the box and through vertical sticks in holes in the box sides. The sticks turn and close the holes not occupied by pins. Pivoted pieces under the bottom turn up vertically when the bottom is in the middle and horizontally when the bottom is down. Courtesy of the United States Patent Office.

C. P. SULLIVAN.
Adding-Machine.

No. 228,416. Patented June 1, 1880.

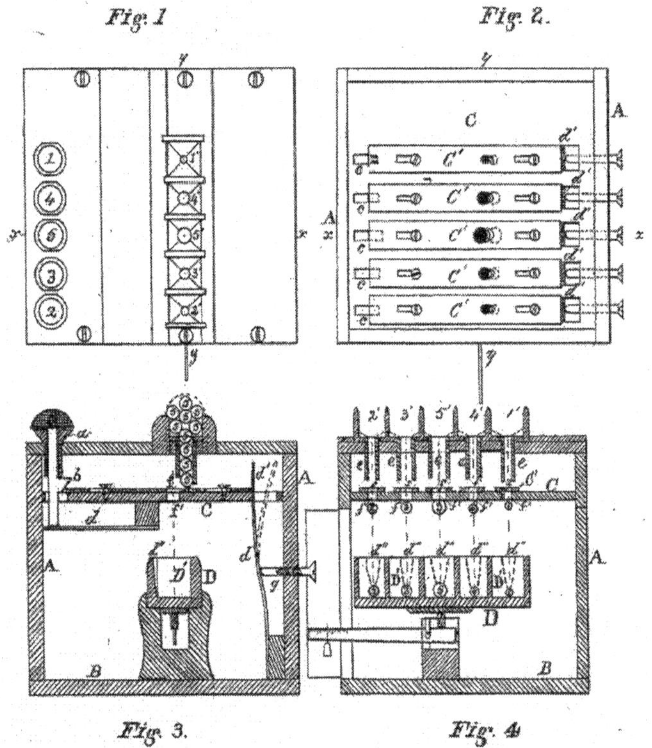

Witnesses
John Lockie
R. P. Edwards

Inventor
Charles P. Sullivan
Per Wm. R. Singleton and Wm. M. Ireland Attys

Charles Pleasant Sullivan's patent number 228,416, dated the 1st of June 1880, for a mechanical adding machine. It operated with balls of various sizes and weights that fell through specific tubes and orifices. The solution was determined by the weight of the balls. Courtesy of the United States Patent Office.

ii Hattie Sullivan. [67] She married Pascal D. Huff on the 13th of August 1866 in Greenville District. [67]

90 **George Washington Sullivan.** [45, 67, 69, 96, 99, 110, 114, 115, 116, 117]
Born on the 27th of September 1809 in Dunklin Township, Greenville County, South Carolina. [45, 67]
Died on the 19th of December 1887 in Charleston Hall, Laurens County, South Carolina. [67]

(Hewlett Sullivan-24, Charles B. Sullivan-23, Owen Sullivan-22, Owen Sullivan-21, John Thomas O'Sullivan-20, Owen Donal O'Sullivan-19, Owen O'Sullivan Beare Lord of Beare and Bantry-18, Sir Owen O'Sullivan Beare, 14th Lord of Beare and Bantry-17, Dermod O'Sullivan Beare, 11th Lord of Beare and Bantry-16, Donal O'Sullivan Beare, the Swarthy, 8th Lord of Beare and Bantry-15, Dermod (aka Dermond) Balluf O'Sullivan Beare-14, Teige O'Sullivan Beare-13, Amhiaffe O'Sullivan Beare-12, Annaidh O'Sullivan, 1st Lord of Beare and Bantry-11, Philip O'Sullivan-10, Giolla na Bhflainn O'Sullivan Mór-9, Donal O'Sullivan Mór, 15th Lord of Knockgraffon-8, MacCraith O'Sullivan Mór, 14th Lord of Knockgraffon-7, Baudhach O'Sullivan, 13th Lord of Knockgraffon-6, Cathal O'Sullivan, 12th Lord of Knockgraffon-5, Aodh O'Sullivan, 11th Lord of Knockgraffon-4, Baudhach O'Sullivan, 10th Lord of Knockgraffon-3, Lorcan MacSullivan, 9th Lord of Knockgraffon-2, Eochaid Súilleabháinn, 8th Lord of Knockgraffon-1)

George Washington Sullivan was a farmer and merchant in Laurens County, South Carolina. He served as a captain in the South Carolina militia and served two terms in the state legislature. In 1865, the South Carolina tax register, division 18, district number 3 showed that Charles Washington Sullivan had an income of $1,283.50 and paid $64.17 in tax at the rate of 5%.

He married **Jane Washington Brooks,** daughter of Littleton A. Brooks and Sarah née unknown [45, 67, 69, 105, 114, 115, 116] on the 14th of January 1836. [67] She died on the 1st of February 1855. [67]

They had the following known children:

100 i **George Washington Sullivan** [69, 114, 145, 146] was born on the 25th of March 1848 in Laurens County, South Carolina. [114] He died on the 17th of November 1928 in Anderson County, South Carolina. [114]
101 ii **Joseph Hewlett Sullivan** [69, 115, 147] was born on the 6th of November 1852 in Laurens County, South Carolina. [115] He died on the 9th of June 1920 in Laurens County, South Carolina of acute dysentery. [115]
iii Euginia Sullivan. [69]
iv Mary Sullivan. [69]
v Jane Sullivan. [69]
vi Charleton Sullivan. [69]
vii Lizzie Sullivan. [69]

He married **Mary Margaret Cunningham** [69]. They had no known children.

91 **Charles Pickney Sullivan.** [45, 67, 96, 99, 110, 118, 119, 120, 121, 122, 123]
Born on the 3rd of October 1811 in Greenville County, South Carolina. [45, 67]

(Hewlett Sullivan-24, Charles B. Sullivan-23, Owen Sullivan-22, Owen Sullivan-21, John Thomas

O'Sullivan-20, Owen Donal O'Sullivan-19, Owen O'Sullivan Beare Lord of Beare and Bantry-18, Sir Owen O'Sullivan Beare, 14th Lord of Beare and Bantry-17, Dermod O'Sullivan Beare, 11th Lord of Beare and Bantry-16, Donal O'Sullivan Beare, the Swarthy, 8th Lord of Beare and Bantry-15, Dermod (aka Dermond) Balluf O'Sullivan Beare-14, Teige O'Sullivan Beare-13, Amhiaffe O'Sullivan Beare-12, Annaidh O'Sullivan, 1st Lord of Beare and Bantry-11, Philip O'Sullivan-10, Giolla na Bhflainn O'Sullivan Mór-9, Donal O'Sullivan Mór, 15th Lord of Knockgraffon-8, MacCraith O'Sullivan Mór, 14th Lord of Knockgraffon-7, Baudhach O'Sullivan, 13th Lord of Knockgraffon-6, Cathal O'Sullivan, 12th Lord of Knockgraffon-5, Aodh O'Sullivan, 11th Lord of Knockgraffon-4, Baudhach O'Sullivan, 10th Lord of Knockgraffon-3, Lorcan MacSullivan, 9th Lord of Knockgraffon-2, Eochaid Súilleabháinn, 8th Lord of Knockgraffon-1)

He married **Sarah Smith.** [45, 67] She died on the 30th of December 1845. [67] They had the following known children:

i John Mims Sullivan [121, 122, 148] was born on the 1st of January 1838. [121, 122]

ii Warren Pickney Sullivan [121, 122, 123] was born in 1840. [121, 122] He died after 1860 in the Civil War.

102 iii **Jared Dunklin Sullivan** [121, 122, 149, 150, 151, 152, 153] was born on the 11th of February. 1841 [121, 122]

iv Marion Sullivan [154] was born in 1844 [154]. She died on the 15th of August 1844. [154]

v James G. Sullivan [121, 122] was born in 1845. [122]

His second wife was **Zelena Boyd** [119, 120, 121, 122] born on the 28th of January 1828 in Laurens County, South Carolina. [121] They had the following daughter:

i Phoebe A. Sullivan [121, 122] was born in 1848. [121]

His third wife was **Mary Charlton Sullivan,** [118] born in England. They had the following known children:

i Charles Boyd Sullivan [118, 121, 122] was born on the 28th of April 1849 in Laurens, South Carolina. [118, 121, 122] He died on the 5th of June 1915 in Laurens County, South Carolina. [118]

ii Mary Charleton Sullivan [120, 123] was born on the 21st of November 1850 in Laurens County, South Carolina. [120] She died on the 5th of July 1932 in Laurens County, South Carolina of gastric carcinoma, fracture of left hip. [120

iii Hewlett Sullivan [119] was born on the 3rd of May 1857. [119] He died on the 14th of July 1936 in Asheville, North Carolina. [119]

92 **Dr. James Madison Sullivan.** [27, 45, 67, 96, 99, 124, 125]
Born on the 11th of March 1816 in Greenville County, South Carolina. [45, 67]
Died on the 9th of April 1875 at home in Warthen, South Carolina. [67]

(Hewlett Sullivan-24, Charles B. Sullivan-23, Owen Sullivan-22, Owen Sullivan-21, John Thomas O'Sullivan-20, Owen Donal O'Sullivan-19, Owen O'Sullivan Beare Lord of Beare and Bantry-18, Sir Owen O'Sullivan Beare, 14th Lord of Beare and Bantry-17, Dermod O'Sullivan Beare, 11th Lord of

Beare and Bantry-16, Donal O'Sullivan Beare, the Swarthy, 8th Lord of Beare and Bantry-15, Dermod (aka Dermond) Balluf O'Sullivan Beare-14, Teige O'Sullivan Beare-13, Amhiaffe O'Sullivan Beare-12, Annaidh O'Sullivan, 1st Lord of Beare and Bantry-11, Philip O'Sullivan-10, Giolla na Bhflainn O'Sullivan Mór-9, Donal O'Sullivan Mór, 15th Lord of Knockgraffon-8, MacCraith O'Sullivan Mór, 14th Lord of Knockgraffon-7, Baudhach O'Sullivan, 13th Lord of Knockgraffon-6, Cathal O'Sullivan, 12th Lord of Knockgraffon-5, Aodh O'Sullivan, 11th Lord of Knockgraffon-4, Baudhach O'Sullivan, 10th Lord of Knockgraffon-3, Lorcan MacSullivan, 9th Lord of Knockgraffon-2, Eochaid Súilleabháinn, 8th Lord of Knockgraffon-1)

He married **Sara Mims** [27, 45, 67]. She died on the 28th of September 1856 [67]. They had no known children.

He married **Elisabeth Vaughn** [27, 124, 125]. They had the following known children:

i Belton O'Neal Sullivan [124] was born on the 10th of May 1866 [124]. He died on the 18th of July 1929 [124].
ii Marian Sullivan [125]. She died on the 12th of May 1937 [125].

94 **Dr. John Landon Sullivan.** [26, 28, 91]
Born on the 9th April 1777 in Saco, Maine. [26, 28, 91]
Died on the 10th of February 1865 in Boston, Massachusetts. [26, 28, 91]

(James Sullivan-24, Owen O'Sullivan-23, Major Philip O'Sullivan of Ardea O'Sullivan-22, Owen O'Sullivan Beare, Lord of Ardea Castle-21, Daniel O'Sullivan. Lord of Ardea Castle-20, Philip O'Sullivan Beare-19, Donal O'Sullivan Beare, Lord of Ardea Castle-18, Sir Philip O'Sullivan Beare, Lord of Ardea Castle-17, Dermod O'Sullivan Beare, 11th Lord of Beare and Bantry-16, Donal O'Sullivan Beare, the Swarthy, 8th Lord of Beare and Bantry-15, Dermod (aka Dermond) Balluf O'Sullivan Beare-14, Teige O'Sullivan Beare-13, Amhiaffe O'Sullivan Beare-12, Annaidh O'Sullivan, 1st Lord of Beare and Bantry-11, Philip O'Sullivan-10, Giolla na Bhflainn O'Sullivan Mór-9, Donal O'Sullivan Mór, 15th Lord of Knockgraffon-8, MacCraith O'Sullivan Mór, 14th Lord of Knockgraffon-7, Baudhach O'Sullivan, 13th Lord of Knockgraffon-6, Cathal O'Sullivan, 12th Lord of Knockgraffon-5, Aodh O'Sullivan, 11th Lord of Knockgraffon-4, Baudhach O'Sullivan, 10th Lord of Knockgraffon-3, Lorcan MacSullivan, 9th Lord of Knockgraffon-2, Eochaid Súilleabháinn, 8th Lord of Knockgraffon-1)

Dr. John Landon Sullivan studied medicine at Yale University.

He married **Elisabeth Russell** [91, 93] on the 10th of October 1797. [26, 91] She was born on the 17th of August 1779. [91] She died on the 16th of April 1854. They had the following children:

103 i **Thomas Russell Sullivan** [26, 28, 91] was born on the 13th of February 1799 in Boston, Massachusetts. He died on the 23rd of December 1862.
ii Elisabeth Sullivan [26, 91] was born on the 27th of January 1800. [26, 91] She died on the 16th of January 1871. [26, 91]
iii Emily Sullivan [91] was born on the 4th of August 1801 in Brookline. [91] She died on the 8th of April 1880. [91]

He married **Susan Macesh** [26, 91, 93] in circa1861. [26, 91] They had no known children.

97 **Sean O'Sullivan MacCragh.** [10, 226]
Born in 1714. [10]

(Dermot O'Sullivan MacCragh-24, Owen O'Sullivan MacCragh-23, Dermot O'Sullivan MacCragh-22, Owen O'Sullivan MacCragh-21, Conor O'Sullivan MacCragh-20, Donogh O'Sullivan MacCragh-19, Buadach O'Suillivan MacCragh-18, Eoghan O'Sullivan MacCragh-17, Conor O'Sullivan MacCragh-16, Donal O'Sullivan MacCragh-15, Cragh O'Sullivan Mór-14, Dunlong O'Sullivan Mór-13, Bernard O'Sullivan Mór-12, Murtagh O'Sullivan-11, Dunlong O'Sullivan-10, Giolla na Bhflainn O'Sullivan Mór-9, Donal O'Sullivan Mór, 15th Lord of Knockgraffon-8, MacCraith O'Sullivan Mór, 14th Lord of Knockgraffon-7, Baudhach O'Sullivan, 13th Lord of Knockgraffon-6, Cathal O'Sullivan, 12th Lord of Knockgraffon-5, Aodh O'Sullivan, 11th Lord of Knockgraffon-4, Baudhach O'Sullivan, 10th Lord of Knockgraffon-3, Lorcan MacSullivan, 9th Lord of Knockgraffon-2, Eochaid Súilleabháinn, 8th Lord of Knockgraffon-1)

Sean was *The O'Sullivan MacCragh* (chief of the O'Sullivan MacCragh sept). He is recorded in the account books of Bantry House, Bantry, County Cork, Ireland.

Sean O'Sullivan MacCragh had the following known son:

104 i **Seamus O'Sullivan MacCragh** [10] was born in 1748. [10]

Generation 26

98 **John Hewlett Sullivan.** [67, 96, 110, 126, 127, 128, 129, 130, 131, 132, 133]
Born on the 8th of March 1821 in Tumbling Shoals, Laurens County, South Carolina. [67, 96]
Died on the 28th of June 1899 in Hickory Tavern, Laurens County, South Carolina. [96]

(Joseph Pickney Sullivan-25, Hewlett Sullivan-24, Charles B. Sullivan-23, Owen Sullivan-22, Owen Sullivan-21, John Thomas O'Sullivan-20, Owen Donal O'Sullivan-19, Owen O'Sullivan Beare Lord of Beare and Bantry-18, Sir Owen O'Sullivan Beare, 14th Lord of Beare and Bantry-17, Dermod O'Sullivan Beare, 11th Lord of Beare and Bantry-16, Donal O'Sullivan Beare, the Swarthy, 8th Lord of Beare and Bantry-15, Dermod (aka Dermond) Balluf O'Sullivan Beare-14, Teige O'Sullivan Beare-13, Amhiaffe O'Sullivan Beare-12, Annaidh O'Sullivan, 1st Lord of Beare and Bantry-11, Philip O'Sullivan-10, Giolla na Bhflainn O'Sullivan Mór-9, Donal O'Sullivan Mór, 15th Lord of Knockgraffon-8, MacCraith O'Sullivan Mór, 14th Lord of Knockgraffon-7, Baudhach O'Sullivan, 13th Lord of Knockgraffon-6, Cathal O'Sullivan, 12th Lord of Knockgraffon-5, Aodh O'Sullivan, 11th Lord of Knockgraffon-4, Baudhach O'Sullivan, 10th Lord of Knockgraffon-3, Lorcan MacSullivan, 9th Lord of Knockgraffon-2, Eochaid Súilleabháinn, 8th Lord of Knockgraffon-1)

According to Dr. Charles McCreight, great-grandson of John Hewlett Sullivan, the Sullivans were large landholders in South Carolina. "*Squire*" Sullivan had a large plantation in Laurens County, owned many slaves, and operated a gristmill and other enterprises. He had an accident that left him an invalid in considerable pain. After the Civil War, the overseer and some of the slaves left and John Hewlett said he could no longer manage the plantations. At the age of twelve, his son Charles Pleasant Washington Sullivan took over the plantation management, hired workers, and saved the plantation for the family.

A trust document shows that part of the estate of John Hewlett Sullivan 's father was held in trust by the executor for his eldest son John Hewlett Sullivan. The will specified that land

and slaves be divided equally among his children. This indicates the value of John Hewlett Sullivan's inheritance was in excess of $14,000. This was a considerable amount of money at that time.

Obituary of John H. Sullivan, transcribed from an original newspaper clipping.

> *"... The subject of this sketch was born in Greenville County, March 8th, 1821. When quite young his parents moved to Tumbling Shoals, in Laurens County, near which place he spent most of his life. on the July 14th, 1884, he was married to Miss Mary L. Cureton and together they lived happily for nearly fifty-four years. Early in life he united himself with the Baptist church and remained a constant member until the time of his death. A few years ago, he met with an accident that caused him to remain a cripple. He suffered a great deal of pain but he bore it with a Christian's fortitude. He was unable for several years to attend church, but his pastor and friends were very kind to him and preaching and prayer meetings were occasionally held at his home and on such occasions he would get full of the Holy ghost and shout God's praises. Only a few days before his death he called his wife to his bed, and in the most tender words told her that he would soon leave her, but that separation would not be long and they would be again united in God's house never to be separated again. On the morning of July 29th just as the sun arose his soul ascended to God whom he loved and served. We miss our father and when we look on the dear old homestead, our hearts sadden, but when we look up to the blue sky we know that father now rests in our heavenly Father's hand. Farewell! Dear father, May thy wife and all thy children meet in heaven and behold Thee awaiting thy loved ones.*
>
> *Daughter ... "*

He married **Mary Dudley Cureton,** daughter of Abner Heath Cureton and Matilda Nelson [96, 126, 128, 129, 130, 131, 132, 133, 156] on the 14th of July 1844. [129, 134] She was born on the 29th of September 1822 in Laurens City, Laurens County, South Carolina. [96] She died on the 6th of July 1903 in Hickory Tavern, Laurens County, South Carolina. [96] They had the following known children:

- i Joseph Pickney Sullivan was born on the 15th of March 1848. He died on the 30th of September 1851 of croup.
- ii Katherine Sullivan [130] was born about 1849.
- iii Mary I. Sullivan [131] was born on the 25th May 1850. She died in Tumbling Shoals, Laurens County, South Carolina. [108]
- iv Temperance A. Sullivan [130, 131, 133, 157, 158, 159, 160, 161] was born on the 21st of August 1851. She died on the 19th of April 1934 in Laurens County, South Carolina.
- v William D. Sullivan was born on the 3rd of September 1853. He died on the 20th of August 1855.
- 105 vi **Charles Pleasant Washington Sullivan** [67, 96, 116, 128, 130, 131, 132, 133, 156, 162, 163, 164, 165, 166, 167, 168, 169, 170, 171, 172, 173, 174, 175, 176, 177, 178, 179, 180, 181, 182, 183, 184,

[185, 186, 187, 188, 189, 190, 191, 192, 193, 194, 195, 196, 197, 198, 199, 200, 201, 202, 203, 204] was born on the 25th of March 1859 in Laurens County, South Carolina. He died on the 20th of October 1946 in Washington, District of Columbia.

106 vii **Benjamin Arnold Sullivan** [133, 205, 206, 207, 208] was born on the 11th of April 1861. He died on the 16th of May 1932 in Laurens County, South Carolina.

99 **Thomas Jefferson Sullivan.** [67, 113, 136, 137, 138, 139, 140, 141, 142, 143, 144]

Born on the 24th of December 1853 in Tumbling Shoals, Laurens County, South Carolina. [67, 113]

Died on the 5th of November 1923 in Mount Bethel, South Carolina of chronic nephritis and contributing factors of arteriosclerosis and arterial hemorrhagic coma. [67, 113]

(Joseph Pickney Sullivan-25, Hewlett Sullivan-24, Charles B. Sullivan-23, Owen Sullivan-22, Owen Sullivan-21, John Thomas O'Sullivan-20, Owen Donal O'Sullivan-19, Owen O'Sullivan Beare Lord of Beare and Bantry-18, Sir Owen O'Sullivan Beare, 14th Lord of Beare and Bantry-17, Dermod O'Sullivan Beare, 11th Lord of Beare and Bantry-16, Donal O'Sullivan Beare, the Swarthy, 8th Lord of Beare and Bantry-15, Dermod (aka Dermond) Balluf O'Sullivan Beare-14, Teige O'Sullivan Beare-13, Amhiaffe O'Sullivan Beare-12, Annaidh O'Sullivan, 1st Lord of Beare and Bantry-11, Philip O'Sullivan-10, Giolla na Bhflainn O'Sullivan Mór-9, Donal O'Sullivan Mór, 15th Lord of Knockgraffon-8, MacCraith O'Sullivan Mór, 14th Lord of Knockgraffon-7, Baudhach O'Sullivan, 13th Lord of Knockgraffon-6, Cathal O'Sullivan, 12th Lord of Knockgraffon-5, Aodh O'Sullivan, 11th Lord of Knockgraffon-4, Baudhach O'Sullivan, 10th Lord of Knockgraffon-3, Lorcan MacSullivan, 9th Lord of Knockgraffon-2, Eochaid Súilleabháinn, 8th Lord of Knockgraffon-1)

He married **Felicia Arnold** [67, 136, 138, 139, 140, 141, 142, 143, 144] on the 11th November 1884. [67] Their pictures are in the group photograph of the 50th wedding anniversary of William Dunklin and Mary Elisabeth Quarles, taken in 1919, in this section. They had the following known children:

i **Sara Lucile Sullivan** [140, 144] was born on the 23rd of May 1886 in Laurens County, South Carolina. [140, 144]

ii **Claudius Arnold Sullivan** [138, 139, 143] was born on the 19th of January 1893 in Laurens County, South Carolina. [138, 139, 143] He died on the 15th of May 1942 in Columbia, South Carolina. [139]

iii **Charles Humbert Sullivan** [136, 142] was born on the 14th of August 1896. [136, 142]

iv **Thomas Cureton Sullivan** [141] was born on the 9th of September 1907. He died on the 14th of August 1916 of infantile paralysis.

100 **George Washington Sullivan.** [69, 114, 145, 146]

Born on the 25th of March 1848 in Laurens County, South Carolina.[114]
Died on the 17th of November 1928 in Anderson County, South Carolina. [114]

(George Washington Sullivan-25, Hewlett Sullivan-24, Charles B. Sullivan-23, Owen Sullivan-22, Owen Sullivan-21, John Thomas O'Sullivan-20, Owen Donal O'Sullivan-19, Owen O'Sullivan Beare Lord of Beare and Bantry-18, Sir Owen O'Sullivan Beare, 14th Lord of Beare and Bantry-17, Dermod O'Sullivan Beare, 11th Lord of Beare and Bantry-16, Donal O'Sullivan Beare, the Swarthy, 8th Lord of Beare and Bantry-15, Dermod (aka Dermond) Balluf O'Sullivan Beare-14, Teige O'Sullivan Beare-

13, Amhiaffe O'Sullivan Beare-12, Annaidh O'Sullivan, 1st Lord of Beare and Bantry-11, Philip O'Sullivan-10, Giolla na Bhflainn O'Sullivan Mór-9, Donal O'Sullivan Mór, 15th Lord of Knockgraffon-8, MacCraith O'Sullivan Mór, 14th Lord of Knockgraffon-7, Baudhach O'Sullivan, 13th Lord of Knockgraffon-6, Cathal O'Sullivan, 12th Lord of Knockgraffon-5, Aodh O'Sullivan, 11th Lord of Knockgraffon-4, Baudhach O'Sullivan, 10th Lord of Knockgraffon-3, Lorcan MacSullivan, 9th Lord of Knockgraffon-2, Eochaid Súilleabháinn, 8th Lord of Knockgraffon-1)

George Washington Sullivan (1848-1928). *From History of South Carolina*, by Yates Snowden, LLD, 1920.

George Washington Sullivan enlisted in the South Carolina militia in 1864 during the Civil War when he was sixteen years old. He was appointed as a cadet in the South Carolina Military Academy by Governor McGrath. After two months, he entered the confederate army state cadets and served until the end of the war. After the war, he enrolled in Wofford College in Spartanburg and received a bachelor of science in 1870. He was employed by the Sullivan Manufacturing Company with his father and brother. In 1870, the company built a cotton mill at Fork Shoals in Greenville County, South Carolina, where he served as treasurer for ten years. In 1880, he sold his interest in the company and bought a farm. In 1885, he opened a general merchandise store. His major interest was agriculture, but he was a man of considerable means with banking interest in Anderson and Greenville Counties. In 1877, he was commissioned the rank of major on the staff of General J. G. Gray. In 1906, he was elected to the state senate and was re-elected in 1910 without opposition. He was a trustee of Lander College and Master of the Masonic Lodge.

He married **Lizzie Chiles.** [69] Their pictures are in the group photograph of the 50th wedding anniversary of William Dunklin Sullivan and Mary Elisabeth Quarles, taken in 1919, in this section. They had the following known children:

i	Hewlett Sullivan. [61]
ii	Janie Brooks Sullivan. [69]
iii	Washington H. Sullivan. [61, 69]
iv	J. Edgar Sullivan. [61]
v	George M. Sullivan. [69]
vi	Joseph Dunklin Sullivan. [69]
vii	Lillian Sullivan. [69]

101 **Joseph Hewlett Sullivan** [69, 115, 147].
Born on the 6th November 1852 in Laurens County, South Carolina [115].
Died on the 9th June 1920 in Laurens County, South Carolina of acute dysentery [115].

(George Washington Sullivan-25, Hewlett Sullivan-24, Charles B. Sullivan-23, Owen Sullivan-22, Owen Sullivan-21, John Thomas O'Sullivan-20, Owen Donal O'Sullivan-19, Owen O'Sullivan Beare Lord of Beare and Bantry-18, Sir Owen O'Sullivan Beare, 14th Lord of Beare and Bantry-17, Dermod O'Sullivan Beare, 11th Lord of Beare and Bantry-16, Donal O'Sullivan Beare, the Swarthy, 8th Lord of Beare and Bantry-15, Dermod (aka Dermond) Balluf O'Sullivan Beare-14, Teige O'Sullivan Beare-13, Amhiaffe O'Sullivan Beare-12, Annaidh O'Sullivan, 1st Lord of Beare and Bantry-11, Philip

O'Sullivan-10, Giolla na Bhflainn O'Sullivan Mór-9, Donal O'Sullivan Mór, 15th Lord of Knockgraffon-8, MacCraith O'Sullivan Mór, 14th Lord of Knockgraffon-7, Baudhach O'Sullivan, 13th Lord of Knockgraffon-6, Cathal O'Sullivan, 12th Lord of Knockgraffon-5, Aodh O'Sullivan, 11th Lord of Knockgraffon-4, Baudhach O'Sullivan, 10th Lord of Knockgraffon-3, Lorcan MacSullivan, 9th Lord of Knockgraffon-2, Eochaid Súilleabháinn, 8th Lord of Knockgraffon-1)

Charles P. Pelham. Courtesy of Pelham Lyles, Director, Fairfield County, South Carolina Museum.

He married **Mary Pelham** daughter of Charles P. Pelham and Jane Dunlap [147, 209, 210, 211, 212] in circa 1879. She was born on the 13th of November 1858 in Columbia, South Carolina. [147] She died on the 27th of December 1919 in Laurens County, South Carolina, of carcinoma of the thyroid. [147] They had the following known children:

i Josephine B. Sullivan [213] was born in November 1882 in Laurens County, South Carolina.

ii Jane Sullivan [213] was born on the 18th of June 1885 in Laurens County, South Carolina. She died in January 1920 in Albemarle, Stanley County, North Carolina.

107 iii **Mary Josephine Sullivan** [213] was born on the 17th of October 1890 in Laurens County, South Carolina. She died on the 18th of June 1924 in Laurens County, South Carolina.

iv William Elleby Sullivan. [213] He died on the 7th of October 1918 in Newberry, South Carolina. He died of influenza and pneumonia.

102 **Jared Dunklin Sullivan** [121, 122, 149, 150, 151, 152, 153].
Born on the 11th of February 1841 [121, 122].

(Charles Pickney Sullivan-25, Hewlett Sullivan-24, Charles B. Sullivan-23, Owen Sullivan-22, Owen Sullivan-21, John Thomas O'Sullivan-20, Owen Donal O'Sullivan-19, Owen O'Sullivan Beare Lord of Beare and Bantry-18, Sir Owen O'Sullivan Beare, 14th Lord of Beare and Bantry-17, Dermod O'Sullivan Beare, 11th Lord of Beare and Bantry-16, Donal O'Sullivan Beare, the Swarthy, 8th Lord of Beare and Bantry-15, Dermod (aka Dermond) Balluf O'Sullivan Beare-14, Teige O'Sullivan Beare-13, Amhiaffe O'Sullivan Beare-12, Annaidh O'Sullivan, 1st Lord of Beare and Bantry-11, Philip O'Sullivan-10, Giolla na Bhflainn O'Sullivan Mór-9, Donal O'Sullivan Mór, 15th Lord of Knockgraffon-8, MacCraith O'Sullivan Mór, 14th Lord of Knockgraffon-7, Baudhach O'Sullivan, 13th Lord of Knockgraffon-6, Cathal O'Sullivan, 12th Lord of Knockgraffon-5, Aodh O'Sullivan, 11th Lord of Knockgraffon-4, Baudhach O'Sullivan, 10th Lord of Knockgraffon-3, Lorcan MacSullivan, 9th Lord of Knockgraffon-2, Eochaid Súilleabháinn, 8th Lord of Knockgraffon-1)

He married **Rosalie Amanda Moore,** daughter of John Moore and Martha Cook [149, 150, 151,

[152, 153, 214] born on the 29th of November 1848. [214] She died on the 17th of August 1929 in Laurens City, Laurens County, South Carolina. [214] They had the following known children:

i Rosalie M. Sullivan [149, 153] was born on the 31st of August 1869. She died on the 25th of April 1931.
ii Lofton Dunklin Sullivan [149, 154] was born on the 20th of August 1871. [154] He died on the 14th of July 1907. [154]
iii Sara Sallie Sullivan [149, 150] was born on the 27th of April 1876. She died on the 4th of December 1940.
iv Lucy Blanche Sullivan [149] was born on the 17th of July 1879. She died on the 29th of October 1963.
v Alice Zelena Sullivan [150] was born on the 3rd of May 1882. She died on the 24th of December 1957.
vi John Moore Sullivan [150, 151, 154] was born on the 7th of June 1885. [154] He died on the 12th of October 1916 [154].
vii James Henry Sullivan. [150]
viii Jared David Sullivan [150, 151, 152, 215] was born on the 15th of October 1892. [152]

103 **Thomas Russell Sullivan.** [26, 28, 91, 155]
Born on the 13th of February 1799 in Boston, Massachusetts.
Died on the 23rd of December 1862.

(Dr. John Landon Sullivan-25, James Sullivan-24, Owen O'Sullivan-23, Major Philip O'Sullivan of Ardea O'Sullivan-22, Owen O'Sullivan Beare, Lord of Ardea Castle-21, Daniel O'Sullivan. Lord of Ardea Castle-20, Philip O'Sullivan Beare-19, Donal O'Sullivan Beare, Lord of Ardea Castle-18, Sir Philip O'Sullivan Beare, Lord of Ardea Castle-17, Dermod O'Sullivan Beare, 11th Lord of Beare and Bantry-16, Donal O'Sullivan Beare, the Swarthy, 8th Lord of Beare and Bantry-15, Dermod (aka Dermond) Balluf O'Sullivan Beare-14, Teige O'Sullivan Beare-13, Amhiaffe O'Sullivan Beare-12, Annaidh O'Sullivan, 1st Lord of Beare and Bantry-11, Philip O'Sullivan-10, Giolla na Bhflainn O'Sullivan Mór-9, Donal O'Sullivan Mór, 15th Lord of Knockgraffon-8, MacCraith O'Sullivan Mór, 14th Lord of Knockgraffon-7, Baudhach O'Sullivan, 13th Lord of Knockgraffon-6, Cathal O'Sullivan, 12th Lord of Knockgraffon-5, Aodh O'Sullivan, 11th Lord of Knockgraffon-4, Baudhach O'Sullivan, 10th Lord of Knockgraffon-3, Lorcan MacSullivan, 9th Lord of Knockgraffon-2, Eochaid Súilleabháinn, 8th Lord of Knockgraffon-1)

Thomas Russell Sullivan graduated from Harvard University in 1817 and was a Unitarian minister at Keene from 1825 to 1835.

He married **Charlotte Caldwell Blake** [91, 155] on the 19th of February 1826. [91, 155] She was born on the 14th of June 1804. [91] She died on the 3rd of July 1863[91, 155]. They had the following known children:

108 i **John Langdon Sullivan** [28, 155] was born on the 8th of March 1827. He died on the 13th July 1905.
ii Jonathan Amory Sullivan [155] was born on the 3rd of October 1830. He died on the 13th of July 1905.
iii Francis Blake Sullivan was born in March 1834. He died in 1834.

iv Henry Dor Sullivan [155] was born on the 20th of June 1841.[155] He died on the 29th of August 1889. [155]

v George Smith Blake Sullivan [155] was born on the 11th of November 1845. He died on the 12th of March 1891.

vi Thomas Russell Sullivan [155].

104 **Seamus O'Sullivan MacCragh.** [10, 226]
Born in 1748. [10]

(Sean O'Sullivan MacCragh-25, Dermot O'Sullivan MacCragh-24, Owen O'Sullivan MacCragh-23, Dermot O'Sullivan MacCragh-22, Owen O'Sullivan MacCragh-21, Conor O'Sullivan MacCragh-20, Donogh O'Sullivan MacCragh-19, Buadach O'Suillivan MacCragh-18, Eoghan O'Sullivan MacCragh-17, Conor O'Sullivan MacCragh-16, Donal O'Sullivan MacCragh-15, Cragh O'Sullivan Mór-14, Dunlong O'Sullivan Mór-13, Bernard O'Sullivan Mór-12, Murtagh O'Sullivan-11, Dunlong O'Sullivan-10, Giolla na Bhflainn O'Sullivan Mór-9, Donal O'Sullivan Mór, 15th Lord of Knockgraffon-8, MacCraith O'Sullivan Mór, 14th Lord of Knockgraffon-7, Baudhach O'Sullivan, 13th Lord of Knockgraffon-6, Cathal O'Sullivan, 12th Lord of Knockgraffon-5, Aodh O'Sullivan, 11th Lord of Knockgraffon-4, Baudhach O'Sullivan, 10th Lord of Knockgraffon-3, Lorcan MacSullivan, 9th Lord of Knockgraffon-2, Eochaid Súilleabháinn, 8th Lord of Knockgraffon-1)

Seamus is recorded in the account books of Bantry House, Bantry, County Cork, Ireland.

Seamus O'Sullivan MacCragh had the following known son:

109 i **Murtagh O'Sullivan MacCragh** [10] was born in 1788. [10]

Generation 27

105 **Charles Pleasant Washington Sullivan.** [67, 96, 116, 128, 130, 131, 132, 133, 156, 162, 163, 164, 165, 166, 167, 168, 169, 170, 171, 172, 173, 174, 175, 176, 177, 178, 179, 180, 181, 182, 183, 184, 185, 186, 187, 188, 189, 190, 191, 192, 193, 194, 195, 196, 197, 198, 199, 200, 201, 202, 203, 204]

Born on the 25th of March 1859 in Laurens County, South Carolina.
Died on the 20th of October 1946 in Washington, District of Columbia.

(John Hewlett Sullivan-26, Joseph Pickney Sullivan-25, Hewlett Sullivan-24, Charles B. Sullivan-23, Owen Sullivan-22, Owen Sullivan-21, John Thomas O'Sullivan-20, Owen Donal O'Sullivan-19, Owen O'Sullivan Beare Lord of Beare and Bantry-18, Sir Owen O'Sullivan Beare, 14th Lord of Beare and Bantry-17, Dermod O'Sullivan Beare, 11th Lord of Beare and Bantry-16, Donal O'Sullivan Beare, the Swarthy, 8th Lord of Beare and Bantry-15, Dermod (aka Dermond) Balluf O'Sullivan Beare-14, Teige O'Sullivan Beare-13, Amhiaffe O'Sullivan Beare-12, Annaidh O'Sullivan, 1st Lord of Beare and Bantry-11, Philip O'Sullivan-10, Giolla na Bhflainn O'Sullivan Mór-9, Donal O'Sullivan Mór, 15th Lord of Knockgraffon-8, MacCraith O'Sullivan Mór, 14th Lord of Knockgraffon-7, Baudhach O'Sullivan, 13th Lord of Knockgraffon-6, Cathal O'Sullivan, 12th Lord of Knockgraffon-5, Aodh O'Sullivan, 11th Lord of Knockgraffon-4, Baudhach O'Sullivan, 10th Lord of Knockgraffon-3, Lorcan MacSullivan, 9th Lord of Knockgraffon-2, Eochaid Súilleabháinn, 8th Lord of Knockgraffon-1)

The house in Newton, North Carolina on Court House Square. A bank now occupies the site. Courtesy Catawba Carolina County Library, Newton, North Carolina

Charles and his wife Sarah were first cousins, their mothers being sisters. According to his grandson Dr. Charles Edward McCreight: " ... *After the Civil War, some of the slaves left the Sullivan plantation and some remained. After a few years the overseer left. Charles' father John had an accident that left him an invalid in great pain and said he could not manage the plantation. Charles took over the management of the plantation at the age of twelve and hired workers. Charles managed to keep the plantation together for the family... .*"

Charles' grandfather owned a half league of land (over 2,000 acres) in the Great Beaumont Country of Hardin County, Texas. Mr. J. R. Davenport obtained powers of attorney from a number of people, including Charles' grandfather, which gave him very generous rights. Mr. Davenport never made any distributions and Charles sent a lawyer named John Kay to investigate. On the 4th of March 1900, John Kay wrote a letter that said a judge in Hardin County told him Mr. Davenport had presented a power of attorney, signed by Sullivan heirs, and had sold a half league of land. Mr. Davenport moved to Houston, Texas and Mr. Kay was unable to locate him. On the 21st of May, John Kay visited Kountze, Hardin County, Texas, and said the town consisted of three or four stores and a frame courthouse. Despite its size, the courthouse employed twenty-one young women as stenographers. "*People were falling over themselves to examine land records*." In the southwest corner of Hardin County, oil had been discovered and land prices had increased many times over in the past few weeks.

John Kay wrote that unfortunately in Texas a power of attorney did not expire on the death of the grantor. Mr. Davenport apparently registered fictitious sales and John Kay wrote that *"it appears we waited too long to make a claim of fraud."* It would be costly to collect evidence and there were so many Sullivan heirs that it would probably not be worth the expense. The outcome is not known, but there was a stock certificate among Charles P. W. Sullivan's papers for now worthless shares in a Texas oil company.

On the 16th of March 1842, Charles Sullivan's grandfather placed land in trust with Thomas J. and George W. Sullivan as Trustees. This trust came into the hands of Charles' father John Hewlett Sullivan, who died intestate. On the 9th of November 1901, John's widow Mary conveyed all rights in the land to her married daughter Temperance Wasson, née Sullivan. On the 20th of November 1901, Charles P. W. Sullivan and his brother Benjamin Arnold Sullivan filed a lawsuit against their mother Mary Sullivan and their sister Temperance Wasson. They claimed that when their father died intestate they became co-owners of the trust. They wanted the land to be sold and the proceeds divided three ways. The outcome of the case is not known, because the court records could not be found. The complaint and summons were found, but the final decision was not found in the South Carolina State Archive.

Charles Pleasant Washington Sullivan was quite an adventurous entrepreneur. From sometime before 1901 until at least 1941, he owned eight known hotels in South Carolina, North Carolina, Virginia, and Florida, some at the same time. Some were bought at the height of the Great Depression when few people had any money to spare and were skeptical of investments. His son-in-law Beverly Randolph McCreight usually lived in the household of Charles Sullivan and was listed at various times as Assistant Hotel Manager and Hotel Manager.

Charles Sullivan apparently owned some of these buildings, but rented others to operate his hotels. This is certainly the case for the hotels in Camden, South Carolina; the one in Newton, North Carolina; and probably the one in Lancaster, South Carolina.

Olwell Hotel in Aiken, South Carolina

Historical Aiken, South Carolina, Main Street. Courtesy of the Aiken County, South Carolina Public Library

Charles Pleasant Washington Sullivan owned the Olwell Hotel in Aiken, South Carolina, from before the 14th of March 1901 until after the 5th of March 1919 and probably until after the 25th of February 1921. Thirteen Aiken Journal articles mention Charles P. W. Sullivan as proprietor of the Olwell Hotel and his son Edmund and his son-in-law Beverly R. McCreight. Charles Sullivan's grandchildren Robert and Minnie Katherine McCreight (children of Sarah Katherine Sullivan and Beverly Randolph McCreight) were born in Aiken, South Carolina, on the 25th of October 1918 and the 25th of February 1921 respectively. The Olwell Hotel is now called the Aiken Hotel.

Camden Hotel, Camden, South Carolina

Charles Pleasant Washington Sullivan was proprietor of the Camden Hotel before the 2nd of November 1910 until it was demolished in 1914. The Camden Hotel was built in 1860. It is listed in the 1914/15 Camden City Directory with C. P. W. Sullivan as proprietor. However he was proprietor of the hotel at least before the 2nd of November 1910 when his daughter was married there. A newspaper article, found in the trunk of Mary McCreight née Randolph, said Sarah Katherine Sullivan married Beverly Randolph McCreight in the Hotel Camden on the 2nd of November 1910 and her father Charles Sullivan. The article describes it as the elegant Hotel Camden with its affable host Charles Sullivan. Their sons Beverly and Charles McCreight were born in Camden on the 3rd of October 1911 and on the 17th of March 1913 respectively.

In 1911, the United States Post Office bought the land at the corner of DeKalb Street and Broad Street from A. N. Sample and J. C. Hough. This indicates that Charles Sullivan did not own the building, but rented it for his hotel. The hotel was demolished in 1914 to build the Camden Post Office.

Camden Hotel on the 3rd of April 1913, before it was demolished to build the post office. Courtesy of the Camden, South Carolina Archive.

The Hotel Stratford. Courtesy of the Roanoke, Virginia Public Library

An article published in 1913 said:

" ..The site of the proposed post office is now occupied by a hostelry that is well known by frequenters of the town - the Camden Hotel, .."

Another Camden Hotel was built, across from the post office on Dekalb Street in 1925, eleven years after the original Hotel Camden was demolished.

Hotel Stratford, Roanoke, Virginia

Charles Pleasant Washington Sullivan and his wife owned the Hotel Stratford, at 102 North Jefferson Avenue on the corner of Central Avenue in Roanoke, Virginia, from 1915 until the 17th of December 1917. They were listed in the Roanoke City Directories of 1915 and 1916 as proprietors. The 1919 Deed Card shows the property was owned by M. F. Posey et al, purchased on the 17th of December 1917.

An article published in 1912 said:

> *"... Of the well-established and popular hotels, for which Roanoke is noted, none are better known or more regularly patronized than the Hotel Stratford, which is most conveniently located for the general traveling public. The building [the hotel] occupied is strictly modern and contains many rooms, all handsome and comfortably furnished, which are kept neat, clean and elegant. The dining room is splendidly equipped. All modern improvements are in service, such as electric lights, hot and cold baths, call bells, local and long distance 'phones, etc. The house has always been favored with the patronage of the best class of the traveling public with special attention given to traveling salesmen, and the very best home*

comforts are provided. The hotel is, indeed one of the most perfect American and European plan hotels in Roanoke and the rates are only two dollars per day for the best service. ..."

Charles Sullivan's granddaughter Ella Elisabeth McCreight, daughter of Beverly Randolph McCreight and Sarah Katherine Sullivan, was born in Roanoke, Virginia on the 6th of February 1916.

Arthur Hotel in High Point, North Carolina

The Arthur Hotel. Courtesy of the High Point, North Carolina Public Library

Charles Pleasant Washington Sullivan owned the Arthur Hotel, at 145-151 West High Street, from the 4th of July 1922 to after the 26th of July 1924 and probably until 1928, when S. E. Corbitt became proprietor. S. E. Corbitt was Shelby Edmund Corbitt, the husband of Charles Sullivan's daughter Minnie Katherine. The hotel was built in 1851 by Jeremiah Pickett (or Piggett). He later sold it to W. G. Barbee. He called it the Barby House. Governor Zebulan Bard Vance declared W. G. Barbee exempt from military service as long as his hotel was used to treat wounded soldiers. Beginning on the 1st of September 1863, the hotel was used as a hospital for wounded confederate soldiers until 1865. Five thousand soldiers were treated in the hotel when it was serving as a hospital. Fifty of them died. This is a 1% death rate, which was very low considering battlefield injuries and the state of medicine at the time.

A newspaper article in 1922 said C. P. W. Sullivan had taken over the Hotel Arthur in High Point, North Carolina and further stated it would be renovated and ready for occupancy on the 1st of April 1922. Charles Sullivan's granddaughter Sarah Pauline McCreight was born in High Point, North Carolina on the 26th of July 1924.

The name Arthur Hotel first appeared in the 1923 Directory at 145-151 West High Avenue, with C. P. W. Sullivan as proprietor. In 1928, S. E. Corbitt was listed as proprietor. An article in 1922 called it the Hotel Arthur, but the name was officially changed to Hotel Arthur by S. E. Corbitt after 1928.

Royal Hotel in Lancaster, South Carolina

There is evidence that Charles Pleasant Washington Sullivan had a hotel in Lancaster, South Carolina before the 1st of March 1927 until at least 1930. The name of the hotel has not been conclusively verified, but it is probably the Royal Hotel at 200 Main Street, Lancaster, in the Springs Block. Charles P. Sullivan was listed on the 1930 census of

Lancaster, South Carolina, as a hotel proprietor, age 71. His wife, Sarah E., his son-in-law Beverly R. McCreight, and his wife, Sarah were listed in the household and Beverly was listed as assistant hotel manager. The daughter of Beverly McCreight, Mary Henry McCreight, was born in Lancaster, South Carolina on the 1st of March 1927, which shows the family was already living in Lancaster in 1927. The residential address was either North Market Street, or North White Street. These two Lancaster city streets are parallel. The earliest city directories were in the 1960's. The library has *The Lancaster News* newspapers on microfilm for the 1920's and 1930's, but the microfilm is not indexed. The Lancaster News also has no index, nor do they have advertisement invoices for this period.

Lancaster, South Carolina Main Street. The Royal Hotel is number 200 on the right. Courtesy of the Lancaster Society for Historical Preservation and Richard Horwege, Donning Company Publishers.

A telegram from H. R. Rice in Lancaster, South Carolina, to C. P W Sullivan in the Montezuma Hotel in Florida dated the 11th of November 1929 asked him to arrange to take charge of the hotel at once. The hotel was not named in the telegram. Mr. H. R. Rice was on the Board of Directors of Lancaster and the Chester Railroad and Colonel Leroy Springs was the primary stockholder. Colonel Springs was among the wealthiest men in South Carolina and he owned the Royal Hotel in the Springs Block at 200 Main Street in Lancaster. An insurance company now occupies the site.

Mr. Lindsay Pettus, President of the Lancaster Historical Society, said the Royal Hotel had a lobby on the ground floor, 23 rooms on the 2nd floor of a large building that Leroy Springs built in 1905/06, and occupied a major portion of an entire block. The 1930 census stated Charles Sullivan was a Lancaster hotel proprietor and his son-in-law, Beverly McCreight, was an assistant hotel manager. He must have acquired the hotel before the 1930 census.

Old Saint Hubert's Inn, Newton, North Carolina

Charles Pleasant Washington Sullivan owned the Old Saint Hubert's Inn at 218 South Main Street in Newton, North Carolina, in circa 1934. The hotel was demolished in 1936 to build the post office.

Saint Hubert's Inn was one of Newton's oldest landmarks. It was among the finest hotels in that part of the state. The three floor hotel was rebuilt in 1885 by the Hickory contractor R. P. Dakin, for a development company owned by George A. Warlick Sr., Bill Williams and others. It was originally called the Bost Hotel. It was later remodeled, virtually replacing the original building. Mr. E. E. Post, from Maine, renamed the hotel the Saint Hubert's Inn at the end of the 19th century. The original building was probably a hotel built and operated by the master carpenter Johannes Bost.

At the beginning of the 20th century, the hotel was noted for *"impressive accommodations, fine food and crisp table linen."* Wealthy northern members of the Continental Hunting Club, came for the bird dog competitions and kept their dogs in kennels behind the hotel.

Mr. C. P. W. Sullivan came from South Carolina and took over the hotel in circa 1934. The United States Post Office selected the site of the Old Saint. Hubert's Inn for a new post office.

The Old Saint Hubert's Inn. The post office now occupied the site.

Dixie Hotel in Jacksonville, Florida

Charles Pleasant Washington Sullivan acquired the Dixie Hotel, at 405 West Forsyth Street, Jacksonville, Florida in 1937. The Dixie hotel had a short life. It was first listed in a City Directory in 1937. The property had been an office building, apparently with some apartments. Charles W. Sullivan was listed as the manager. The following year in 1938, the hotel was under new management: Mrs. Margaret J. Heiss and Mrs. Eleanor W. Copeland.

Montezuma Hotel in Sanford, Florida

Charles Pleasant Washington Sullivan bought the Montezuma Hotel at 300 South Magnolia Ave, Sanford, Florida, on the 22nd of December 1937. He was in the Montezuma Hotel in 1929 when H. R. Rice sent him a telegram there to arrange to take charge of a hotel in Lancaster, South Carolina at once, but he did not buy the Montezuma hotel until 1937. He may have been there investigating a possible purchase and had to leave to take charge of the hotel in Lancaster.

Montezuma Hotel. Courtesy Alecia Clark, Sanford, Florida Museum.

He and his sister-in-law Mattie bought the hotel from W. H.

Schmidt on the 14th of December 1937, and the price was $9,200.00 according to the documentary tax stamps affixed to the deed. The deed recorded Mattie's full name as Martha Georgiana Garrison.

A newspaper article dated the 22nd of December 1937 said:

> *" .. The Montezuma Hotel was sold today [by the former owner Mr. W. H. Schmidt] to C. [P.] W. Sullivan, a Jacksonville hotel man. In making the announcement Mr. Sullivan added that he expects to reopen the dining room just as soon as satisfactory arrangements can be completed and that he expects to cater in every possible way to the tourist business and the home people. He said he was throwing the hotel open to bridge parties and expects to cooperate in every way possible with civic clubs and various women's organizations. The Montezuma, one of Sanford's oldest hotels was purchased by Mr. Schmidt from J. R. Owens on October the 13th 1936... "*

Charles Sullivan and Mattie sold the hotel to Reconstruction Finance Corp on the 29th of May 1941.

Charles P. W. Sullivan married **Sarah Elisabeth Garrison,** daughter of Edward G. Garrison and Sarah Moon Cureton. [194, 197, 198, 199, 204, 216, 217] She was born on the 16th of February 1856 in Greenville, South Carolina. [198, 217]. She died on the 14th of June 1940. [198 217] According to the 1900 U. S. census, Sarah Elisabeth Garrison had seven children, but only three had survived in 1900. These three children were:

110 i **Sarah Katherine Sullivan** [196, 197, 199, 204, 218] was born on the 30th of November 1886 in Laurens County, South Carolina. She died on the 14th of January 1955 in Washington City, District of Columbia.

111 ii **Minnie Pauline Sullivan** [197, 199, 218] was born in 1888. She died in 1972 in Winston Salem, North Carolina.

112 iii **Charles Edmund Sullivan** [194, 197, 199, 218, 219] was born on the 4th November 1891. [194] He died on the 11th July 1970 in Lumberton, North Carolina. [194]

106 **Benjamin Arnold Sullivan.** [133, 205, 206, 207, 208]
Born on the 11th of April 1861.
Died on the 16th of May 1932 in Laurens County, South Carolina.

(John Hewlett Sullivan-26, Joseph Pickney Sullivan-25, Hewlett Sullivan-24, Charles B. Sullivan-23, Owen Sullivan-22, Owen Sullivan-21, John Thomas O'Sullivan-20, Owen Donal O'Sullivan-19, Owen O'Sullivan Beare Lord of Beare and Bantry-18, Sir Owen O'Sullivan Beare, 14th Lord of Beare and Bantry-17, Dermod O'Sullivan Beare, 11th Lord of Beare and Bantry-16, Donal O'Sullivan Beare, the Swarthy, 8th Lord of Beare and Bantry-15, Dermod (aka Dermond) Balluf O'Sullivan Beare-14, Teige O'Sullivan Beare-13, Amhiaffe O'Sullivan Beare-12, Annaidh O'Sullivan, 1st Lord of Beare and Bantry-11, Philip O'Sullivan-10, Giolla na Bhflainn O'Sullivan Mór-9, Donal O'Sullivan Mór, 15th Lord of Knockgraffon-8, MacCraith O'Sullivan Mór, 14th Lord of Knockgraffon-7, Baudhach O'Sullivan, 13th Lord of Knockgraffon-6, Cathal O'Sullivan, 12th Lord of Knockgraffon-5, Aodh O'Sullivan, 11th Lord of Knockgraffon-4, Baudhach O'Sullivan, 10th Lord of Knockgraffon-3, Lorcan MacSullivan, 9th Lord of Knockgraffon-2, Eochaid Súilleabháinn, 8th Lord of Knockgraffon-

1)

He married **Nannie Brooks** [133, 206, 207, 208] on the 26th of January 1882. [133] She was born in 1860 and died in 1952. Their pictures are shown in the 50th wedding anniversary photograph of William Dunklin Sullivan and Mary Elisabeth Quarles, taken in 1919, in this section.

They had the following known children:

i	James Duncan Sullivan [133, 206] was born in 1888.[206]
ii	Benjamin A. Sullivan [133, 206] was born in 1890. [206]
iii	Kathleen Sullivan [133, 206] was born in 1893.[206]
iv	Mary Dudley Sullivan [133, 206, 207] was born on the 3rd of June 1897. [206]
v	Virginia Sullivan [133, 206, 208] was born on the 17th of June 1899. [208]
vi	Isabella Sullivan [133, 206] was born in 1902.

107 **Mary Josephine Sullivan.** [213]
Born on the 17th of October 1890 in Laurens County, South Carolina.
Died on the 18th June of 1924 in Laurens County, South Carolina.

(Joseph Hewlett-26, George Washington Sullivan-25, Hewlett Sullivan-24, Charles B. Sullivan-23, Owen Sullivan-22, Owen Sullivan-21, John Thomas O'Sullivan-20, Owen Donal O'Sullivan-19, Owen O'Sullivan Beare Lord of Beare and Bantry-18, Sir Owen O'Sullivan Beare, 14th Lord of Beare and Bantry-17, Dermod O'Sullivan Beare, 11th Lord of Beare and Bantry-16, Donal O'Sullivan Beare, the Swarthy, 8th Lord of Beare and Bantry-15, Dermod (aka Dermond) Balluf O'Sullivan Beare-14, Teige O'Sullivan Beare-13, Amhiaffe O'Sullivan Beare-12, Annaidh O'Sullivan, 1st Lord of Beare and Bantry-11, Philip O'Sullivan-10, Giolla na Bhflainn O'Sullivan Mór-9, Donal O'Sullivan Mór, 15th Lord of Knockgraffon-8, MacCraith O'Sullivan Mór, 14th Lord of Knockgraffon-7, Baudhach O'Sullivan, 13th Lord of Knockgraffon-6, Cathal O'Sullivan, 12th Lord of Knockgraffon-5, Aodh O'Sullivan, 11th Lord of Knockgraffon-4, Baudhach O'Sullivan, 10th Lord of Knockgraffon-3, Lorcan MacSullivan, 9th Lord of Knockgraffon-2, Eochaid Súilleabháinn, 8th Lord of Knockgraffon-1)

She married **William Whitley,** born on the 10th of July 1886 in Stanley County, North Carolina. They had the following known children:

i	Pauline Whitley [213] was born in circa 1917.
ii	Josephine Whitley [213] was born in July 1923.
iii	Mary Pelham Whitley [213] was born in 1927. Either her mother Mary Josephine Sullivan's death date or this birthdate is not correct.

108 **John Langdon Sullivan.** [28, 155]
Born on the 8th of March 1827.
Died on the 13th of July 1905.

(Thomas Russell Sullivan-26, Dr. John Landon Sullivan-25, James Sullivan-24, Owen O'Sullivan-23, Major Philip O'Sullivan of Ardea O'Sullivan-22, Owen O'Sullivan Beare, Lord of Ardea Castle-21, Daniel O'Sullivan. Lord of Ardea Castle-20, Philip O'Sullivan Beare-19, Donal O'Sullivan Beare, Lord of Ardea Castle-18, Sir Philip O'Sullivan Beare, Lord of Ardea Castle-17, Dermod O'Sullivan

Beare, 11th Lord of Beare and Bantry-16, Donal O'Sullivan Beare, the Swarthy, 8th Lord of Beare and Bantry-15, Dermod (aka Dermond) Balluf O'Sullivan Beare-14, Teige O'Sullivan Beare-13, Amhiaffe O'Sullivan Beare-12, Annaidh O'Sullivan, 1st Lord of Beare and Bantry-11, Philip O'Sullivan-10, Giolla na Bhflainn O'Sullivan Mór-9, Donal O'Sullivan Mór, 15th Lord of Knockgraffon-8, MacCraith O'Sullivan Mór, 14th Lord of Knockgraffon-7, Baudhach O'Sullivan, 13th Lord of Knockgraffon-6, Cathal O'Sullivan, 12th Lord of Knockgraffon-5, Aodh O'Sullivan, 11th Lord of Knockgraffon-4, Baudhach O'Sullivan, 10th Lord of Knockgraffon-3, Lorcan MacSullivan, 9th Lord of Knockgraffon-2, Eochaid Súilleabháinn, 8th Lord of Knockgraffon-1)

He married **Mary Lynde** [[155] in 1848[155]. She died in 1857. [155] They had the following known children:

i	Mary Lynde Sullivan [155] was born in 1850. [155] She married Alexander Cockrane in 1867. [155]
ii	Seth Lynde Sullivan [155] was born in 1853. [155]

He married **Helen Lynde** [155] in 1860.[155] She died on the 5th of September 1900. [155] They had the following known children:

i	Elisabeth Sullivan[155] was born in 1862. [155]
ii	Lynde Sullivan [155] was born in 1865. [155] He married Katherine Baldwin in 1898.
iii	Helen Lynde Sullivan [155] was born in 1870. [155]
iv	James Amory Sullivan [155] was born in 1875. [155] He married Lavina Kaufman in 1900.

109 **Murtagh O'Sullivan MacCragh** [10, 226].
Born in 1788 [10].

(Seamus O'Sullivan MacCragh-26, Sean O'Sullivan MacCragh-25, Dermot O'Sullivan MacCragh-24, Owen O'Sullivan MacCragh-23, Dermot O'Sullivan MacCragh-22, Owen O'Sullivan MacCragh-21, Conor O'Sullivan MacCragh-20, Donogh O'Sullivan MacCragh-19, Buadach O'Suillivan MacCragh-18, Eoghan O'Sullivan MacCragh-17, Conor O'Sullivan MacCragh-16, Donal O'Sullivan MacCragh-15, Cragh O'Sullivan Mór-14, Dunlong O'Sullivan Mór-13, Bernard O'Sullivan Mór-12, Murtagh O'Sullivan-11, Dunlong O'Sullivan-10, Giolla na Bhflainn O'Sullivan Mór-9, Donal O'Sullivan Mór, 15th Lord of Knockgraffon-8, MacCraith O'Sullivan Mór, 14th Lord of Knockgraffon-7, Baudhach O'Sullivan, 13th Lord of Knockgraffon-6, Cathal O'Sullivan, 12th Lord of Knockgraffon-5, Aodh O'Sullivan, 11th Lord of Knockgraffon-4, Baudhach O'Sullivan, 10th Lord of Knockgraffon-3, Lorcan MacSullivan, 9th Lord of Knockgraffon-2, Eochaid Súilleabháinn, 8th Lord of Knockgraffon-1)

Murtagh is recorded in Griffith's valuation. Richard John Griffith was appointed by the British government to established Irish town, county, parish and barony boundaries in 1844. Between 1830 and 1855, he valued Irish land and buildings.

Murtagh O'Sullivan MacCragh had the following known son:

113 i **Murtagh O'Sullivan MacCragh** [10] was born in 1816. [10]

Generation 28

110 **Sarah Katherine Sullivan.** [196, 197, 199, 204, 218]
Born on the 30th of November 1886 in Laurens County, South Carolina.
Died on the 14th of January 1955 in Washington City, District of Columbia.

Chicora College, now part of Furman University.
Courtesy of Greensville, South Carolina Library.

Sarah Katherine Sullivan and her husband Beverly Randolph McCreight

(Charles Pleasant Washington Sullivan-27, John Hewlett Sullivan-26, Joseph Pickney Sullivan-25, Hewlett Sullivan-24, Charles B. Sullivan-23, Owen Sullivan-22, Owen Sullivan-21, John Thomas O'Sullivan-20, Owen Donal O'Sullivan-19, Owen O'Sullivan Beare Lord of Beare and Bantry-18, Sir Owen O'Sullivan Beare, 14th Lord of Beare and Bantry-17, Dermod O'Sullivan Beare, 11th Lord of Beare and Bantry-16, Donal O'Sullivan Beare, the Swarthy, 8th Lord of Beare and Bantry-15, Dermod (aka Dermond) Balluf O'Sullivan Beare-14, Teige O'Sullivan Beare-13, Amhiaffe O'Sullivan Beare-12, Annaidh O'Sullivan, 1st Lord of Beare and Bantry-11, Philip O'Sullivan-10, Giolla na Bhflainn O'Sullivan Mór-9, Donal O'Sullivan Mór, 15th Lord of Knockgraffon-8, MacCraith O'Sullivan Mór, 14th Lord of Knockgraffon-7, Baudhach O'Sullivan, 13th Lord of Knockgraffon-6, Cathal O'Sullivan, 12th Lord of Knockgraffon-5, Aodh O'Sullivan, 11th Lord of Knockgraffon-4, Baudhach O'Sullivan, 10th Lord of Knockgraffon-3, Lorcan MacSullivan, 9th Lord of Knockgraffon-2, Eochaid Súilleabháinn, 8th Lord of Knockgraffon-1)

Sarah Catherine Sullivan graduated from Chicora College, now part of Furman University. It was unusual for a woman born in the late 19th century to have the opportunity to graduate from college.

The marriage announcement of Beverly Randolph McCreight and Sarah Katherine Sullivan, transcribed from the original Camden newspaper clipping:

" … Marriage of a popular young couple

> *Mr. Beverly R. McCreight and Miss Sarah Katherine Sullivan both of this city [Camden South Carolina] were married Wednesday evening last in the spacious parlor of the Hotel Camden in the presence of relatives and a few intimate friends. There were no attendants and the marriage was in every way quiet owing to a recent bereavement in the family.*
>
> *The parlor was decorated with beautiful ferns and simlax and the soft light was shed by numerous colored candles, leading up to and during the ceremony Mendelsohn's Wedding March and "Hearts and Flowers" were beautifully rendered by Miss Mary Nicholson. The matrimonial bans were pronounced by Rev. M. L. Lawson, Pastor of the Camden Baptist church, after which the happy young couple received the warm congratulations of all present and took their departure for an extended northern bridal tour…"*

The McCreight House in Camden, South Carolina, built by Edward Oscar McCreight, Beverly's father. Charles Sullivan's granddaughter now lives in this house.

In several newspapers and business directories Beverly Randolph McCreight was listed as assistant manager and manager of his father-in-law's hotels in South Carolina, Virginia, Florida, and North Carolina.

She married **Beverly Randolph McCreight** [196, 197] on the 2nd of November 1910 in Camden, South Carolina. He was born on the 2nd November 1886.

They had the following known children:

i   Beverly Randolph McCreight Jr. [197, 199, 204] was born on the 31st of October 1911 in Camden, South Carolina. He died on the 3rd of February

1955 in Washington, District of Columbia.

ii Dr. Charles Edward McCreight [197, 204] was born on the 17th March 1913 in Camden, South Carolina. He died on the 1st of November 2010 in Camden, South Carolina. He was Professor Emeritus of Anatomy at Bowman Grey Medical School in Winston Salem, North Carolina and continued working into his eighties.

iii Ella Elisabeth McCreight [197, 199, 204] was born on the 6th of February 1916 in Roanoke, Virginia. She died on the 28th of August 1982 in Newton, North Carolina. She married Harold Hartsoe.

iv Robert Sullivan McCreight [197, 199, 204] was born on the 25th of October 1918 in Aiken, South Carolina. He died on the 25th of April 2002 in the Veterans Administration Hospital in North Carolina. He married Drusilla Hobs.

v Minnie Katherine McCreight [199, 204, 220] was born on the 25th February 1921 in Aiken, South Carolina. She died on the 21st of March 2010 in Warrenton, Virginia. She married Louis Jennings.

vi Sarah Pauline McCreight [199, 204] was born on the 29th of July 1924 in High Point, North Carolina. She married Bernard Grozbean.

vii Mary Henry McCreight [204] was born on the 1st of March 1927 in Lancaster, South Carolina. She married Shep Goodman.

111 **Minnie Pauline Sullivan** [197, 199, 218].

Greenville Women's College class of 1897. Courtesy of Greenville County, South

Greenville Women's College, now part of Furman University. Courtesy of Greensville, South Carolina Library.

Born in 1888.
Died in 1972 in Winston Salem, North Carolina.

(Charles Pleasant Washington Sullivan-27, John Hewlett Sullivan-26, Joseph Pickney Sullivan-25, Hewlett Sullivan-24, Charles B. Sullivan-23, Owen Sullivan-22, Owen Sullivan-21, John Thomas O'Sullivan-20, Owen Donal O'Sullivan-19, Owen O'Sullivan Beare Lord of Beare and Bantry-18, Sir Owen O'Sullivan Beare, 14th Lord of Beare and Bantry-17, Dermod O'Sullivan Beare, 11th Lord of Beare and Bantry-16, Donal O'Sullivan Beare, the Swarthy, 8th Lord of Beare and Bantry-15, Dermod (aka Dermond) Balluf O'Sullivan Beare-14, Teige O'Sullivan Beare-13, Amhiaffe O'Sullivan Beare-12, Annaidh O'Sullivan, 1st Lord of Beare and Bantry-11, Philip O'Sullivan-10, Giolla na Bhflainn O'Sullivan Mór-9, Donal O'Sullivan Mór, 15th Lord of Knockgraffon-8, MacCraith O'Sullivan Mór, 14th Lord of Knockgraffon-7, Baudhach O'Sullivan, 13th Lord of Knockgraffon-6, Cathal O'Sullivan, 12th Lord of Knockgraffon-5, Aodh O'Sullivan, 11th Lord of Knockgraffon-4, Baudhach O'Sullivan, 10th Lord of Knockgraffon-3, Lorcan MacSullivan, 9th Lord of Knockgraffon-2, Eochaid Súilleabháinn, 8th Lord of Knockgraffon- 1)

Minnie Pauline Sullivan graduated from Greenville Women's College, now part of Furman University.

She married **Shelby Edmund Corbitt**. They had the following Daughter:

i Jean Corbitt. [199]

112 **Charles Edmund Sullivan.** [194, 197, 199, 218, 219]
Born on the 4th of November 1891.[194].
Died on the 11th of July 1970 in Lumberton, North Carolina. [194]

Beverly Randolph McCreight and Charles Edmund Sullivan.

(Charles Pleasant Washington Sullivan-27, John Hewlett Sullivan-26, Joseph Pickney Sullivan-25, Hewlett Sullivan-24, Charles B. Sullivan-23, Owen Sullivan-22, Owen Sullivan-21, John Thomas O'Sullivan-20, Owen Donal O'Sullivan-19, Owen O'Sullivan Beare Lord of Beare and Bantry-18, Sir Owen O'Sullivan Beare, 14th Lord of Beare and Bantry-17, Dermod O'Sullivan Beare, 11th Lord of Beare and Bantry-16, Donal O'Sullivan Beare, the Swarthy, 8th Lord of Beare and Bantry-15, Dermod (aka Dermond) Balluf O'Sullivan Beare-14, Teige O'Sullivan Beare-13, Amhiaffe O'Sullivan Beare-12, Annaidh O'Sullivan, 1st Lord of Beare and Bantry-11, Philip O'Sullivan-10, Giolla na Bhflainn O'Sullivan Mór-9, Donal O'Sullivan Mór, 15th Lord of Knockgraffon-8, MacCraith O'Sullivan Mór, 14th Lord of Knockgraffon-7, Baudhach O'Sullivan, 13th Lord of Knockgraffon-6, Cathal O'Sullivan, 12th Lord of Knockgraffon-5, Aodh O'Sullivan, 11th Lord of Knockgraffon-4, Baudhach O'Sullivan, 10th Lord of Knockgraffon-3, Lorcan MacSullivan, 9th Lord of Knockgraffon-2, Eochaid Súilleabháinn, 8th Lord of Knockgraffon- 1)

He married **Ethleen Amanda Peacock,** daughter of Elijah Felton Peacock and Hattie Caroline Kennedy [194, 219, 221] in 1922. She was born on the 10th of February 1900 [221]. They had the following daughter:

i Peggy Sullivan. [199]

113 **Murtagh O'Sullivan MacCragh** [10] was born in 1816. [10, 226]

(Murtagh O'Sullivan MacCragh-27, Seamus O'Sullivan MacCragh-26, Sean O'Sullivan MacCragh-25, Dermot O'Sullivan MacCragh-24, Owen O'Sullivan MacCragh-23, Dermot O'Sullivan MacCragh-22, Owen O'Sullivan MacCragh-21, Conor O'Sullivan MacCragh-20, Donogh O'Sullivan MacCragh-19, Buadach O'Suillivan MacCragh-18, Eoghan O'Sullivan MacCragh-17, Conor O'Sullivan MacCragh-16, Donal O'Sullivan MacCragh-15, Cragh O'Sullivan Mór-14, Dunlong O'Sullivan Mór-13, Bernard O'Sullivan Mór-12, Murtagh O'Sullivan-11, Dunlong O'Sullivan-10, Giolla na Bhflainn O'Sullivan Mór-9, Donal O'Sullivan Mór, 15th Lord of Knockgraffon-8, MacCraith O'Sullivan Mór, 14th Lord of Knockgraffon-7, Baudhach O'Sullivan, 13th Lord of Knockgraffon-6, Cathal O'Sullivan, 12th Lord of Knockgraffon-5, Aodh O'Sullivan, 11th Lord of Knockgraffon-4, Baudhach O'Sullivan, 10th Lord of Knockgraffon-3, Lorcan MacSullivan, 9th Lord of Knockgraffon-2, Eochaid Súilleabháinn, 8th Lord of Knockgraffon-1)

Murtagh is recorded in Griffith's valuation. Richard John Griffith was appointed by the British government to established Irish town, county, parish and barony boundaries in 1844. Between 1830 and 1855, he valued Irish land and buildings.

Murtagh O'Sullivan MacCragh had the following known son:

114 i **Mortimer James O'Sullivan MacCragh** [222] was born in 1857. [222]

Generation 29

114 **Mortimer James O'Sullivan MacCragh.** [222, 228]
Born in 1857. [222]
Died in Derryconnery, Ireland on the 7th of February 1940 at the age of 82.

(Murtagh O'Sullivan MacCragh-28, Murtagh O'Sullivan MacCragh-27, Seamus O'Sullivan MacCragh-26, Sean O'Sullivan MacCragh-25, Dermot O'Sullivan MacCragh-24, Owen O'Sullivan MacCragh-23, Dermot O'Sullivan MacCragh-22, Owen O'Sullivan MacCragh-21, Conor O'Sullivan MacCragh-20, Donogh O'Sullivan MacCragh-19, Buadach O'Suillivan MacCragh-18, Eoghan O'Sullivan MacCragh-17, Conor O'Sullivan MacCragh-16, Donal O'Sullivan MacCragh-15, Cragh O'Sullivan Mór-14, Dunlong O'Sullivan Mór-13, Bernard O'Sullivan Mór-12, Murtagh O'Sullivan-11, Dunlong O'Sullivan-10, Giolla na Bhflainn O'Sullivan Mór-9, Donal O'Sullivan Mór, 15th Lord of Knockgraffon-8, MacCraith O'Sullivan Mór, 14th Lord of Knockgraffon-7, Baudhach O'Sullivan, 13th Lord of Knockgraffon-6, Cathal O'Sullivan, 12th Lord of Knockgraffon-5, Aodh O'Sullivan, 11th Lord of Knockgraffon-4, Baudhach O'Sullivan, 10th Lord of Knockgraffon-3, Lorcan MacSullivan, 9th Lord of Knockgraffon-2, Eochaid Súilleabháinn, 8th Lord of Knockgraffon-1)

Mortimer is recorded in the church records of the parish Kilcasken, County Cork, Ireland. The baptismal record of his son Daniel list him as a farmer. He married Catherine Daily, who died on the 14th of January 1945. When they both died only one of their eleven children, their youngest son William, was still in Ireland.

Mortimer James O'Sullivan MacCragh had the following known sons:

115 i **Daniel Joseph O'Sullivan MacCragh** [222] was born in 1890. [222]
ii William O'Sullivan MacCragh was the youngest of 11 children. He married Julia Lynch and they had eight children. He remained in Ireland and inherited the family farm in Derryconnery, Ireland.

Generation 30

115 **Daniel Joseph O'Sullivan MacCragh.** [222, 226]
Born on the 9th of February 1890 [222] in Derryconnery, Glengarriff, Ireland.

(Mortimer James O'Sullivan MacCragh-29, Murtagh O'Sullivan MacCragh-28, Murtagh O'Sullivan MacCragh-27, Seamus O'Sullivan MacCragh-26, Sean O'Sullivan MacCragh-25, Dermot O'Sullivan MacCragh-24, Owen O'Sullivan MacCragh-23, Dermot O'Sullivan MacCragh-22, Owen O'Sullivan MacCragh-21, Conor O'Sullivan MacCragh-20, Donogh O'Sullivan MacCragh-19, Buadach O'Suillivan MacCragh-18, Eoghan O'Sullivan MacCragh-17, Conor O'Sullivan MacCragh-16, Donal

O'Sullivan MacCragh-15, Cragh O'Sullivan Mór-14, Dunlong O'Sullivan Mór-13, Bernard O'Sullivan Mór-12, Murtagh O'Sullivan-11, Dunlong O'Sullivan-10, Giolla na Bhflainn O'Sullivan Mór-9, Donal O'Sullivan Mór, 15th Lord of Knockgraffon-8, MacCraith O'Sullivan Mór, 14th Lord of Knockgraffon-7, Baudhach O'Sullivan, 13th Lord of Knockgraffon-6, Cathal O'Sullivan, 12th Lord of Knockgraffon-5, Aodh O'Sullivan, 11th Lord of Knockgraffon-4, Baudhach O'Sullivan, 10th Lord of Knockgraffon-3, Lorcan MacSullivan, 9th Lord of Knockgraffon-2, Eochaid Súilleabháinn, 8th Lord of Knockgraffon-1)

Daniel is recorded in the church records of the parish Kilcasken, County Cork, Ireland. There was little opportunity for Daniel in Ireland. In 1908, he left Cobb Port, Queenstown, onboard the H.M.S. Oceanic and landed at Ellis Island, New York on the 29th of April 1908. He was naturalized a United States Citizen on the 26th of September 1916. He joined the naval reserves on the 24th of April 1918 and served as seaman second class for four years. On the 29th of December 1918, he married **Rose Cowley**, daughter of James Cowley (MacCowley) and Mary McGovern. In 1919, he became an officer in the New York Police force.

Daniel Joseph O'Sullivan MacCragh had the following known children:

116 i **Daniel Joseph O'Sullivan MacCragh** [222] was born in 1920. [222]

ii Mortimer O'Sullivan MacCragh was born on the 1st of August 1923. He married (Bertie) Geiger.

iii Rosemary O'Sullivan was born on the 20th of June 1929. She married Zolton Varga.

Generation 31

116 **Daniel Joseph O'Sullivan MacCragh.** [222, 226]
Born on the 28th of December 1920 [222] in New York City.

(Daniel Joseph O'Sullivan MacCragh-30, Mortimer James O'Sullivan MacCragh-29, Murtagh O'Sullivan MacCragh-28, Murtagh O'Sullivan MacCragh-27, Seamus O'Sullivan MacCragh-26, Sean O'Sullivan MacCragh-25, Dermot O'Sullivan MacCragh-24, Owen O'Sullivan MacCragh-23, Dermot O'Sullivan MacCragh-22, Owen O'Sullivan MacCragh-21, Conor O'Sullivan MacCragh-20, Donogh O'Sullivan MacCragh-19, Buadach O'Suillivan MacCragh-18, Eoghan O'Sullivan MacCragh-17, Conor O'Sullivan MacCragh-16, Donal O'Sullivan MacCragh-15, Cragh O'Sullivan Mór-14, Dunlong O'Sullivan Mór-13, Bernard O'Sullivan Mór-12, Murtagh O'Sullivan-11, Dunlong O'Sullivan-10, Giolla na Bhflainn O'Sullivan Mór-9, Donal O'Sullivan Mór, 15th Lord of Knockgraffon-8, MacCraith O'Sullivan Mór, 14th Lord of Knockgraffon-7, Baudhach O'Sullivan, 13th Lord of Knockgraffon-6, Cathal O'Sullivan, 12th Lord of Knockgraffon-5, Aodh O'Sullivan, 11th Lord of Knockgraffon-4, Baudhach O'Sullivan, 10th Lord of Knockgraffon-3, Lorcan MacSullivan, 9th Lord of Knockgraffon-2, Eochaid Súilleabháinn, 8th Lord of Knockgraffon-1)

He married **Helen Elisabeth Culver**, born on the 24th of April 1929. On the eve of World War II, Daniel joined the army and passed the examinations for flight training. He was wounded in the invasion of Okinawa and was shipped to Valley Forge Army Hospital. His injuries later resulted in total blindness. Daniel Joseph O'Sullivan MacCragh and Helen Elisabeth Culver had the following known son:

i **Dr. Gary Brian O'Sullivan MacCragh** [222, 226] was born on the 11th of October 1955 [222] in Montebello, California. Dr. O'Sullivan is the present elected chief of the O'Sullivan MacCragh sept. He is a direct male descendent of Cragh and therefore of King Finghin of Munster, Ireland and King Milesius in Spain. The O'Sullivan clan is the oldest of the Irish royal lines and the MacCragh sept is the senior line of the O'Sullivan clan. Dr. O'Sullivan is a Fellow of the American College of Obstetricians and Gynecologists and a Fellow of the American College of Surgeons. His primary residence is Château du Gravier, La Guerche sur L'Aubois, in Cher, France, also known as Dunberry Castle (see the picture in Part I). His other residence is Beare Haven House in Statesboro, Georgia, U.S.A. He has written two books about the history of the O'Sullivan clan: *The Oak and the Serpent* and *History of the O'Sullivan Clan, the Royal Blood of Gaelic Ireland.*

Part II Sources

1. Materials For a History of the Family of John Sullivan of Berwick, New England, and of the O'Sullivans of Ardea, Ireland, partially taken from Sir J. Bernard Burke 1893, page 90, Gertrude Euphemia Meredith and Thomas Coffin Amory.
2. *The Oak and the Serpent*, Gary B. Sullivan MD FACOG FACS, Gold Stag Communications 2007, page 57.
3. *Eóghanacht Genealogies Book of Munster,* Reverend Eugene O'Keeffe, 1702, page 244.
4. *Linea Antiqua Genealogica*, Roger O'Ferrall, Office Dublin 1709.
5. *Book of Genealogies, Cú Choigcríche* Ó Cléirigh (O'Clery) one of the four masters, written before 1664.
6. *Eóghanacht Genealogies - Book of Munster,* Rev. Eugene O'Keeffe, 1703.
7. Analecta Hibernica #18, the O'Clery Book of Genealogies.
8. *The Oak and the Serpent*, Gary B. Sullivan MD FACOG FACS, Gold Stag Communications 2007, page 58.
9. *History of the O'Sullivan Clan, The Royal Blood of Gaelic Ireland,* Gary B. Sullivan MD, FACOG FACS, page 30.
10. The Oak and the Serpent, Gary B. Sullivan MD FACOG FACS, Gold Stag Communications 2007, page 58.
11. *Irish Pedigrees, the Origin and Stem,* Volume 1, 5th edition, John O'Hart, Burns & Oats, London, 1892, page 245.
12. *The Annals of the Kingdom of Ireland (Annála Ríoghachta Éireann)* also known as *The Annals of the Four Masters (Annála nag Ceithre Máistrí)*, 1632, annotations by Philip MacDermott, translation by Bryan Geraghty, 1846, M1563.2.
13. *Materials for a History of the Family of John Sullivan of Berwick New England: and of the O'Sullivans of Ardea, Ireland*, taken from Sir J. Bernard Burke 1893, page 104, Gertrude Euphemia Meredith and Thomas Coffin Amory.
14. *The New England Historical and Genealogical Register*, 1865.
15. Supplement to *Index of the 1800 Census of NC*, Elisabeth Petty Bently and Sarah Sullivan, Genealogical.
16. *The New England Historical and Genealogical Register*, 1865.
17. *The Annals of the Kingdom of Ireland (Annála Ríoghachta Éireann)* also known as *The Annals of the Four Masters (Annála nag Ceithre Máistrí)*, 1632, annotations by Philip MacDermott, translation by Bryan Geraghty, 1846, M 1594.2.
18. *The Prominent Families of the United States of America,* Arthur Meredith Burke, 1908, Sackville Press, page 264.
19. *Materials for a History of the Family of John Sullivan of Berwick New England: and of the O'Sullivans of Ardea, Ireland,* taken from Sir J. Bernard Burke 1893, page 91, Gertrude Euphemia Meredith and Thomas Coffin Amory.
20. *The Annals of the Kingdom of Ireland (Annála Ríoghachta Éireann)* also known as *The Annals of the Four Masters (Annála nag Ceithre Máistrí)*, 1632, annotations by Philip MacDermott, translation by Bryan Geraghty, 1846.
21. Materials For a History of the Family of John Sullivan of Berwick, New England, and of the O'Sullivans of Ardea, Ireland, partially taken from Sir J. Bernard Burke 1893, page 94, Gertrude Euphemia Meredith and Thomas Coffin Amory.
22. *Lodge's Peerage of Ireland,* volume IV, 1754.
23. *The New England Historical and Genealogical Register*, 1865, pages 289-305.

24. *The Annals of the Kingdom of Ireland (Annála Ríoghachta Éireann)* also known as The Annals of the Four Masters (Annála nag Ceithre Máistrí), 1632, annotations by Philip MacDermott, translation by Bryan Geraghty, 1846, M1549.8.
25. *New England Historical and Genealogical Register,* Volume XIX, October 1865, Number 4, page 296.
26. *The Prominent Families of the United States of America,* Arthur Meredith Burke, 1908, Sackville Press, page 265.
27. Supplement to *Index of the 1800 Census of NC*, Elisabeth Petty Bently and Sarah Sullivan, Genealogical, page 186C.
28. *Magna Charta Barons and Their Descendants*, Charles H. Browning, 1898, republished in 1915, Genealogical Publishing Company, page 157.
29. *Irish Pedigrees, the Origin and Stem*, Volume 1, 5th edition, John O'Hart, Burns & Oats, London, 1892, page 94.
30. The Annals of the Kingdom of Ireland (Annála Ríoghachta Éireann) also known as The Annals of the Four Masters (Annála nag Ceithre Máistrí), 1632, annotations by Philip MacDermott, translation by Bryan Geraghty, 1846, M1549.10.
31. The Annals of the Kingdom of Ireland (Annála Ríoghachta Éireann) also known as The Annals of the Four Masters (Annála nag Ceithre Máistrí), 1632, annotations by Philip MacDermott, translation by Bryan Geraghty, 1846, M1593.8.
32. *Historiae Catholicae Hiberniae Compendium,* Philip O'Sullivan, 1621, introduction by M. Kelly.
33. *Materials for a History of the Family of John Sullivan of Berwick, New England, and of the O'Sullivans of Ardea, Ireland*, 1893, letter from Mrs. John Louis O'Sullivan letter dated 1885, page 100.
34. *Materials for a History of the Family of John Sullivan of Berwick, New England, and of the O'Sullivans of Ardea, Ireland,* 1893, letter from Mrs. John Louis O'Sullivan letter dated 1885, page 100.
35. *New England Historical and Genealogical Register*, Volume XIX, October 1865, Number 4, page 297.
36. *Burke's Irish Family Records* (London, U.K.: Burkes Peerage Ltd, 1976), Barry Hugh.
37. *The Annals of the Kingdom of Ireland (Annála Ríoghachta Éireann)* also known as *The Annals of the Four Masters (Annála nag Ceithre Máistrí)*, 1632, annotations by Philip MacDermott, translation by Bryan Geraghty, 1846, M1585.
38. *Catholic Encyclopedia*, search key Philip O'Sullivan Beare.
39. *Catholic Encyclopedia*, search key Philip O'Sullivan Beare.
40. *The Oak and the Serpent,* Gary B. Sullivan MD FACOG FACS, Gold Stag Communications 2007.
41. *Pacata Hiberna*, Sir George Carew, Lowney & Company, 1896.
42. *The Oak and the Serpent*, Gary B. Sullivan MD FACOG FACS, Gold Stag Communications 2007, pages 268, 270, 271, 273, 279.
43. *The Annals of the Kingdom of Ireland (Annála Ríoghachta Éireann)* also known as *The Annals of the Four Masters (Annála nag Ceithre Máistrí)*, 1632, annotations by Philip MacDermott, translation by Bryan Geraghty, 1846, M1600.11 to M1602.18.
44. *The Annals of the Kingdom of Ireland (Annála Ríoghachta Éireann)* also known as *The Annals of the Four Masters (Annála nag Ceithre Máistrí)*, 1632, annotations by Philip MacDermott, translation by Bryan Geraghty, 1846, M1581.20.
45. Supplement to *Index of the 1800 Census of NC*, Elisabeth Petty Bently and Sarah Sullivan, Genealogica 186dl.

46. *Materials For a History of the Family of John Sullivan of Berwick, New England, and of the O'Sullivans of Ardea, Ireland*, partially taken from Sir J. Bernard Burke 1893, Gertrude Euphemia Meredith and Thomas Coffin Amory.
47. *Materials For a History of the Family of John Sullivan of Berwick, New England, and of the O'Sullivans of Ardea, Ireland*, partially taken from Sir J. Bernard Burke 1893, Gertrude Euphemia Meredith and Thomas Coffin Amory.
48. *Magazine of Virginia, James Sullivan of Charlotte County and the problem of entrenched misinformation, volume* 25, number 4, pages 3 to13, November 1987, by Carolyn Copeland Bland.
49. Patent Book 3, page 392, land office Richmond, Virginia.
50. Book 1, page 194; and State Library, Richmond.
51. *Journal of Irish-Americans* Soc. 25/103. Abstract of will of Owen Hayes, 25, 99.
52. John Thomas O'Sullivan 's will dated the 12th of May 1698, proven the 7th of September 1698, Book 1, page 194 Lynhaven.
53. Princess Anne County, Virginia, Deed Book 1, 1691-1708, microfilm publication, Central Library, Virginia, page 87, on the 16th of December 1694, Esther Sullivan, widow of John Sullivan Jr., gave her power of attorney to her father-in-law John Sullivan.
54. Princess Anne County, Virginia, Deed Book 1, 1691-1708, microfilm publication, Central Library, Virginia, page 194, on the 7th of September 1698, the court proved the will of John Sullivan, written on the 12th of May 1693.
55. Princess Anne County, Virginia, Deed Book 1, 1691-1708, microfilm publication, Central Library, Virginia, page 446, on the 3rd of January 1705/6, Owen Sullivan and his wife Ruth deeded 120 acres from his father John Sullivan to his brother Morris Sullivan.
56. Princess Anne County, Virginia, Deed Book 1, 1691-1708, microfilm publication, Central Library, Virginia, page 528, on the 2nd of January 1708 Morris Sullivan deeded to Joseph Lane twenty acres known as Cow Pen Ridge from the patent of Owen Sullivan dated the 7th of November 1700.
57. Princess Anne County, Virginia, Book 4, fol. 126.
58. Lunenburg County, the 10th of September 1755 Pat. Book. 32, 631.
59. *William and Mary Quarterly*. 11, 57.
60. Will, Owen Sullivan, proved in Charlotte County, Virginia on the 6th of February 1769.
61. *Materials For a History of the Family of John Sullivan of Berwick, New England, and of the O'Sullivans of Ardea, Ireland,* partially taken from Sir J. Bernard Burke 1893, page 93, Gertrude Euphemia Meredith and Thomas Coffin Amory.
62. *Materials For a History of the Family of John Sullivan of Berwick, New England, and of the O'Sullivans of Ardea, Ireland,* partially taken from Sir J. Bernard Burke 1893, page 92, Gertrude Euphemia Meredith and Thomas Coffin Amory.
63. *New England Historical and Genealogical Register,* Volume XIX, October 1865, Number 4.
64. *Materials For a History of the Family of John Sullivan of Berwick, New England, and of the O'Sullivans of Ardea, Ireland,* 1893, Philip O'Sullivan letter dated 1796.
65. *A History of the Sullivan Family*, compiled in1882, published by William D. Sullivan 1913.
66. Charlotte County, Virginia Deed Book 3, page 571.
67. Family Bible of Jefferson Sullivan, older parts written by Mary Sullivan née Charlton, born in 1722, died in 1837, North Carolina State Archive.
68. *History of the Sullivan Family,* William D. Sullivan, 1882.
69. *History of South Carolina*, Volume 3, Yates Snowden, Harry Gardner Cutler Lewis Publishing Company, 1920, pages 137-138.

70. United States Census, 1790 Greenville County South Carolina.
71. Will, John Sullivan, Twitty's Creek, Lunenburg County, Virginia, proved 1750.
72. *Materials For a History of the Family of John Sullivan of Berwick, New England, and of the O'Sullivans of Ardea, Ireland,* 1893, Philip O'Sullivan letter dated 1796.
73. *New England Historical and Genealogical Register*, Volume XIX, October 1865, Number 4, page 298.
74. *Materials For a History of the Family of John Sullivan of Berwick, New England, and of the O'Sullivans of Ardea, Ireland,* partially taken from Sir J. Bernard Burke 1893, page 149, Gertrude Euphemia Meredith and Thomas Coffin Amory.
75. *Materials For a History of the Family of John Sullivan of Berwick, New England, and of the O'Sullivans of Ardea, Ireland* 1893, letter from Mortimer O'Sullivan of Kenmare dated 1887, page 87.
76. *New England Historical and Genealogical Register*, Volume XIX, October 1865, Number 4, Page 98, John Sullivan 's own account of his genealogy.
77. United States Census, 1800, Greenville County, South Carolina.
78. United States Census, 1810, Greenville County, South Carolina.
79. South Carolina land grant, Charles Sullivan, 170 acres, the 4th of December 1780, volume 8, page 359.
80. South Carolina land grant, Charles Sullivan, 200 acres, the 11th of February 1788, volume 22, page 86.
81. South Carolina land grant, Charles Sullivan, 400 acres, the 4th of December 1785, volume 6, page 310.
82. South Carolina land grant, Charles Sullivan, 100 acres, the 4th of December 1785, volume 22, page 86.
83. Lunenburg County, Virginia deed book, book 4, page 329, the 5th ,of October 1758, James Sullivan sold land to James Land and his wife Sarah relinquished her right of dower to the land and premises.
84. Charlotte County, Virginia Deed Book, book 5, page 55, the 26th of April 1783, James Sullivan deeded 500 acres of land to Francis Barns and his wife Sarah relinquished her right of dower to the land and premises.
85. South Carolina Archive, Equity Court papers, Washington District, Laurens County.
86. *South Carolinians in the Revolution,* Sara Sullivan Ervin, 1949, Parts of this book have been discredited, in particular the validity of a transcript of Sullivan family details from the James Sullivan Bible used as proof that James was the son of Owen.
87. *Materials For a History of the Family of John Sullivan of Berwick, New England, and of the O'Sullivans of Ardea, Ireland,* partially taken from Sir J. Bernard Burke 1893, page 150, Gertrude Euphemia Meredith and Thomas Coffin Amory.
88. *Military Services and Public Life of Major General John Sullivan*, Thomas Coffin Amory, Bedford, Massachusetts, Applewood Books, originally published 1868.
89. *Materials For a History of the Family of John Sullivan of Berwick, New England, and of the O'Sullivans of Ardea, Ireland,* partially taken from Sir J. Bernard Burke 1893, page 151, Gertrude Euphemia Meredith and Thomas Coffin Amory.
90. *Military Services and Public Life of Major General John Sullivan*, Thomas Coffin Amory, Bedford, Massachusetts, Applewood Books, originally published 1868.
91. *Materials For a History of the Family of John Sullivan of Berwick, New England, and of the O'Sullivans of Ardea, Ireland*, Gertrude Euphemia Meredith and Thomas Coffin Amory, partially taken from Sir J. Bernard Burke 1893, page 152.
92. *Materials For a History of the Family of John Sullivan of Berwick, New England, and of*

the O'Sullivans of Ardea, Ireland, Gertrude Euphemia Meredith and Thomas Coffin Amory, partially taken from Sir J. Bernard Burke 1893, page 153.

93. *Materials For a History of the Family of John Sullivan of Berwick, New England, and of the O'Sullivans of Ardea, Ireland*, Gertrude Euphemia Meredith and Thomas Coffin Amory, partially taken from Sir J. Bernard Burke 1893, page 154.
94. Supplement to Index of the 1800 Census of NC, Elisabeth Petty Bently and Sarah Sullivan, Genealogical, page 186D.
95. Two Obituaries of Hewlett Sullivan dated the 16th of July 1830 and the 6th of August 1630.
96. Letter to Sarah Katherine Sullivan.
97. United States Census, 1820, Greenville County, South Carolina.
98. United States Census, 1830, Greenville County, South Carolina.
99. Will of Hewlett Sullivan, signed the 21st of August 1829, AP 7, file 434, probated the 13th of September 1830.
100. South Carolina land grant, Hewlett Sullivan, the 9th of July 1808, volume 54, page 393 and a surveyor's map in volume 41, page 376.
101. South Carolina land grant, Hewlett Sullivan, the 11th of June 1784, volume 10, page 533.
102. Will, Joseph Perrin, Charlotte County, Virginia, probated 1773.
103. *Scruggs & Dunklin Genealogies,* Ethel Hastings Scruggs Dunklin.
104. United States. Census 1810, 1820 and1850 Greenville County, South Carolina.
105. United States Census, 1850, Greenville County, South Carolina.
106. South Carolina land grant, John Sullivan, the 24th of November 1842, volume P, number 6, page 85.
107. John Sullivan, land grant issued on the 3rd of March 1845, volume P, number 6, page 186.
108. Obituary, Charles Pickney Sullivan died in Charleston, South Carolina on the 24th of October 1849.
109. South Carolina death certificate, Greycourt, William Dunklin Sullivan the 2nd of September 1931.
110. Land deed, 1842 from Joseph Sullivan to Thomas J. and G. W. Sullivan, 287 acres with wagon, tools, buildings, furnishing and slaves in trust for his son John H. Sullivan.
111. Obituary, Temperance Hamilton Sullivan née Arnold dated the 24th of October 1857.
112. South Carolina death certificate, Sullivan Township, Laurens County, William Dunklin Sullivan, the 2nd of September 1931.
113. South Carolina death certificate, Sullivan Township, Laurens County, Thomas Jefferson Sullivan Jr. the 9th of November 1923.
114. South Carolina death certificate, Anderson County, George Washington Sullivan Jr. the 17th of November 1928.
115. South Carolina death certificate, Laurens County, Joseph Hewlett Sullivan died the 9th of June 1920.
116. United States Census, 1850, Laurens County, South Carolina, 1910 Camden, Kershaw County, Camden South Carolina, 1920, Aiken County South Carolina.
117. South Carolina tax register, 1865 Division 19, district 3.
118. South Carolina death certificate, Lauren County, Charles Boyd Sullivan the 5th of June 1915.
119. North Carolina Death Certificate, Asheville, Hewlett Sullivan the 14th of July 1936.
120. South Carolina death certificate, Hunter Township, Laurens County, Mary Charleton Sullivan, the 5th of July 1932, registration number 32.
121. United States Census, 1850, Laurens County, South Carolina.

122. United States Census, 1850, Laurens County, South Carolina.
123. United States Census, 1860, Laurens County, South Carolina.
124. Tennessee death record, Jackson, Madison County, Belton O'Neal Sullivan, the 18th of July 1929.
125. South Carolina death certificate, Greenville, Greenville County, Marian Agnew, née Sullivan the 12th of May 1937.
126. Obituary, John Hewlett Sullivan on the 8th of March 1821 died the 28th of June 1899.
127. Marriage announcement.
128. Obituary, Mary Dudley Cureton.
129. Obituary, John Hewlett Sullivan on the 28th of July 1899.
130. United States Census, 1860, Greenville County, South Carolina.
131. United States Census, 1870, Greenville County, South Carolina.
132. United States Census, 1880, Greenville County, South Carolina.
133. Obituary, Benjamin Arnold Sullivan, died the 16th of May 1932 in Laurens County, South Carolina.
134. South Carolina Magazine of Ancestral Research, volume 5, number 3.
135. Obituary, Sally Clinkscales, aka Ellen, born the 15th of April 1859.
136. South Carolina birth certificate, Charles Humbert Sullivan the 14th of August 1895.
137. South Carolina birth certificate, Thomas Jefferson Sullivan, Laurens County, the 24th of December 1853.
138. South Carolina birth certificate, Laurens County, Claudius Arnold Sullivan, the 19th of January 1893.
139. South Carolina death certificate, Laurens County, Claudius Arnold Sullivan, the 9th of May 1942.
140. South Carolina birth certificate, Laurens County, Sarah Lucile Sullivan, the 23rd of May 1886.
141. South Carolina death certificate, Sullivan Township, Laurens County, Thomas Cureton Sullivan, the 14th of August 1916.
142. South Carolina birth certificate, Sullivan Township, Laurens County, Charles Humbert Sullivan, the 14th of August 1895.
143. South Carolina birth certificate, Laurens County, Claudius Arnold Sullivan, the 19th of January 1893.
144. South Carolina birth certificate, Laurens County, Sara Lucile Sullivan, the 23rd of May 1886.
145. Laurens County, South Carolina Surveyor, George Washington Sullivan land map.
146. United States Census, 1850 Laurens County, South Carolina.
147. South Carolina death certificate, Laurens County, Mary Pelham, the 27th of December 1919.
148. United States National Park Service, U.S. Civil War soldiers.
149. United States Census, 1880, Laurens County, South Carolina.
150. United States Census, 1900, Laurens County, South Carolina.
151. United States Census, 1910, Laurens County, South Carolina.
152. South Carolina birth certificate, Laurens County, Jared David, the 15th of October 1892.
153. South Carolina death certificate, Greenville County, Rosalie Burnside née Sullivan, the 25th of April 1931.
154. Gravestone inscription.
155. *The Prominent Families of the United States of America,* Arthur Meredith Burke, 1908, Sackville Press, page 266.

156. Obituary, Mary Cureton.
157. South Carolina death certificate, Temperance Wasson, née Sullivan, Laurens County the 19th of April 1934.
158. United States Census, 1880, Lauren County, Joseph Wesson head of Household.
159. United States Census, 1900, Laurens County, South Carolina, Joseph Wesson head of Household.
160. United States Census Laurens County, 1920 Laurens County, South Carolina, Joseph Wesson head of Household.
161. United States Census, 1930 Laurens County, South Carolina, Joseph Wesson head of Household.
162. Letter from John P. West, legal attorney to John C. Kay, legal attorney in Graham Texas dated the 14th of March 1901 on Olwell Hotel letterhead, Aiken, South Carolina.
163. Aiken Journal and Review 13 articles from the 5th of March 1919 to the 5th of July 1922.
164. Register of Deeds, Kershaw County, South Carolina.
165. Columbia Record Saturday the 5th of April 1913, page 3 provided by the Camden Archive.
166. Camden, South Carolina City Archive.
167. Roanoke City Directories 1915 and 1916, provided by Roanoke, Virginia Public Library, The Virginia Room.
168. Sanborn Insurance of Roanoke Virginia, map, dated 1907, provided by Roanoke, Virginia Public Library, The Virginia Room.
169. Roanoke City Directory 1914, provided by Roanoke, Virginia Public Library, The Virginia Room.
170. Illustrated Story of Roanoke: The "Magic City", circa 1912, provided by Roanoke, Virginia Public Library Virginia Room.
171. High Point, North Carolina city directory 1922 and 1928, provided by the High Point, N.C. Public Library.
172. High Point Enterprise, on July 4th 1976, provided by the High Point, North Carolina Public Library.
173. High Point: A Pictorial History, Roy Shipman, provided by the High Point, North Carolina Public Library.
174. Aiken Journal and Review on the 4th of July 1922, Aiken, South Carolina.
175. Aiken South Carolina city directory 1923, provided by the Aiken, South Carolina City Library.
176. High Point, North Carolina city directory 1923, provided by the High Point, North Carolina City Library.
177. High Point North Carolina city directory 1928, provided by the High Point, North Carolina City Library.
178. High Point North Carolina city directory 1933, provided by the High Point, North Carolina City Library.
179. High Point North Carolina city directory 1935, provided by the High Point, North Carolina City Library.
180. Lancaster County Library, South Carolina, genealogy department.
181. Western Union telegram JN36 10 Lancaster So Car 11 1018A the 11th of November 1929 AM 10 51 H. H. Rice to C. P. W. Sullivan Montezuma Hotel, Stanford, Florida.
182. Mr. Lindsay Pettus, President of the Lancaster Historical Society.
183. Catawba News Enterprise the 7th of August 1936.
184. The Catawbans, Pioneers in Progress, volume two, 2002, by Gary R. Freeze, Catawba County Historical Association.

185. Catawba News Enterprise the 14th of July 1936.
186. Catawba News Enterprise the 20th of October 1936.
187. Catawba News Enterprise the 3rd of November 1936.
188. Jacksonville, Florida City Directory 1937, provided by the Jacksonville City Library.
189. Jacksonville City Library, Florida, research report.
190. Land records department of the Seminole County, Florida Records Department the 2nd of July 2012.
191. The Stanford Herald on the 22nd of December 1937, provided by the Stanford Florida City Archive.
192. Stanford Florida City Archive, research report.
193. Camden City Directory 1925-1926, provided by the Camden, South Carolina City Archive.
194. North Carolina Death Certificate, Lumberton, Charles Edmund Sullivan the 11th of July 1970.
195. Obituary, Charles Pleasant Washington Sullivan, the 4th of October 1946.
196. Marriage announcement, Beverly Randolph McCreight and Sarah Katherine Sullivan, daughter of Charles P. W. Sullivan, the 2nd of November 1910.
197. United States Census, 1920, Aiken, Aiken County, South Carolina.
198. North Carolina Death Certificate, Sarah Elisabeth Garrison 1940.
199. Obituary, Sarah Elisabeth Sullivan née Garrison dated the 15th of January 1940.
200. United States Census, 1900, Laurens County, South Carolina.
201. United States Census, 1910, Greenville County, South Carolina.
202. United States Census, 1910, Camden, Kershaw County, South Carolina.
203. United States Census, 1920, Aiken, South Carolina.
204. United States Census, 1930, Lancaster, Lancaster County, South Carolina.
205. United States Census Laurens County, 1910, Laurens County, South Carolina.
206. United States Census, 1910, Laurens County, South Carolina, Ben Sullivan head of household.
207. South Carolina birth certificate, Laurens, Laurens County, Mary Dudley Sullivan the 3rd of June 1897.
208. South Carolina birth certificate, Laurens County, Virginia Sullivan, the 17th of June 1899.
209. Pelham Lyles, Director The Fairfield County Museum, South Carolina, and Steve Beaty.
210. Census, Laurens County, South Carolina 1880.
211. Census, Laurens County, South Carolina 1900.
212. Census, Columbia, Richland County, South Carolina 1860.
213. Pelham Lyles, Director The Fairfield County Museum, South Carolina, and Steve Beaty.
214. South Carolina death certificate, Laurens County, Rosalie Sullivan née Moore the 17th of August 1929.
215. Military record, was accepted for officers training at Camp Gordon, Atlanta, Georgia to enter on the 15th of November 1918, but cancelled on the 12th of November 1918, because World War I ended.
216. United States Census, 1910, Camden, Kershaw County, South Carolina, 1920, Aiken County South Carolina.
217. North Carolina Death Certificate, Newton, Catawba County, Sarah Elisabeth Garrison, the 14th of January 1940.
218. United States Census, 1910, Camden, Kershaw County, South Carolina.
219. South Carolina birth certificate, Aiken County, Ethleen Amanda Peacock, the 10th of February 1900.
220. Obituary, Minnie Katherine Jennings, née McCreight the 21st of March 2010, Warrenton,

Virginia.
221. South Carolina birth certificate, Aiken, Ethleen Peacock, the 10th of February 1900.
222. *The Oak and the Serpent*, Gary B. Sullivan MD FACOG FACS, Gold Stag Communications 2007, page 59.
223. *History of the O'Sullivan Clan, The Royal Blood of Gaelic Ireland*, Dr. Gary Sullivan, page 110.
224. Ibidem page 122.
225. Ibidem page 123.
226. *The Oak and the Serpent*, Gary B. Sullivan MD FACOG FACS, Gold Stag Communications 2007, page 224.
227. Caroline County order book 1732-1740, pages 50, 74, book 1740-1746, page 67, transactions the 11th of October 1733, the 15th of January 1736 and the 13th of July 1744.
228. Virginia land office and patents, patent number 9, 1697-1706, volumes 1-2, page 1-742, page 271, reel 9, Library of Virginia.
229. Virginia land office and patents, patent number 32, 1752-1756, volumes 1-2, page 1-715, page 631, reel 30, Virginia Library.

Index of Names

D

E

F

G

H

www.ingramcontent.com/pod-product-compliance
Lightning Source LLC
Chambersburg PA
CBHW080422270326
41929CB00018B/3131